Prentice Hall LITERATURE

PENGUIN EDITION

D1450346

Reader's Notebook

Grade Six

PEARSON

Upper Saddle River, New Jersey
Boston, Massachusetts
Chandler, Arizona
Glenview, Illinois

ISBN 13: 978-0-13-366673-1
ISBN 10: 0-13-366673-5

8 9 10 V011 17 16 15 14 13 12

ACKNOWLEDGMENTS

Grateful acknowledgment is made to the following for copyrighted material:

Airmont Publishing Company, Inc.
"Water" by Helen Keller from *The Story of My Life.* Copyright © 1965 by Airmont Publishing Company, Inc.

Ricardo E. Alegría
"The Three Wishes" selected and adapted by Ricardo E. Alegría from *The Three Wishes: A Collection of Puerto Rican Folktales.* Copyright © 1969 by Ricardo E. Alegría. Used by permission of Ricardo E. Alegría.

ASPCA
ASPCA Animaland from *http://www.aspca.org.* Copyright © 2007 by The American Society for the Prevention of Cruelty to Animals. Used by permission.

Atheneum Books for Young Readers, an imprint of Simon & Schuster
"Stray" by Cynthia Rylant from *Every Living Thing.* Copyright © 1985 by Cynthia Rylant. Used by permission of Atheneum Books for Young Readers, an imprint of Simon & Schuster Children's Publishing Division.

Susan Bergholz Literary Services
"Names/Nombres" by Julia Alvarez from *Nuestro, March, 1985.* Copyright © 1985 by Julia Alvarez. First published in *Nuestro. March, 1985.* Used by permission of Susan Bergholz Literary Services, New York, NY and Lamy, NM. All rights reserved.

Brandt & Hochman Literary Agents, Inc.
"Wilbur Wright and Orville Wright" by Rosemary and Stephen Vincent Benét, from *A Book of Americans* by Rosemary and Stephen Vincent Benét. Copyright © 1933 by Rosemary and Stephen Vincent Benét. Copyright © renewed 1961 by Rosemary Carr Benét.

John Brewton, George M. Blackburn & Lorraine A. Blackburn
"Limerick (Accidents—More or Less Fatal)" from *Laughable Limericks.* Copyright © 1965 by Sara and John E. Brewton. Used by permission of Brewton, Blackburn and Blackburn.

Curtis Brown Ltd.
"Adventures of Isabel" by Ogden Nash from *Parents Keep Out.* Originally published by *Nash's Pall Mall Magazine.* Copyright © 1936 by Ogden Nash. All rights reserved. "Greyling" by Jane Yolen from *Greyling: A Picture Story from the Islands.* Copyright © 1968, 1996 by Jane Yolen. First published by Penguin Putnam. Used by permission of Curtis Brown, Ltd.

Chronicle Books
"Oranges" from *New and Selected Poems* by Gary Soto. Copyright © 1995 by Gary Soto. Visit *www.chroniclebooks.com.* Used with permission of Chronicle Books LLC, San Francisco.

(Acknowledgments continue on page V71)

PART 1

UNIT 1 Fiction and Nonfiction

CONTENTS

UNIT 2 Short Stories

CONTENTS

CONTENTS

CONTENTS

UNIT 4 Poetry

MODEL SELECTIONS

"Oranges" by Gary Soto
"Ode to Family Photographs" by Gary Soto

© Pearson Education

CONTENTS

CONTENTS

UNIT 5 Drama

CONTENTS

UNIT 6 Folk Literature

MODEL SELECTIONS

"Black Cowboy, Wild Horses" by Julius Lester

Before You Read "The Tiger Who Would Be King" • "The Ant and the Dove" • "The Lion and the Bulls" • "A Crippled Boy"

"The Tiger Who Would Be King" by James Thurber

"The Ant and the Dove" by Leo Tolstoy

"The Lion and the Bulls" by Aesop

"A Crippled Boy" by My-Van Tran

Before You Read "Arachne" • Prologue *from* The Whale Rider

"Arachne" by Olivia E. Coolidge

Prologue *from* The Whale Rider by Witi Ihimaera

INFORMATIONAL TEXT

Satellites and Sea Lions

CONTENTS

As you read your hardcover student edition of *Prentice Hall Literature* use the **Reader's Notebook** to guide you in learning and practicing the skills presented. In addition, many selections in your student edition are presented here in an interactive format. The notes and instruction will guide you in applying reading and literary skills and in thinking about the selection. The examples on these pages show you how to use the notes as a companion when you read.

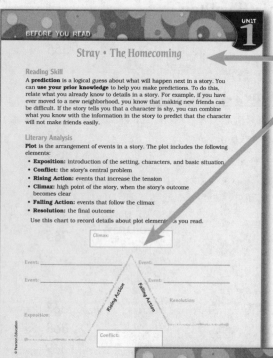

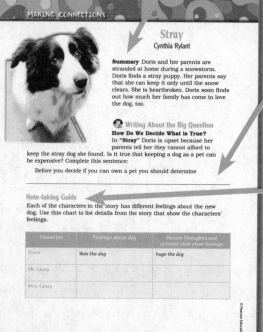

Get Ready to Learn

Use the *Before You Read* page to learn about the Reading Skill and Literary Analysis you will be studying.

To practice the skills, you can write directly in the graphic organizer as you read.

Get the Big Idea

A *Making Connections* page for every selection presents a selection summary, which lets you know what the selection is about before you read.

Make a Big Question Connection

Sentence starters help you think about the Big Question.

Be an Active Reader

A *Note-taking Guide* helps you organize the main ideas of the selection. Complete the guide as you read to track your understanding.

Doris was sitting alone in the living room, hugging a pillow and rocking back and forth on the edge of a chair. She was trying not to cry but she was not strong enough. Her face was wet and red, her eyes full of distress.

Mrs. Lacey looked into the room from the doorway.

"Mama," Doris said in a small voice. "Please."

Mrs. Lacey shook her head.

"You know we can't afford a dog, Doris. You try to act more grown-up about this."

Doris pressed her face into the pillow.

Outside, she heard the trunk of the car slam shut, one of the doors open and close, the old engine cough and choke and finally start up.

"Daddy," she whispered. "Please."

She heard the car travel down the road, and, though it was early afternoon, she could do nothing but go to her bed. She cried herself to sleep, and her dreams were full of searching and searching for things lost.

It was nearly night when she finally woke up. Lying there, like stone, still exhausted, she wondered if she would ever in her life have anything. She stared at the wall for a while.

But she started feeling hungry, and she knew she'd have to make herself get out of bed and eat some dinner. She wanted not to go into the kitchen, past the basement door. She wanted not to face her parents.

But she rose up heavily.

Her parents were sitting at the table, dinner over, drinking coffee. They looked at her when she came in, but she kept her head down. No one spoke.

Doris made herself a glass of powdered milk and drank it all down. Then she picked up a cold biscuit and started out of the room.

"You'd better feed that mutt before it dies of starvation," Mr. Lacey said.

Doris turned around.

"What?"

"I said, you'd better feed your dog. I figure it's looking for you."

Doris put her hand to her mouth.

"You didn't take her?" she asked.

TAKE NOTES

Stop to Reflect
What would ___
___

Literary Analysis 🔎
Read the first bracketed paragraph. What element of the **plot** occurs when Doris's father takes the dog to the car? Circle the correct answer.

a **exposition**, or introduction of the basic situation
b **rising action**, or an event that deepens the conflict
c **climax**, or the high point of the story
d **falling action**, or events that follow the climax

Reading Skill
Read the second bracketed paragraph. **Predict** what will happen when Doris next sees her parents.

___
___
___

© Pearson Education

Stray 19

AFTER YOU READ

Stray

1. **Analyze:** Why does Mr. Lacey change his mind about keeping the dog?

___
___

2. **Take a Position:** Doris does not make a strong case for keeping the dog. How could she have made a stronger case?

___
___

SUPPORT FOR WRITING AND EXTEND YOUR LEARNING

Writing: News Report
Write a **news report** about Doris's rescue of the dog and her family's decision to keep it. A news report gives information about a story. Use details from the story to write your article. Focus on these questions:

• **Who** found the dog? ___
• **When** was it found? ___
• **Where** was it found? ___
• **Why** did Doris want to keep the dog? ___
___
• **Why** did her father keep it? ___

Use your notes to write your article.

Listening and Speaking: Speech
The animal shelter in Doris's hometown needs to be improved. Prepare a **speech** about ways to make it better. You will need to list the problems as well as solutions for each problem. Answer these questions for ideas.

• What are the problems at the animal shelter?
___
___

• What is a way that you can get people involved in improving an animal shelter?
___
___

Use your notes to prepare your speech.

show how you **used prior knowledge**
nswer to each of these questions. One
Example: What will Doris do with the

ut the puppy?
the weather finally clears?

From Story	Predictions
e abandoned.	Doris will want to keep it.

climax, or high point, in the **plot** of the

___
___

Stray 21

© Pearson Education

© Pearson Education

Read the Text
Text set in a wider margin provides the author's actual words.

Text set in a narrow margin provides a summary of selection events or details.

Take Notes
Side-column questions accompany the selections that appear in the Reader's Notebooks. These questions are a built-in tutor to help you practice the skills and understand what you read.

Mark the Text
Use write-on lines to answer questions in the side column. You may also want to use the lines for your own notes.

When you see a pencil, you should underline, circle, or mark the text as indicated.

Check Your Understanding
Questions after every selection help you think about the selection. You can use the write-on lines and charts to answer the questions. Then, share your ideas in class discussions.

Go Beyond the Selection
This page provides step-by-step guidance for completing the Writing and Extend Your Learning activities presented in your student edition.

Selections and Skills Support

The pages in your *Reader's Notebook* go with the pages in the hardcover student edition. The pages in the *Reader's Notebook* allow you to participate in class instruction and take notes on the concepts and selections.

Before You Read

Build Skills Follow along in your *Reader's Notebook* as your teacher introduces the **Reading Skill** and **Literary Analysis** instruction. The graphic organizer is provided on this page so that you can take notes right in your *Reader's Notebook*.

Preview Use this page for the selection your teacher assigns.

- The **Summary** gives you an outline of the selection.
- Use the **Reading-Writing Connection** to understand the big idea of the selection and join in the class discussion about the ideas.
- Use the **Note-taking Guide** while you read the story. This will help you organize and remember information you will need to answer questions about the story later.

While You Read

Selection Text and Sidenotes You can read the full text of one selection in each pair in your *Reader's Notebook*.

- You can write in the *Reader's Notebook*. Underline important details to help you find them later.
- Use the **Take Notes** column to jot down your reactions, ideas, and answers to questions about the text. If your assigned selection is not the one that is included in the *Reader's Notebook*, use sticky notes to make your own **Take Notes** section in the side column as you read the selection in the hardcover student edition.

After You Read

Apply the Skills Use this page to answer questions about the selection right in your *Reader's Notebook*. For example, you can complete the graphic organizer that is in the hardcover student edition right on the page in your *Reader's Notebook*.

Support for Writing and Extend Your Learning Use this page to help you jot down notes and ideas as you prepare to do one or more of the projects assigned with the selection.

Other Features in the *Reader's Notebook* You will also find note-taking opportunities for these features:

- Learning About the Genre
- Support for the Model Selection
- Support for Reading Informational Materials

Greyling

Fiction is a form of writing that tells a story about made-up characters and events. Fiction always has the same features:

- people or animals called **characters**
- a group of events called the **plot**
- a time and place called **setting**
- someone called the **narrator** who tells the story
- a message or idea about life called a **theme**
- a **point of view**

There are two basic kinds of point of view.

First-person point of view means that the narrator is part of the story. This narrator uses the word *I* to tell what happened.

Third-person point of view means that the narrator is **not** part of the story. This narrator uses the words *he* and *she* to tell what happened to others.

The purpose of fiction is to entertain.

Examples of Fiction		
Type	Length	Characteristics
Novel	long, with many chapters	• a **plot** with many events • several **characters** who face challenges • often more than one **setting** • often more than one **theme**
Novella	shorter than a novel but longer than a short story	• a **plot**, often with fewer events than a novel • several **characters** who face challenges • often more than one **setting** • sometimes more than one **theme**
Short story	brief enough to be read in one sitting	• a **plot** with a few connected events • one or more **characters** • usually one main **setting** • usually one main **theme**

My Heart Is in the Highlands

Nonfiction is writing that gives information or states the author's opinion about a subject.

- Nonfiction is about real people, events, or ideas.
- Nonfiction gives information from the **author's perspective**, or the way the author sees things. The author's attitude or feelings about a topic is called **tone**.
- Nonfiction writers may have several reasons for writing, called the **writer's purpose**.

Nonfiction is written to do the following:

- explain
- persuade
- inform
- entertain

Examples of Nonfiction	
Examples	Characteristics
Biography	the story of a person's life told by someone else
Autobiography	the story of the author's life
Letter	written message from one person to another to share information, thoughts, or feelings
Journal or diary	written record of daily events and of the writer's thoughts and feelings
Essay	a brief written work that tells the author's opinion
Informational text	written work that gives information. Textbooks, applications, instructions, manuals are examples.
Speech	written work meant to be spoken to an audience

Greyling
Jane Yolen

Summary A fisherman and his wife cannot have a child. One day the fisherman brings home a seal pup. The seal turns into a child they name Greyling. They do not let Greyling go into the sea. One day Greyling has to save his father. He finds out what he really is when he jumps into the sea.

Note-taking Guide

Characters in fiction have wants and needs. Fill in this chart to record what the characters in this story want.

What the Wife Wants	What the Fisherman Wants	What Greyling Wants
She wants a child.		

Greyling
Jane Yolen

Once on a time when wishes were aplenty, a fisherman and his wife lived by the side of the sea. All that they ate came out of the sea. Their hut was covered with the finest mosses that kept them cool in the summer and warm in the winter. And there was nothing they needed or wanted except a child.

Each morning, when the moon touched down behind the water and the sun rose up behind the plains, the wife would say to the fisherman, "You have your boat and your nets and your lines. But I have no baby to hold in my arms." And again, in the evening, it was the same. She would weep and wail and rock the cradle that stood by the hearth. But year in and year out the cradle stayed empty.

Now the fisherman was also sad that they had no child. But he kept his sorrow to himself so that his wife would not know his grief and thus double her own. Indeed, he would leave the hut each morning with a breath of song and return each night with a whistle on his lips. His nets were full but his heart was empty, yet he never told his wife.

One sunny day, when the beach was a tan thread spun between sea and plain, the fisherman as usual went down to his boat. But this day he found a small grey seal stranded on the sandbar, crying for its own.

The fisherman looked up the beach and down. He looked in front of him and behind. And he looked to the town on the great grey cliffs that sheared off into the sea. But there were no other seals in sight.

So he shrugged his shoulders and took off his shirt. Then he dipped it into the water and wrapped the seal pup carefully in its folds.

"You have no father and you have no mother," he said. "And I have no child. So you shall come home with me."

And the fisherman did no fishing that day but brought the seal pup, wrapped in his shirt, straight home to his wife.

© Pearson Education

Vocabulary Development

grief (GREEF) *n.* deep sadness
sheared (SHEERD) *v.* cut off sharply

Activate Prior Knowledge

What do you know about seals? Write two facts about them.

1. _____

   _____

2. _____

   _____

Fiction

The **setting** in fiction is the location where the story takes place. What is the setting of this story? Underline the text that tells the location.

Fiction

Readers of fiction learn about **characters** by reading:
• what the characters say
• what the characters do
• what the characters think and feel

What do you learn about the fisherman's wife in the bracketed paragraph?

_____

_____

_____

_____

Fiction

Point of view shows who tells the story. A narrator who is inside the story uses **first-person point of view.** A **narrator** who is outside the story uses **third-person point of view.** What point of view does the writer use in this story?

_____

_____

How can you tell?

_____

_____

_____

_____

Stop to Reflect

Why do you think Greyling is sad in the bracketed paragraph? Explain.

_____

_____

_____

_____

_____

Reading Check ✎

What happens to the seal that the fisherman brings home? Underline the answer in the text.

When she saw him coming home early with no shirt on, the fisherman's wife ran out of the hut, fear riding in her heart. Then she looked wonderingly at the bundle which he held in his arms.

"It's nothing," he said, "but a seal pup I found stranded in the shallows and longing for its own. I thought we could give it love and care until it is old enough to seek its kin."

The fisherman's wife nodded and took the bundle. Then she uncovered the wrapping and gave a loud cry. "Nothing!" she said. "You call this nothing?"

The fisherman looked. Instead of a seal lying in the folds, there was a strange child with great grey eyes and silvery grey hair, smiling up at him.

The fisherman wrung his hands. "It is a <u>selchie</u>," he cried. "I have heard of them. They are men upon the land and seals in the sea. I thought it was but a tale."

"Then he shall remain a man upon the land," said the fisherman's wife, clasping the child in her arms, "for I shall never let him return to the sea."

"Never," agreed the fisherman, for he knew how his wife had wanted a child. And in his secret heart, he wanted one, too. Yet he felt, somehow, it was wrong.

"We shall call him Greyling," said the fisherman's wife, "for his eyes and hair are the color of a storm-coming sky. Greyling, though he has brought sunlight into our home."

And though they still lived by the side of the water in a hut covered with mosses that kept them warm in the winter and cool in the summer, the boy Greyling was never allowed into the sea.

He grew from a child to a lad. He grew from a lad to a young man. He gathered driftwood for his mother's hearth and searched the tide pools for shells for her mantel. He mended his father's nets and tended his father's boat. But though he often stood by the shore or high in the town on the great grey cliffs, looking and longing and grieving in his heart for what he did not really know, he never went into the sea.

Vocabulary Development

selchie (SEL kee) *n.* magical creature that looks like a seal when in water and a human when on land

Then one wind-wailing morning just fifteen years from the day that Greyling had been found, a great storm blew up suddenly in the North. It was such a storm as had never been seen before: the sky turned nearly black and even the fish had trouble swimming. The wind pushed huge waves onto the shore. The waters gobbled up the little hut on the beach. And Greyling and the fisherman's wife were forced to flee to the town high on the great grey cliffs. There they looked down at the roiling, boiling, sea. Far from shore they spied the fisherman's boat, its sails flapping like the wings of a wounded gull. And clinging to the broken mast was the fisherman himself, sinking deeper with every wave.

The fisherman's wife gave a terrible cry. "Will no one save him?" she called to the people of the town who had gathered on the edge of the cliff. "Will no one save my own dear husband who is all of life to me?"

But the townsmen looked away. There was no man there who dared risk his life in that sea, even to save a drowning soul.

"Will no one at all save him?" she cried out again.

"Let the boy go," said one old man, pointing at Greyling with his stick. "He looks strong enough."

But the fisherman's wife clasped Greyling in her arms and held his ears with her hands. She did not want him to go into the sea. She was afraid he would never return.

"Will no one save my own dear heart?" cried the fisherman's wife for a third and last time.

But shaking their heads, the people of the town edged to their houses and shut their doors and locked their windows and set their backs to the ocean and their faces to the fires that glowed in every hearth.

"I will save him, Mother," cried Greyling, "or die as I try."

And before she could tell him no, he broke from her grasp and dived from the top of the great cliffs, down, down, down into the tumbling sea.

"He will surely sink," whispered the women as they ran from their warm fires to watch.

"He will certainly drown," called the men as they took down their spyglasses from the shelves.

 TAKE NOTES

Fiction

The **plot** is the series of events in a story. What causes a sudden change in the **plot** of "Greyling"?

_____

_____

_____

Fiction

It is possible to learn about **characters** from very little information. What do you learn in the bracketed paragraph about the people of the town?

_____

_____

_____

_____

Reading Check

Why does the fisherman's wife not want Greyling to go into the sea? Underline the text that tells what she fears.

Fiction

Fiction is writing that tells about made-up characters and events. What happens when Greyling dives into the water that tells you the story is **fiction**?

_____

_____

_____

Fiction

Do the other characters in the town know that Greyling is a seal?

_____

How do you know?

_____

_____

_____

Stop to Reflect

What does the fisherman's wife realize after Greyling turns back into a seal?

_____

_____

_____

_____

_____

They gathered on the cliffs and watched the boy dive down into the sea.

As Greyling disappeared beneath the waves, little fingers of foam tore at his clothes. They snatched his shirt and his pants and his shoes and sent them bubbling away to the shore. And as Greyling went deeper beneath the waves, even his skin seemed to <u>slough</u> off till he swam, free at last, in the sleek grey coat of a great grey seal.

The selchie had returned to the sea.

But the people of the town did not see this. All they saw was the diving boy disappearing under the waves and then, farther out, a large seal swimming toward the boat that <u>wallowed</u> in the sea. The sleek grey seal, with no effort at all, eased the fisherman to the shore though the waves were wild and bright with foam. And then, with a final salute, it turned its back on the land and headed joyously out to sea.

The fisherman's wife hurried down to the sand. And behind her followed the people of the town. They searched up the beach and down, but they did not find the boy.

"A brave son," said the men when they found his shirt, for they thought he was certainly drowned.

"A very brave son," said the women when they found his shoes, for they thought him lost for sure.

"Has he really gone?" asked the fisherman's wife of her husband when at last they were alone.

"Yes, quite gone," the fisherman said to her. "Gone where his heart calls, gone to the great wide sea. And though my heart grieves at his leaving, it tells me this way is best."

The fisherman's wife sighed. And then she cried. But at last she agreed that, perhaps, it was best. "For he is both man and seal," she said. "And though we cared for him for a while, now he must care for himself." And she never cried again. So once more they lived alone by the side of the sea in a new little hut which was covered with mosses to keep them warm in the winter and cool in the summer.

Vocabulary Development

slough (SLUF) *v.* be cast off; be gotten rid of

wallowed (WAHL ohd) *v.* rolled and tilted

Yet, once a year, a great grey seal is seen at night near the fisherman's home. And the people in town talk of it, and wonder. But seals do come to the shore and men do go to the sea; and so the townfolk do not dwell upon it very long.

But it is no ordinary seal. It is Greyling himself come home—come to tell his parents tales of the lands that lie far beyond the waters, and to sing them songs of the wonders that lie far beneath the sea.

Reader's Response: Do you think that Greyling is better off living in the sea as a seal? Why?

_____

_____

_____

TAKE NOTES

Fiction

The **theme** is a message about life. The couple goes back to their lives after Greyling goes back to the sea. How does this show the theme of the story?

_____

_____

_____

_____

Fiction

What does the **narrator** know about the seal that the townspeople do not know?

_____

_____

_____

_____

Reading Check ✏️

Why does Greyling return every year? Circle the answer in the text.

My Heart Is in the Highlands
Jane Yolen

Summary The author describes her first visit to Scotland. The stone houses amaze her. She sees new homes built from the stones of very old homes and castles. She thinks that this is like writing. Memories from her past become part of everything new that she writes.

Note-taking Guide

Fill in this chart to record how the author uses memories to write.

What writers do with "stones from the past"	What the writer is "made up of"	What the writer does with "story stones"
reshape and rebuild with them		

My Heart Is in the Highlands
Jane Yolen

I first set foot on Scottish soil in the mid '80s, when my husband and I—between conferences (science fiction for me, computer science for him)—took a trip north from Brighton.

We drove, being used to long road trips and camping vacations with our children, and were predictably stunned by Edinburgh and its looming castle on the hill. None of America, and blessed little of Brighton, had prepared us for such a sight.

But it was when we began our ascent through the Highlands that it became clear to us that here was the home of the heart. . . .

I love the white-washed stone cottages here in Scotland, small cozy homes that seem to have grown rough hewn right up from the land. I love the gray stone mansions and the tall stone tower houses, too.

If you search the histories of any individual town here, or a particular street, you will find that these homes and walled gardens have often been built upon older, vanished buildings. Where a kirk or a tollbooth or a great hall once stood, now a townsman's seven-room house with mod cons squats.[1]

But it is not just the site that has been <u>cannibalized</u>. The very stones have been reused. So in Scotland history lies upon history. As a wonderful little book on the royal burgh of Falkland in the Kingdom of Fife[2] puts it: "Absorbing stones from an old building into the fabric of the later one is . . . a way of holding on to the past."

After the stones have been pulled together and balanced and mortared into place, the walls are harled, or <u>roughcast</u> so as to protect the soft stone and mortar from the winter winds and heavy gales.

Vocabulary Development

cannibalized (KAN uh buhl yzd) *v.* used parts of one thing to build up another

roughcast (RUF kast) *v.* covered with a coarse stucco

---

1. **kirk** (KERK) **... mod cons squats** Where churches or other structures were, now there are houses with modern conveniences.

2. **royal burgh** (BERG) **... Fife** Falkland, once the home of the Earls of Fife, is a Scottish town created by royal charter.

Activate Prior Knowledge

Have you ever written about something from your memory? If so, what did you write about?

_____

_____

_____

_____

Nonfiction

The **author's perspective** is the point of view of the author. How do you know that this piece of nonfiction is told from the author's perspective?

_____

_____

_____

Nonfiction

This piece of writing was first a **speech**. Yolen talked about this information to an audience.

Autobiographies are about the author's life. Why might the reader think that this piece of writing is an autobiography?

_____

_____

_____

Nonfiction

A **writer's purpose** can be to explain, persuade, inform, or entertain. What might be the writer's purpose here? Explain your answer.

_____

_____

_____

_____

_____

Stop to Reflect

What does the writer mean by using her "own private history" to write fiction?

_____

_____

_____

_____

_____

Reading Check

What does the writer warn the reader about? Underline the answer in the text.

Stones, harling, a way of holding on to the past. It's all a perfect metaphor for writing a book, especially books set here in Scotland.

Writers use stones from the past, reshaping and rebuilding with them. And then they protect the soft memories with a harling of technique.

How can it be otherwise? All fiction uses memory. Or re-memory for those of us whose grasp of the past is exceeded by the need to embellish, decorate, deepen, widen and otherwise change what was actual.

As a writer, I am made up of the little building blocks of my own private history, and what I know of the world that has already been rebuilt upon. My infancy told to me so often by my parents in delicious anecdote, my childhood captured in photos and catchlines, my adolescence in letters and journals, my young adulthood in poetry and prose.

I simply take those story-stones and use them again in any new building. Or I thieve from my closest friends and relatives, from my husband's life and my children. They don't just endure such thievery—they expect it. A warning—get to know me well and you will most certainly find yourself enshrined in one of my books.

But even those closest to me sometimes have trouble identifying themselves when next they meet themselves in fiction. For they will have been metamorphosed[3] into a toad or a selchie or a wind blowing in over the wall. Even I don't always know whose bones lie beneath a particular character's skin.

That's because fiction (to mix this metaphor hopelessly) is a magic mirror that gives back a changed self.

Reader's Response: Why do you think the author takes information from the people around her for her writing?

_____

_____

Vocabulary Development

enshrined (in SHRYND) *v.* put in a special place so that people can see

---

3. **metamorphosed** (met uh MAWR fohzd) *v.* changed in form or shape.

Fiction and Nonfiction

1. **Evaluate:** Should the fisherman and his wife have kept Greyling from the sea? Why or why not?

_____

_____

2. **Compare:** How does the author in "My Heart Is in the Highlands" compare writing a book to reusing old stones?

_____

_____

_____

3. **Fiction:** Fill in this chart with details that show that "Greyling" is **fiction**.

Fictional Details	Importance to the Story

4. **Nonfiction:** What do you think is the **purpose** of "My Heart Is in the Highlands"? Explain.

_____

_____

_____

Bulletin Board Display

- Other fiction by Jane Yolen includes *Dream Weaver, The Faery Flag, Here There Be Dragons,* and *Mightier than the Sword.* Her nonfiction work includes *A Letter From Phoenix Farm. A Letter From Phoenix Farm* is about the author's writing life at the farm. It is also an autobiography.

- Search the Internet for words and phrases such as "Jane Yolen family" or "Jane Yolen education." Search the author's Web site for information about her writing: www.janeyolen.com.

   What I learned: _____

   _____

   _____

   _____

   _____

- Search the library and the Internet for photographs of the author. You may even find photographs or drawings of her subjects. You can also display the book jackets or photocopies of the book jackets.

- Search through a few of Jane Yolen's fiction and nonfiction books to find the ones that you like best. Write a summary of each book that includes the most important information.

- Watch the video interview with Jane Yolen, and review your source material. Use this information to answer the following questions.

1. What did you learn about Yolen's life?

   _____

   _____

2. What did you learn about why Yolen writes?

   _____

   _____

Stray • The Homecoming

Reading Skill

A **prediction** is a logical guess about what will happen next in a story. You can **use your prior knowledge** to help you make predictions. To do this, relate what you already know to details in a story. For example, if you have ever moved to a new neighborhood, you know that making new friends can be difficult. If the story tells you that a character is shy, you can combine what you know with the information in the story to predict that the character will not make friends easily.

Literary Analysis

Plot is the arrangement of events in a story. The plot includes the following elements:

- **Exposition:** introduction of the setting, characters, and basic situation
- **Conflict:** the story's central problem
- **Rising Action:** events that increase the tension
- **Climax:** high point of the story, when the story's outcome becomes clear
- **Falling Action:** events that follow the climax
- **Resolution:** the final outcome

Use this chart to record details about plot elements as you read.

Climax:

Event: _____   Event: _____

Event: _____   Event: _____

Rising Action   Falling Action

Resolution:

Exposition:

Conflict:

Stray
Cynthia Rylant

Summary Doris and her parents are stranded at home during a snowstorm. Doris finds a stray puppy. Her parents say that she can keep it only until the snow clears. She is heartbroken. Doris soon finds out how much her family has come to love the dog, too.

Writing About the Big Question
How Do We Decide What is True?
In **"Stray"** Doris is upset because her parents tell her they cannot afford to keep the stray dog she found. Is it true that keeping a dog as a pet can be expensive? Complete this sentence:

Before you decide if you can own a pet you should determine

_____.

Note-taking Guide
Each of the characters in the story has different feelings about the new dog. Use this chart to list details from the story that show the characters' feelings.

Character	Feelings about dog	Details (thoughts and actions) that show feelings
Doris	likes the dog	hugs the dog
Mr. Lacey		
Mrs. Lacey		

Stray
Cynthia Rylant

In January, a puppy wandered onto the property of Mr. Amos Lacey and his wife, Mamie, and their daughter, Doris. Icicles hung three feet or more from the eaves of houses, snowdrifts swallowed up automobiles and the birds were so fluffed up they looked comic.

The puppy had been abandoned, and it made its way down the road toward the Laceys' small house, its ears tucked, its tail between its legs, shivering.

Doris, whose school had been called off because of the snow, was out shoveling the cinderblock front steps when she spotted the pup on the road. She set down the shovel.

"Hey! Come on!" she called.

The puppy stopped in the road, wagging its tail timidly, trembling with shyness and cold.

Doris trudged[1] through the yard, went up the shoveled drive and met the dog.

"Come on, Pooch."

"Where did *that* come from?" Mrs. Lacey asked as soon as Doris put the dog down in the kitchen.

Mr. Lacey was at the table, cleaning his fingernails with his pocketknife. The snow was keeping him home from his job at the warehouse.

"I don't know where it came from," he said mildly, "but I know for sure where it's going."

Doris hugged the puppy hard against her. She said nothing.

Because the roads would be too bad for travel for many days, Mr. Lacey couldn't get out to take the puppy to the pound[2] in the city right away. He agreed to let it sleep in the basement while Mrs. Lacey grudgingly let Doris feed it table scraps. The woman was sensitive about throwing out food.

© Pearson Education

Activate Prior Knowledge

Think about people you know who have adopted animals. Where did they get the animals?

_____

_____

What do you know about animal shelters?

_____

_____

_____

Literary Analysis

Exposition introduces the setting, characters, and basic situation of a story. Circle the exposition paragraph on this page. What are the names of the main characters in the story?

_____

_____

_____

Reading Check

What is Doris doing when she sees the puppy? Underline the text that tells you.

Vocabulary Development

timidly (TIM id lee) *adv.* in a way that shows fear or shyness

grudgingly (GRUJ ing lee) *adv.* in an unwilling or resentful way

1. **trudged** (TRUJD) *v.* walked as if tired or with effort.
2. **pound** (POWND) *n.* animal shelter.

Reading Skill

You can make **predictions**, or guesses, by **using prior knowledge**, or what you already know. Circle the kind of dog Doris thinks the puppy might be. List what you know about how much room and food this dog might need.

_____

_____

Do you predict that Mr. Lacey will let Doris keep the dog? Why or why not?

_____

_____

_____

Literary Analysis

Part of a story's **plot** is the **conflict** or problem that characters face. What is the conflict in the story?

_____

_____

_____

Reading Check

Why doesn't Doris give the dog a name? Underline the text that tells you.

By the looks of it, Doris figured the puppy was about six months old, and on its way to being a big dog. She thought it might have some shepherd in it.

Four days passed and the puppy did not complain. It never cried in the night or howled at the wind. It didn't tear up everything in the basement. It wouldn't even follow Doris up the basement steps unless it was invited.

It was a good dog.

Several times Doris had opened the door in the kitchen that led to the basement and the puppy had been there, all stretched out, on the top step. Doris knew it had wanted some company and that it had lain against the door, listening to the talk in the kitchen, smelling the food, being a part of things. It always wagged its tail, eyes all sleepy, when she found it there.

Even after a week had gone by, Doris didn't name the dog. She knew her parents wouldn't let her keep it, that her father made so little money any pets were out of the question, and that the pup would definitely go to the pound when the weather cleared.

Still, she tried talking to them about the dog at dinner one night.

"She's a good dog, isn't she?" Doris said, hoping one of them would agree with her.

Her parents glanced at each other and went on eating.

"She's not much trouble," Doris added. "I like her." She smiled at them, but they continued to <u>ignore</u> her.

"I figure she's real smart," Doris said to her mother. "I could teach her things."

Mrs. Lacey just shook her head and stuffed a forkful of sweet potato in her mouth. Doris fell silent, praying the weather would never clear.

But on Saturday, nine days after the dog had arrived, the sun was shining and the roads were plowed. Mr. Lacey opened up the trunk of his car and came into the house.

Vocabulary Development

ignore (ig NAWR) *v.* pay no attention to

Doris was sitting alone in the living room, hugging a pillow and rocking back and forth on the edge of a chair. She was trying not to cry but she was not strong enough. Her face was wet and red, her eyes full of distress.

Mrs. Lacey looked into the room from the doorway.

"Mama," Doris said in a small voice. "Please."

Mrs. Lacey shook her head.

"You know we can't afford a dog, Doris. You try to act more grown-up about this."

Doris pressed her face into the pillow.

Outside, she heard the trunk of the car slam shut, one of the doors open and close, the old engine cough and choke and finally start up.

"Daddy," she whispered. "Please."

She heard the car travel down the road, and, though it was early afternoon, she could do nothing but go to her bed. She cried herself to sleep, and her dreams were full of searching and searching for things lost.

It was nearly night when she finally woke up. Lying there, like stone, still exhausted, she wondered if she would ever in her life have anything. She stared at the wall for a while.

But she started feeling hungry, and she knew she'd have to make herself get out of bed and eat some dinner. She wanted not to go into the kitchen, past the basement door. She wanted not to face her parents.

But she rose up heavily.

Her parents were sitting at the table, dinner over, drinking coffee. They looked at her when she came in, but she kept her head down. No one spoke.

Doris made herself a glass of powdered milk and drank it all down. Then she picked up a cold biscuit and started out of the room.

"You'd better feed that mutt before it dies of starvation," Mr. Lacey said.

Doris turned around.

"What?"

"I said, you'd better feed your dog. I figure it's looking for you."

Doris put her hand to her mouth.

"You didn't take her?" she asked.

© Pearson Education

Stop to Reflect

What would you do if you found a stray dog?

_____

_____

Literary Analysis

Read the first bracketed paragraph. What element of the **plot** occurs when Doris's father takes the dog to the car? Circle the correct answer.

a **exposition**, or introduction of the basic situation

b **rising action**, or an event that deepens the conflict

c **climax**, or the high point of the story

d **falling action**, or events that follow the climax

Reading Skill

Read the second bracketed paragraph. **Predict** what will happen when Doris next sees her parents.

_____

_____

_____

_____

Literary Analysis 🔍

A **resolution** is the part of the **plot** that comes after the **climax** of a story. What happens to the puppy?

_____

_____

What is surprising about the **resolution** of the **conflict** between Doris and her parents?

_____

_____

_____

Reading Skill 📖

What **prior knowledge** do you have about how Mrs. Lacey feels about the dog?

_____

_____

_____

Read the underlined sentence. Do you **predict** that Mrs. Lacey will be upset with her husband for keeping the dog? Why or why not?

_____

_____

_____

_____

"Oh, I took her all right," her father answered. "Worst looking place I've ever seen. Ten dogs to a cage. Smell was enough to knock you down. And they give an animal six days to live. Then they kill it with some kind of a shot."

Doris stared at her father.

"I wouldn't leave an *ant* in that place," he said. "So I brought the dog back."

Mrs. Lacey was smiling at him and shaking her head as if she would never, ever, understand him.

Mr. Lacey sipped his coffee.

"Well," he said, "are you going to feed it or not?"

> **Reader's Response:** Do you think Doris's father will regret his decision to keep the dog? Explain your answer.
>
> _____
>
> _____
>
> _____

Stray

1. **Analyze:** Why does Mr. Lacey change his mind about keeping the dog?

   _____

   _____

2. **Take a Position:** Doris does not make a strong case for keeping the dog. How could she have made a stronger case?

   _____

   _____

   _____

3. **Reading Skill:** Use this chart to show how you **used prior knowledge** and story clues to **predict** the answer to each of these questions. One question has been done for you. Example: What will Doris do with the puppy she finds?

   a) What will her parents say about the puppy?
   b) What will her father do when the weather finally clears?

Prior Knowledge	Details From Story	Predictions
Puppies are cute.	The puppy is abandoned.	Doris will want to keep it.
a)		
b)		

4. **Literary Analysis:** What is the **climax**, or high point, in the **plot** of the story? Explain.

   _____

   _____

Writing: News Report

Write a **news report** about Doris's rescue of the dog and her family's decision to keep it. A news report gives information about a story. Use details from the story to write your article. Focus on these questions:

- **Who** found the dog?_____

- **When** was it found?_____

- **Where** was it found?_____

- **Why** did Doris want to keep the dog?_____

  _____

- **Why** did her father keep it?_____

  _____

Use your notes to write your article.

Listening and Speaking: Speech

The animal shelter in Doris's hometown needs to be improved. Prepare a **speech** about ways to make it better. You will need to list the problems as well as solutions for each problem. Answer these questions for ideas.

- What are the problems at the animal shelter?

  _____

  _____

- What is a way that you can get people involved in improving an animal shelter?

  _____

  _____

Use your notes to prepare your speech.

The Homecoming
Laurence Yep

Summary A woodcutter gets sidetracked and forgets his work. He promises his wife he will cut wood. She reminds him not to talk to anyone. He finds two chess players in the woods. The time he spends with the chess players results in a surprise.

Writing About the Big Question

How Do We Decide What is True? "The Homecoming" is a fictional story, but it contains a "truth" or a lesson about life. Complete this sentence:

Even if a story is fiction, I can learn lessons by _____.

Note-taking Guide

Fill in this chart with details about the woodcutter.

Why the woodcutter goes to the woods	What is his wife's advice?	What does the woodcutter do?	What the woodcutter finds when he returns to his village
He wants to cut tall oaks.			

The Homecoming

1. **Interpret:** What do the villagers mean by saying that the woodcutter "knew a little of everything and most of nothing"?

_____

_____

2. **Analyze:** What lesson is expressed in this story?

_____

_____

3. **Reading Skill:** Fill in this chart to show how you made a **prediction** to answer each question. The first one has been done for you. Example: What will the woodcutter do in the forest?

   a) What will the woodcutter do when he sees the two men playing chess?

   b) What will happen when the woodcutter leaves the forest?

Prior Knowledge	Details From Story	Prediction
Busybodies like talking to people.	The woodcutter is a busybody.	The woodcutter will stop to talk.
a)		
b)		

4. **Literary Analysis:** What is the **conflict** in the **plot** of this story?

_____

_____

Writing: News Report

Prepare a **news report** about the woodcutter's return. Often witnesses, or people who have seen an event, are interviewed for news reports. What these people say is quoted in the report. Fill in this chart to help you record what the witnesses saw and heard. Then, write a quote from each witness in the last column.

People who saw the woodcutter	What they saw the woodcutter do	What they heard the woodcutter say	Quote
Two children			
A woman			
The schoolteacher			

Listening and Speaking: Speech

Imagine that you are the woodcutter. Prepare a **speech** about why you like being a busybody. Use this chart to describe busybodies.

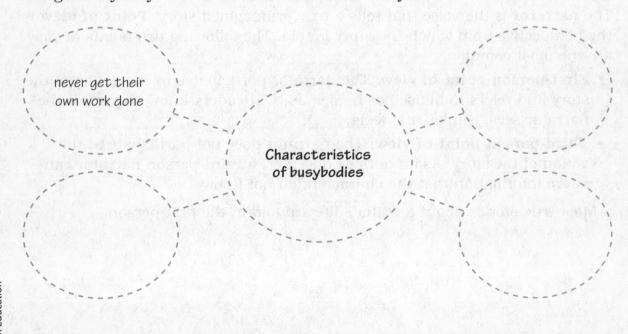

never get their own work done

Characteristics of busybodies

The Drive-In Movies • The Market Square Dog

Reading Skill

Predictions are reasonable guesses about what is most likely to happen next. Base your predictions on details in the literature and on your own experience. Use this diagram to keep track of your predictions. Then, **read ahead to check your prediction**.

Clues From the Story	What I Know

Prediction

Literary Analysis

The **narrator** is the voice that tells a true or imagined story. **Point of view** is the perspective from which the story is told. The following two points of view are the most common:

- **First-person point of view:** The narrator participates in the action of the story and refers to himself or herself as "I." Readers know only what the narrator sees, thinks, and feels.

- **Third-person point of view:** The narrator does not participate in the action of the story. As an outside observer, a third-person narrator can share information that the characters do not know.

Most true stories about a writer's life are told in the first person.

The Drive-In Movies
Gary Soto

Summary Gary Soto remembers a Saturday from his childhood. He and his brother and sister want to go to the drive-in movies. They know that their mother is more likely to take them if she is happy. Soto does his chores without being asked. All of his hard work catches up with him at the movies that night.

 Writing About the Big Question

How Do We Decide What is True? In "The Drive-In Movies," a boy tries to be "extra good" in order to please his mother and win a reward. Complete this sentence:

A person's opinion about a reward will affect _____.

Note-taking Guide

Use this chart to record the main actions of each character in the story.

Characters	Actions
the author	
his brother	helps wax the car
his sister	
his mom	

Activate Prior Knowledge

Suppose that you want a friend or family member to take you to the movies. List one way that you might persuade him or her.

_____

_____

Literary Analysis

The **narrator** is the voice that tells the story. **Point of view** is the angle or perspective from which the story is told. Read the bracketed passage. What clues indicate that the narrator is telling the story from **first-person point of view?**

_____

_____

Reading Skill

You can make **predictions**, or guesses, about the end of a story. Do you predict that Soto's plan will work? Why or why not?

_____

_____

Reading Check

Why does Soto leave cereal out for his mother? Circle the answer in the text.

The Drive-In Movies
Gary Soto

For our family, moviegoing was rare. But if our mom, tired from a week of candling eggs,[1] woke up happy on a Saturday morning, there was a chance we might later scramble to our blue Chevy and beat nightfall to the Starlight Drive-In. My brother and sister knew this. I knew this. So on Saturday we tried to be good. We sat in the cool shadows of the TV with the volume low and watched cartoons, a prelude of what was to come.

One Saturday I decided to be extra good. When she came out of the bedroom tying her robe, she yawned a hat-sized yawn and blinked red eyes at the weak brew of coffee I had fixed for her. I made her toast with strawberry jam spread to all the corners and set the three boxes of cereal in front of her. If she didn't care to eat cereal, she could always look at the back of the boxes as she drank her coffee.

I went outside. The lawn was tall but too wet with dew to mow. I picked up a trowel[2] and began to weed the flower bed. The weeds were really bermuda grass, long stringers that ran finger-deep in the ground. I got to work quickly and in no time crescents of earth began rising under my fingernails. I was sweaty hot. My knees hurt from kneeling, and my brain was dull from making the trowel go up and down, dribbling crumbs of earth. I dug for half an hour, then stopped to play with the neighbor's dog and pop ticks from his poor snout.

I then mowed the lawn, which was still beaded with dew and noisy with bees hovering over clover. This job was less dull because as I pushed the mower over the shaggy lawn, I could see it looked tidier. My brother and sister watched from the window. Their faces were fat with cereal, a third

Vocabulary Development

prelude (PRAY lood) _n._ introduction to a main event

1. **candling eggs** examining uncooked eggs for freshness by placing them in front of a burning candle.
2. **trowel** (TROW uhl) _n._ a small hand tool used by gardeners to weed or dig.

helping. I made a face at them when they asked how come I was working. Rick pointed to part of the lawn. "You missed some over there." I ignored him and kept my attention on the windmill of grassy blades.

While I was emptying the catcher, a bee stung the bottom of my foot. I danced on one leg and was ready to cry when Mother showed her face at the window. I sat down on the grass and examined my foot: the stinger was pulsating. I pulled it out quickly, ran water over the sting and packed it with mud, Grandmother's remedy.

Hobbling, I returned to the flower bed where I pulled more stringers and again played with the dog. More ticks had migrated to his snout. I swept the front steps, took out the garbage, cleaned the lint filter to the dryer (easy), plucked hair from the industrial wash basin in the garage (also easy), hosed off the patio, smashed three snails sucking paint from the house (disgusting but fun), tied a bundle of newspapers, put away toys, and, finally, seeing that almost everything was done and the sun was not too high, started waxing the car.

My brother joined me with an old gym sock, and our sister watched us while sucking on a cherry Kool-Aid ice cube. The liquid wax drooled onto the sock, and we began to swirl the white slop on the chrome. My arms ached from buffing, which though less boring than weeding, was harder. But the beauty was <u>evident</u>. The shine, hurting our eyes and glinting like an armful of dimes, brought Mother out. <u>She looked around the yard and said, "Pretty good." She winced</u> at the grille and returned inside the house.

We began to wax the paint. My brother applied the liquid and I followed him rubbing hard in wide circles as we moved around the car. I began to hurry because my arms were hurting and my stung foot looked like a water balloon. We were working around the trunk when Rick pounded on the bottle of wax.

 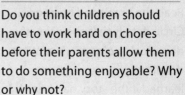

Stop to Reflect

Do you think children should have to work hard on chores before their parents allow them to do something enjoyable? Why or why not?

_____

_____

_____

Literary Analysis

Read the bracketed passage. How would it be different if it were written from the **point of view** of the narrator's brother?

_____

_____

_____

Reading Skill

What chores does the narrator do? Underline at least two chores.

Vocabulary Development

evident (EV uh duhnt) *adj.* easy to see; very clear

winced (winst) *v.* drew back slightly, as if in pain; cringed

© Pearson Education

He squeezed the bottle and it sneezed a few more white drops.

We looked at each other. "There's some on the sock," I said. "Let's keep going."

We polished and buffed, sweat weeping on our brows. We got scared when we noticed that the gym sock was now blue. The paint was coming off. Our sister fit ice cubes into our mouths and we worked harder, more intently, more dedicated to the car and our mother. We ran the sock over the chrome, trying to pick up extra wax. But there wasn't enough to cover the entire car. Only half got waxed, but we thought it was better than nothing and went inside for lunch. After lunch, we returned outside with tasty sandwiches.

Rick and I nearly jumped. The waxed side of the car was foggy white. We took a rag and began to polish vigorously and nearly in tears, but the fog wouldn't come off. I blamed Rick and he blamed me. Debra stood at the window, not wanting to get involved. Now, not only would we not go to the movies, but Mom would surely snap a branch from the plum tree and chase us around the yard.

Mom came out and looked at us with hands on her aproned hips. Finally, she said, "You boys worked so hard." She turned on the garden hose and washed the car. That night we did go to the drive-in. The first feature was about nothing, and the second feature, starring Jerry Lewis, was *Cinderfella*. I tried to stay awake. I kept a wad of homemade popcorn in my cheek and laughed when Jerry Lewis fit golf tees in his nose. I rubbed my watery eyes. I laughed and looked at my mom. I promised myself I would remember that scene with the golf tees and promised myself not to work so hard the coming Saturday. Twenty minutes into the movie, I fell asleep with one hand in the popcorn.

The Drive-In Movies

1. **Draw Conclusions:** Why do you think Soto's mother does not get angry with the children for making a mess with the car wax?

_____

_____

_____

2. **Infer:** Do you think Soto still has fond memories of that day and night? Explain.

_____

_____

_____

3. **Reading Skill:** As you read, did you change any **predictions** that you made about the story? Explain.

_____

_____

_____

4. **Literary Analysis:** Use this chart to note how Soto's **point of view** affects what the readers know about some events in the story.

Event	Details Provided by Narrator
The narrator is stung by a bee.	The sting hurts.

Writing: Autobiographical Narrative

Write an **autobiographical narrative** that describes an event, a person, or a certain time in your life. Answer each question in this chart. Then, list details about the event, the place, and the people. Use your notes to help you write your narrative.

Questions to Ask Yourself	Answers	More Details
Where was the event?		
What happened first at the event?		
What happened last at the event?		
Who was at the event?		

Listening and Speaking: Dialogue

Prepare a **dialogue** between you are your partner. Use the space below to write details that you and your partner want to include in your conversation.

_____

_____

_____

_____

_____

_____

_____

_____

_____

The Market Square Dog
James Herriot

Summary A veterinarian, or animal doctor, sees a dog begging for food in a market square. Later, the dog is injured in an accident. A policeman brings the injured dog to the veterinarian. They become worried when no one comes to claim the dog.

 Writing About the Big Question

How Do We Decide What is True?

In "The Market Square Dog," a stray dog is available for adoption, but people pass him by. The veterinarian believes that he is not wanted because he's a mixed breed, and people are looking for a "more elegant" dog. What do you think? Complete this sentence:

To be a truly great pet, a dog needs to be _____.

Note-taking Guide

Answer the questions in this chart. Record details from the story.

Who is the narrator?	The narrator is a veterinarian.
Where does he first see the dog?	
What does the policeman do when he finds the hurt dog?	
How does the veterinarian help the dog?	
Who adopts the dog? Why?	

The Market Square Dog

1. **Draw Conclusions:** Why do you think the narrator visits the dog at the police station?

   _____

   _____

2. **Interpret:** At the beginning of the story, why does the dog run away from people who try to pet him?

   _____

   _____

3. **Reading Skill:** What did you **predict** would happen to the dog?

   _____

   _____

4. **Literary Analysis:** Use this chart to note how Herriot's **point of view** affects what readers know about some events in the story.

Event	Details Provided by Narrator
The dog is begging for food in front of a stall.	The narrator thinks that dogs look very appealing when they sit up.

Writing: Autobiographical Narrative

Write an **autobiographical narrative** about an animal that you know. Use this chart to help you. First, answer each question. Then, list other details about the event. Use your notes to help you write your narrative.

Questions to Ask Yourself	Answers	More Details
Where was the event?		
What happened first at the event?		
What happened last at the event?		
Who was at the event?		

Listening and Speaking: Conversation

With a partner, act out a **conversation** between the narrator and his wife. The narrator tells his wife that the police officer has adopted the dog. Use the chart to describe how the narrator and his wife will discuss events.

Event	How the narrator describes the event	How the wife responds to narrator's description
The police officer tells the narrator that the dog has been arrested.		
The narrator finds out that the police officer has adopted the dog.		

Web Sites

About Web Sites

Web sites are pages of information you find on the Internet. Each Web site has an address called a Universal Resource Locator (URL).

- **.edu**—The site belongs to an educational institution.
- **.gov**—The site belongs to a government office.
- **.org**—The site belongs to a nonprofit organization.
- **.com**—The site belongs to a commercial organization.

A Web site can have many Web pages. You can move from one page to another by clicking your mouse on a *link*.

Not all Web sites give you good information. Always make sure that your information comes from sources you can trust.

Reading Skill

Web sites are important sources for research. They have special features that help you move quickly around the site. When you find information on the Internet, begin by **analyzing the structural features** of the resources you find. This chart shows some of the features on a Web site.

Web Site Features	
Universal Resource Locator (URL)	The Web site's address. Its ending give information about who maintains the site.
Home Page	The Web site's opening page. It often provides an introduction to the topic and buttons, or links, that lead to more pages.
Link	A connection to another spot on the same Web page or to a different Web page or Web site. A link can be underlined or highlighted text, an image, or a photograph. Links are what make the Web a "web."
Icon	An image or small drawing that may appear by itself or with text. Icons are often links as well.
Graphics	Pictures, maps, tables, and other graphic sources often featured on a Web site. These graphics often provide information, but they may also be links to other Web pages.

This is a recent home page for Animaland®, a Web site published by the American Society for the Prevention of Cruelty to Animals (ASPCA). It is a starting point that will lead you to other pages within the site.

Web Site

Features:

- home page with links to other pages
- informative text
- photos or other images
- may include audio or video content

http://www.aspca.org/site/PageServer?pagename=kids_home

ANIMALAND

Each of these buttons leads to more information on a topic. By clicking on the button, you will open up a new page of the Web site.

| Nose for News | Pet Care | Ask Azula | Animal Careers | Animal ABCs | Real Issues | Cartoons | Activities | Pet of the Week | Home |

SPOTLIGHT ON...

THINK YOU'VE GOT HORSE POWER?
Do you know about equines or are you just horsing around? Saddle up and take our quiz!

"MOO"VE OVER!
Meet the 1,500-pound manatee, also known as a sea cow.

SUMMER'S HERE!
How to keep your pets cool when it's hot.

Another way to navigate a Web site is to click on an underlined item, or link. Like buttons, links take you to specific types of information.

ASK AZULA

Why do some frogs have teeth?
— *Tenille*

I'd be *hoppy* to answer your question, Tenille!

Learn More

PET OF THE WEEK

Meet Caya
Submitted by Jaime, age 11

Favorite Trick: "Playing with her kitty fishing pole with a fuzzy mouse on the hook"

Favorite Treat: Tuna

Why I Love Caya: "She's silly and spunky, just like her owner!"

Send in your pet's photo!

PET CARE CARTOON
Learn why it's important to keep your cat indoors!

PLAY ▶

http://www.aspca.org/site/PageServer?pagename=kids_home

ANIMALAND

This page appears when you click on the button labeled "Pet Care" and then click on "Dog Care."

These buttons are the same as the ones found on the Web site's home page. At any time, you can click on a button to go to a different Web page.

Nose for News | Pet Care | Ask Azula | Animal Careers | Animal ABCs | Real Issues | Cartoons | Activities | Pet of the Week | Home

PET CARE

Dog Care: The 411

Scientific name: *Canis familiaris*

Size: XS, S, M, L, XL!! Dogs range in size from tiny four-pound tea cup poodles to Irish wolfhounds, the tallest dogs at almost three feet high.

Lifespan: As a rule, smaller dogs tend to live longer than larger ones. A compact Chihuahua can live to be 16, while giant breeds like bull mastiffs usually live to be about eight years old. And somewhere in the middle, the average, All-American mixed-breed pooch has a lifespan of about 12 to 14 years.

Colors/varieties: There are more than 400 different breeds of dogs —spotted Dalmatians, shiny black Labrador retrievers, brindle-coated boxers...to name just a few! But the most popular pooches of all are non-pedigree—that includes shaggy dogs, dogs with hairy ears, dogs with all-white socks, dogs with fluffy tails, and everything in between. You may have heard people call these dogs "mutts," but we prefer *one-of-a-kind*!

Parents and teachers, click here [link] for more dog care information to share with your students and children.

LEARN MORE
- The 411
- Chow Time!
- Home Sweet Home
- Fun & Games

Dog Care
Cat Care
Bird Care
Rabbit Care
Fish Care
Gerbil Care
Hamster Care
Guinea Pig Care
Mouse Care
Rat Care

This is a list of links that connect to the different animals that are discussed in the Web site's "Pet Care" guide.

THE BIG ? **How do we decide what is true?**
(a) What does the Web site's URL suggest about its reliability? **(b)** What other sources might you use to check the facts presented by this Web site? **(c)** How does checking facts help you to test an online Web site's reliability?

Thinking About the Web Site

1. Why should you analyze sources of information on the Internet?

_____

2. Why would the ASPCA (an organization that gives away homeless pets) Web site be a more reliable source of information on pet care than the Web site for a pet store?

_____

Reading Skill

3. What is the URL of the Website?

_____

4. Go to the home page for www.aspca.org. What button would you click on if you wanted to find out about jobs related to animal care?

_____

WRITE ABOUT IT ▷ **Timed Writing: Explanation (15 minutes)**

Summarize the features of www.aspca.org to explain how to care for cats. Use the answers to these questions to help write your explanation.

• What is the first thing a cat owner should do to find information about cats on www.aspca.org?

_____

• What kinds of information might the Web site give about cats?

_____

My Papa, Mark Twain • Stage Fright

Reading Skill

Nonfiction works often include an author's opinion as well as facts. A **fact** is information that can be proved. An **opinion** is a person's judgment or belief. To **recognize clues that indicate an opinion**, do the following:

- Look for phrases that indicate an opinion, such as *I believe* or *in my opinion.*
- Look for words that indicate a personal judgment, such as *wonderful* or *terrible.*
- Be aware of words such as *always, nobody, worst,* and *all,* which might indicate a personal judgment or viewpoint.

Literary Analysis

An **author's perspective** is the viewpoint from which he or she writes. This perspective is based on the writer's beliefs and background. The author's perspective reveals his or her feelings or personal interest in a subject.

Use this diagram to look for and record details that reveal the author's perspective.

Detail	Detail

Author's Perspective

My Papa, Mark Twain
Susy Clemens

Summary Thirteen-year-old Susy Clemens writes about her famous father, Mark Twain. Her kind descriptions of her father's looks, actions, and writing show how she feels about him.

 Writing About the Big Question

How Do We Decide What is True?

In "My Papa, Mark Twain," a girl gives a personal view of her father that differs in many ways from the public's image of Mark Twain. Complete this sentence:

To find out what a person is really like, you must _____.

Note-taking Guide

Use this chart to record Susy Clemens's thoughts and feelings about her father.

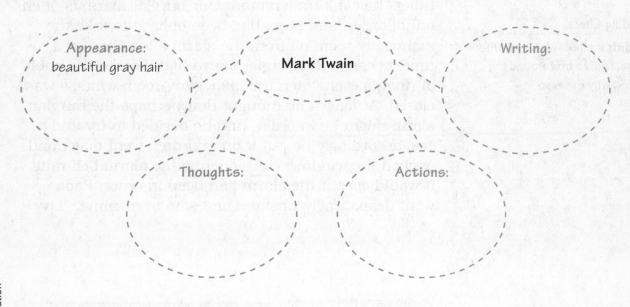

Appearance:
beautiful gray hair

Mark Twain

Writing:

Thoughts:

Actions:

My Papa, Mark Twain
Susy Clemens

Activate Prior Knowledge

Think about someone you admire. What do you like about this person?

_____

_____

Literary Analysis

An author's **perspective** shows the writer's personal feelings and interest in a subject. Susy shows her feelings for her father in this essay. Circle two good characteristics Susy lists about Twain. Underline two bad characteristics Susy lists about Twain. Why do you think Susy wrote both good and bad things about her father?

_____

_____

Reading Check ✎

Billiards is Mark Twain's favorite game. Draw a box around the reason why this is so.

We are a very happy family. We consist of Papa, Mamma, Jean, Clara and me. It is papa I am writing about, and I shall have no trouble in not knowing what to say about him, as he is a very striking character.

Papa's appearance has been described many times, but very incorrectly. He has beautiful gray hair, not any too thick or any too long, but just right; a Roman nose which greatly improves the beauty of his features; kind blue eyes and a small mustache. He has a wonderfully shaped head and profile. He has a very good figure—in short, he is an extrodinarily fine looking man. All his features are perfect except that he hasn't extrodinary teeth. His complexion is very fair, and he doesn't ware a beard. He is a very good man and a very funny one. He has got a temper, but we all of us have in this family. He is the loveliest man I ever saw or ever hope to see—and oh, so <u>absentminded</u>.

Papa's favorite game is billiards, and when he is tired and wishes to rest himself he stays up all night and plays billiards, it seems to rest his head. He smokes a great deal almost <u>incessantly</u>. He has the mind of an author exactly, some of the simplest things he can't understand. Our burglar alarm is often out of order, and papa had been obliged to take the mahogany room off from the alarm altogether for a time, because the burglar alarm had been in the habit of ringing even when the mahogany-room window was closed. At length he thought that perhaps the burglar alarm might be in order, and he decided to try and see; accordingly he put it on and then went down and opened the window; <u>consequently</u> the alarm bell rang, it would even if the alarm had been in order. Papa went despairingly upstairs and said to mamma, "Livy

Vocabulary Development

absentminded (ab suhnt MYND id) *adj.* forgetful
incessantly (in SES uhnt lee) *adv.* constantly; continually
consequently (KAHN suh kwent lee) *adv.* as a result

the mahogany room won't go on. I have just opened the window to see."

"Why, Youth," mamma replied. "If you've opened the window, why of course the alarm will ring!"

"That's what I've opened it for, why I just went down to see if it would ring!"

Mamma tried to explain to papa that when he wanted to go and see whether the alarm would ring while the window was closed he *mustn't go* and open the window—but in vain, papa couldn't understand, and got very impatient with mamma for trying to make him believe an impossible thing true.

Papa has a peculiar gait we like, it seems just to suit him, but most people do not; he always walks up and down the room while thinking and between each coarse at meals.

Papa is very fond of animals particularly of cats, we had a dear little gray kitten once that he named "Lazy" (papa always wears gray to match his hair and eyes) and he would carry him around on his shoulder, it was a mighty pretty sight! the gray cat sound asleep against papa's gray coat and hair. The names that he has give our different cats are really remarkably funny, they are named Stray Kit, Abner, Motley, Fraeulein, Lazy, Buffalo Bill, Soapy Sall, Cleveland, Sour Mash, and Pestilence and Famine.

Papa uses very strong language, but I have an idea not nearly so strong as when he first married mamma. A lady acquaintance of his is rather apt to interrupt what one is saying, and papa told mamma he thought he should say to the lady's husband "I am glad your wife wasn't present when the Deity said Let there be light."

Papa said the other day, "I am a mugwump[1] and a mugwump is pure from the marrow out." (Papa knows that I am writing this biography of him, and he said this for it.) He doesn't like to go to church at all, why I never understood, until just now, he told us the other day that he couldn't bear to hear anyone talk but himself, but that he could listen to himself talk for hours without getting tired, of course

1. **mugwump** (MUG wump) *n.* Republican who refused to support the candidates of the party in the 1884 election.

Reading Skill

What **opinion** does Susy have in the first bracketed paragraph?

_____

_____

Underline the word or words that tell you that this is an opinion.

Literary Analysis

Read the second bracketed paragraph. What new thing does Susy learn that changes her **perspective** of her father in this passage?

_____

_____

_____

Reading Check

What color does Twain always wear?

_____

Circle the reason in the text.

Stop to Reflect

How do you think this biography would be different if Susy had written it when she was an adult?

_____

_____

_____

_____

Reading Skill

Susy says that *The Prince and the Pauper* is "unquestioningly the best book he has ever written." Is this a **fact** or an **opinion**? How do you know?

_____

_____

_____

Reading Check

What does Susy think is "perfect" about *The Prince and the Pauper*? Circle the answer in the text.

he said this in joke, but I've no dought it was founded on truth.

One of papa's latest books is "The Prince and the Pauper" and it is unquestionably the best book he has ever written, some people want him to keep to his old style, some gentleman wrote him, "I enjoyed Huckleberry Finn immensely and am glad to see that you have returned to your old style." That enoyed me, that enoyed me greatly, because it trobles me to have so few people know papa, I mean realy know him, they think of Mark Twain as a humorist joking at everything; "And with a mop of reddish brown hair which sorely needs the barbar brush, a roman nose, short stubby mustache, a sad care-worn face, with maney crows' feet" etc. That is the way people picture papa, I have wanted papa to write a book that would reveal something of his kind sympathetic nature, and "The Prince and the Pauper" partly does it. The book is full of lovely charming ideas, and oh the language! It is perfect. I think that one of the most touching scenes in it is where the pauper is riding on horseback with his nobles in the "recognition procession" and he sees his mother oh and then what followed! How she runs to his side, when she sees him throw up his hand palm outward, and is rudely pushed off by one of the King's officers, and then how the little pauper's conscience troubles him when he remembers the shameful words that were falling from his lips when she was turned from his side "I know you not woman" and how his grandeurs were stricken valueless and his pride consumed to ashes. It is a wonderfully beautiful and touching little scene, and papa has described it so wonderfully. I never saw a man with so much variety of feeling as papa has; now the "Prince and the Pauper" is full of touching places, but there is always a streak of humor in them somewhere. Papa very seldom writes a passage without some humor in it somewhere and I don't think he ever will.

Clara and I are sure that papa played the trick on Grandma about the whipping that is related in "The Adventures of Tom Sawyer": "Hand me that switch." The switch hovered in the air, the peril was desperate—"My, look behind you Aunt!" The old lady whirled around and snatched her skirts out of danger. The lad fled on the instant, scrambling up the high board fence and disappeared over it.

We know papa played "Hookey" all the time. And how readily would papa pretend to be dying so as not to have to go to school! Grandma wouldn't make papa go to school, so she let him go into a printing office to learn the trade. He did so, and gradually picked up enough education to enable him to do about as well as those who were more studious in early life.

Reader's Response: What opinion do you think Susy has about her father as a writer? Explain.

_____

_____

_____

Reading Skill

Susy states the **opinion** that her father did about as well as those who were more studious. What **facts** support Susy Clemens's **opinion**?

_____

_____

Reading Check

Underline the sentence that tells how Susy's father would get out of having to go to school.

My Papa, Mark Twain

1. **Deduce:** Explain how you think Susy feels about her father's lack of formal education.

_____

_____

2. **Speculate:** This essay contains many misspelled words. Why do you think it was published without the errors being corrected?

_____

_____

3. **Reading Skill:** In this chart, record three **opinions** that Susy gives about her father. Then, list the clue words that helped you identify each opinion.

Opinion	Clue Word

4. **Literary Analysis:** Identify two details from Susy Clemens's life that help you see **author's perspective**.

_____

_____

Writing: Dramatic Scene

Turn a passage from "My Papa, Mark Twain" into a **dramatic scene**. Answer the following questions to help you write your dramatic scene.

- First, you must choose a passage from the essay for your scene. Your passage should have at least two characters. What is your passage about?

  _____

  _____

- Which characters are speaking?

  _____

- How do the characters feel as they are talking?

  _____

  _____

Research and Technology: Research for Charts

Create a **poster** that shows some of Mark Twain's best-known works and characters. Use this chart to list details about the stories and characters you choose to put on your poster.

Title of Work	Important Character(s)	Description of Work	Description of Character(s)

Stage Fright
Mark Twain

Summary Mark Twain tells about his first time in front of an audience. He was so scared that he had friends scattered around the audience. One friend was to laugh when Twain looked at her. The way his plan works has a funnier result than he intended.

Writing About the Big Question

How Do We Decide What is True? In "Stage Fright," a well-known humorist must hide his true feelings. He must appear calm before an audience, even though he suffers from stage fright. His friends try to help him. Complete this sentence:

A person's behavior (does / does not) always prove that he or she is

being truthful because _____.

Note-taking Guide

Mark Twain was known for being funny. Fill in this chart with details that show how he is funny in this speech.

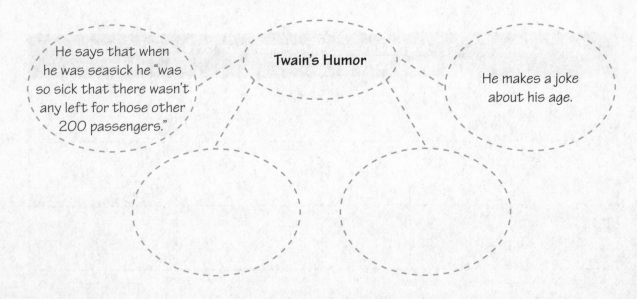

He says that when he was seasick he "was so sick that there wasn't any left for those other 200 passengers."

Twain's Humor

He makes a joke about his age.

Stage Fright

1. **Draw Conclusions:** How might a little bit of stage fright help the author?

   _____

   _____

2. **Speculate:** Twain prearranged a signal with the governor's wife. What probably happened when Twain delivered the "gem" in his speech?

   _____

   _____

3. **Reading Skill:** Use this chart to record three **opinions** that Twain gives. Then, list clue words that helped you identify each opinion.

Opinion	Clue Word

4. **Literary Analysis:** How might the **author's perspective** be different if Mark Twain's daughter had written "Stage Fright"?

   _____

   _____

Writing: Dramatic Scene

Write a **dramatic scene** using Twain's description of his first public appearance. Answer the following questions to help you write your dramatic scene.

- What might two audience members have talked about after Twain's first speech?

_____

_____

- What might Twain's daughter have said to him after his speech at her recital?

_____

_____

Research and Technology: Poster

Use the following questions to guide your research on stage fright.

- What causes stage fright?

_____

_____

- How does a person with stage fright feel?

_____

_____

- What are some suggestions for coping with stage fright?

_____

_____

Names/Nombres • The Lady and the Spider

Reading Skill

To evaluate a work of nonfiction, you must understand the difference between **fact and opinion**. A *fact*, unlike an opinion, can be proved. An *opinion* expresses a judgment that can be supported but not proved. You can **check facts by using resources** such as the following:

- dictionaries
- encyclopedias
- reliable Web sites

Use this chart to help you keep track of facts in these selections.

Fact	Reference Source	True	False
Tigers live in only cold climates.	Internet		✓

Literary Analysis

The **tone** of a literary work is the writer's attitude toward his or her audience and subject. The tone can often be described in one word, such as *playful*, *serious*, or *humorous*. Factors that contribute to the tone are word choice, sentence structure, and sentence length. Notice how word choice can create a friendly tone:

If you plan ahead, I promise you, you'll have the best party ever!

As you read, look for details that convey a certain tone.

Names/Nombres
Julia Alvarez

Summary Young Julia Alvarez and her family are called by different names when they come to America. The names are not the Spanish names they use at home. Julia wonders what name she will use when she becomes a well-known writer.

 Writing About the Big Question

How Do We Decide What is True? In "Names/Nombres," a girl hesitates to correct people who mispronounce her name, even though it hurts. She hides her feelings in order to "fit in." Complete this sentence:

Sometimes it takes courage to show your true feelings because

_____.

Note-taking Guide

Julia Alvarez describes names in this essay. Her name is mispronounced. Her friends call her names other than Julia. She also has nicknames. Use this chart to list the different names or pronunciations of names in Alvarez's essay.

What people call her father	What people call her mother	What people call Julia
Mister Elbures, Mister Alberase		

Names/Nombres
Julia Alvarez

When we arrived in New York City, our names changed almost immediately. At Immigration,[1] the officer asked my father, Mister Elbures, if he had anything to declare. My father shook his head, "No," and we were waved through. I was too afraid we wouldn't be let in if I corrected the man's pronunciation, but I said our name to myself, opening my mouth wide for the organ blast of the a, trilling my tongue for the drum-roll of the r, All-vah-rrr-es! How could anyone get Elbures out of that orchestra of sound?

At the hotel my mother was Missus Alburest, and I was little girl, as in, "Hey, little girl, stop riding the elevator up and down. It's not a toy."

When we moved into our new apartment building, the super[2] called my father Mister Alberase, and the neighbors who became mother's friends pronounced her name Jew-lee-ah instead of Hoo-lee-ah. I, her name-sake, was known as Hoo-lee-tah at home. But at school, I was Judy or Judith, and once an English teacher mistook me for Juliet.

It took awhile to get used to my new names. I wondered if I shouldn't correct my teachers and new friends. But my mother argued that it didn't matter. "You know what your friend Shakespeare said, 'A rose by any other name would smell as sweet.' " My father had gotten into the habit of calling any famous author "my friend" because I had begun to write poems and stories in English class.

By the time I was in high school, I was a popular kid, and it showed in my name. Friends called me Jules or Hey Jude, and once a group of troublemaking friends my mother forbade me to hang out with called me Alcatraz. I was Hoo-lee-tah only to Mami and Papi and uncles and aunts who came over to eat sancocho on Sunday afternoons—old world folk whom I would just as soon go back to where they came from and leave me to pursue whatever mischief I wanted to in America. JUDY ALCATRAZ:

---

1. **Immigration** government agency that processes immigrants.

2. **super** superintendent; the person who manages an apartment building.

TAKE NOTES

Activate Prior Knowledge

Think of a time when you joined a new team or group. Maybe you moved to a new neighborhood or school. What did it feel like to be the new person?

_____

_____

Literary Analysis 🔍

Tone shows the writer's feelings about the audience and subject. Read the bracketed paragraph. What tone, or attitude, does Alvarez have toward her different names?

_____

_____

_____

Underline words that support your answer.

Reading Check

Circle the mispronunciations of the family's last name that Julia and her family hear when they arrive in New York City.

A **fact** can be proved. An **opinion** can be supported but not proved. What opinion does the narrator give in the first bracketed paragraph?

_____

_____

Circle the clue word that helps you know that this is an **opinion**.

Literary Analysis

What **tone** does Alvarez use when writing about her mother in the second bracketed paragraph?

_____

_____

Circle words that support your answer.

Reading Check 🖉

Underline the reason Alvarez's mother does not want to tell the women Mauricia's name.

the name on the Wanted Poster would read. Who would ever trace her to me?

My older sister had the hardest time getting an American name for herself because Mauricia did not translate into English. Ironically, although she had the most foreign-sounding name, she and I were the Americans in the family. We had been born in New York City when our parents had first tried immigration and then gone back "home," too homesick to stay. My mother often told the story of how she had almost changed my sister's name in the hospital.

After the delivery, Mami and some other new mothers were cooing over their new baby sons and daughters and exchanging names and weights and delivery stories. My mother was embarrassed among the Sallys and Janes and Georges and Johns to reveal the rich, noisy name of Mauricia, so when her turn came to brag, she gave her baby's name as Maureen.

"Why'd ya give her an Irish name with so many pretty Spanish names to choose from?" one of the women asked.

My mother blushed and admitted her baby's real name to the group. Her mother-in-law had recently died, she apologized, and her husband had insisted that the first daughter be named after his mother, Mauran. My mother thought it the ugliest name she had ever heard, and she talked my father into what she believed was an improvement, a combination of Mauran and her own mother's name, Felicia.

"Her name is Mao-ree-shee-ah," my mother said to the group of women.

"Why that's a beautiful name," the new mothers cried. "Moor-ee-sha, Moor-ee-sha," they cooed into the pink blanket. Moor-ee-sha it was when we returned to the States eleven years later. Sometimes, American tongues found even that mispronunciation tough to say and called her Maria or Marsha or Maudy from her nickname Maury. I pitied her. What an awful name to have to <u>transport</u> across borders!

Vocabulary Development

transport (trans POHRT) *v.* carry from one place to another

My little sister, Ana, had the easiest time of all. She was plain Anne—that is, only her name was plain, for she turned out to be the pale, blond "American beauty" in the family. The only Hispanic thing about her was the affectionate nicknames her boyfriends sometimes gave her. Anita, or as one goofy guy used to sing to her to the tune of the banana advertisement, Anita Banana.[3]

Later, during her college years in the late '60s, there was a push to pronounce Third World names correctly. I remember calling her long distance at her group house and a roommate answering.

"Can I speak to Ana?" I asked, pronouncing her name the American way.

"Ana?" The man's voice hesitated. "Oh! you must mean Ah-nah!"

Our first few years in the States, though, ethnicity was not yet "in." Those were the blond, blue-eyed, bobby sock years of junior high and high school before the '60s ushered in peasant blouses, hoop earrings, serapes.[4] My initial desire to be known by my correct Dominican name faded. I just wanted to be Judy and merge with the Sallys and Janes in my class. But inevitably, my accent and coloring gave me away. "So where are you from, Judy?"

"New York," I told my classmates. After all, I had been born blocks away at Columbia Presbyterian Hospital.

"I mean, originally."

"From the Caribbean," I answered vaguely, for if I specified, no one was quite sure on what continent our island was located.

"Really? I've been to Bermuda. We went last April for spring vacation. I got the worst sunburn! So, are you from Portoriko?"

"No," I sighed. "From the Dominican Republic."

"Where's that?"

"South of Bermuda."

© Pearson Education

Vocabulary Development

inevitably (in EV i tuh blee) *adv.* unavoidably

---

3. **Anita Banana** a play on the Chiquita Banana name.

4. **serapes** (suh RAH peez) *n.* colorful shawls worn in Latin America.

Stop to Reflect

Why are names important to Julia and the other people she meets?

_____

_____

_____

_____

Reading Skill

What **fact** does Julia give in the bracketed text?

_____

_____

_____

How could you prove this **fact**?

_____

_____

_____

Reading Check 🖉

Circle the reasons that Julia thinks that Ana had it the easiest.

Alvarez gives her full name in the bracketed passage. Why does she say that her name is so long?

_____

_____

Is this a **fact** or an **opinion**? Explain.

_____

_____

Literary Analysis

What **tone** does Julia use to write about her family coming to school events?

_____

_____

Reading Check ✏

Why does Alvarez's family sit in the front row for school occasions? Put a box around the answer.

_____

_____

They were just being curious, I knew, but I burned with shame whenever they singled me out as a "foreigner," a rare, exotic friend.

"Say your name in Spanish, oh please say it!" I had made mouths drop one day by rattling off my full name, which according to Dominican custom, included my middle names, Mother's and Father's surnames for four generations back.

"Julia Altagracia María Teresa Álvarez Tavares Perello Espaillat Julia Pérez Rochet González," I pronounced it slowly, a name as chaotic with sounds as a Middle Eastern bazaar[5] or market day in a South American village.

My Dominican heritage was never more apparent than when my extended family attended school occasions. For my graduation, they all came, the whole lot of aunts and uncles and the many little cousins who snuck in without tickets. They sat in the first row in order to better understand the Americans' fast-spoken English. But how could they listen when they were constantly speaking among themselves in florid-sounding phrases, rococo[6] consonants, rich, rhyming vowels?

Introducing them to my friends was a further trial to me. These relatives had such complicated names and there were so many of them, and their relationships to myself were so convoluted. There was my Tía Josefina, who was not really an aunt but a much older cousin. And her daughter, Aida Margarita, who was adopted, una hija de crianza. My uncle of affection, Tío José, brought my madrina Tía Amelia and her comadre Tía Pilar. My friends rarely had more than a "Mom and Dad" to introduce.

After the commencement ceremony my family waited outside in the parking lot while my friends and I signed yearbooks with nicknames which recalled our high school good times: "Beans" and

Vocabulary Development
chaotic (kay AHT ik) *adj.* completely confused

5. **bazaar** (buh ZAHR) *n.* marketplace; frequently, one held outdoors.
6. **rococo** (ruh KOH koh) *adj.* fancy and ornate; similar to a style of art of the early eighteenth century.

"Pepperoni" and "Alcatraz." We hugged and cried and promised to keep in touch.

Our goodbyes went on too long. I heard my father's voice calling out across the parking lot, "Hoo-lee-tah! Vamonos!"

Back home, my tíos and tías and primas, Mami and Papi, and mis hermanas had a party for me with sancocho and a store-bought pudín, <u>inscribed</u> with Happy Graduation, Julie. There were many gifts—that was a plus to a large family! I got several wallets and a suitcase with my initials and a graduation charm from my godmother and money from my uncles. The biggest gift was a portable typewriter from my parents for writing my stories and poems.

Someday, the family predicted, my name would be well-known throughout the United States. I laughed to myself, wondering which one I would go by.

Reader's Response: How important is someone's name?

_____

_____

Does a name change the way a person feels about himself or herself?

_____

_____

Does a name change the way other people feel about a person?

_____

_____

Reading Skill

What **opinion** does Alvarez express about large families in the bracketed paragraph?

_____

_____

_____

_____

Literary Analysis

Read the last paragraph. What **tone** does Alvarez use?

_____

_____

_____

Reading Skill

Circle the gifts that Alvarez receives for graduation.

Vocabulary Development

inscribed (in SKRYBD) *adj.* written on

Names/Nombres

1. **Draw Conclusions:** A classmate asks Julia where she is from. Julia tells her classmate she is from New York. Why does she respond as she does?

   _____

   _____

2. **Analyze:** How do Julia's feelings about her name change over time?

   _____

   _____

3. **Reading Skill:** Alvarez relates the story of her sister's name by saying, "My mother thought it was the ugliest name she had ever heard." Is her mother stating a **fact** or an **opinion**? Explain.

   _____

   _____

4. **Literary Analysis:** "Names/Nombres" is written in an informal, or friendly, **tone**. In this chart, rewrite the two sentences in a more serious, or formal, tone.

Informal Tone	Formal Tone
"It took a while to get used to my new names." "My mother blushed and admitted her baby's real name to the group."	

Writing: Personal Anecdote

Write a **personal anecdote** about your family. First, choose the experience you plan to write about. Answer the following questions to help you write your anecdote.

- Where does the story take place? _____

  _____

- When does the story take place? _____

  _____

- Who is in the story? _____

  _____

- What is the most important event in the story? _____

  _____

  _____

Listening and Speaking: Monologue

Answer the following questions to prepare your **monologue.** Remember that you should imagine what Alvarez thinks when she hears her name mispronounced.

- How do you feel the first time that you hear your name mispronounced?

  _____

  _____

- What thoughts do you have when you hear your name mispronounced? Describe three thoughts.

  _____

  _____

  _____

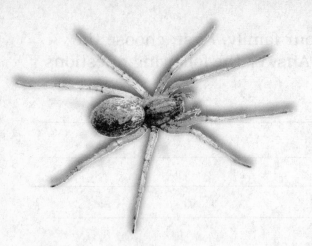

The Lady and the Spider
Robert Fulghum

Summary The narrator sees his neighbor walk into a spider's web. She screams. The narrator writes about the event from the lady's point of view and from the spider's point of view.

? Writing About the Big Question

How Do We Decide What is True? "The Lady and the Spider" presents both true statements and opinions about spiders. Complete this sentence:

An important fact about spiders is _____.

Note-taking Guide

Use this chart to record each character's reactions when the neighbor walks into the spider web.

The Lady	The Spider	The Narrator
She screams.		

The Lady and the Spider

1. **Infer:** What do the lady's actions show about her feelings toward spiders?

   _____

   _____

2. **Analyze:** Why do you think the narrator tells what both the lady and the spider are thinking?

   _____

   _____

3. **Reading Skill:** What are two **facts** from the essay that you could prove true or false by checking on the Internet?

   _____

   _____

4. **Literary Analysis:** The passage in this chart has an informal, or friendly, **tone**. In the space provided, rewrite the passage in a more serious, or formal, tone.

Informal Tone	Formal Tone
Spiders. Amazing creatures. Been around maybe 350 million years, so they can cope with just about anything. Lots of them, too—sixty or seventy thousand per suburban acre. It's the web thing that I envy.	

Writing: Personal Anecdote

Write a **personal anecdote** about your encounter with something in nature. First, choose the experience you plan to write about. Answer the following questions to help you write your anecdote.

- Where does the story take place? _____

_____

- When does the story take place? _____

_____

- Who is in the story? _____

_____

- What is the most important event in the story?_____

_____

_____

Listening and Speaking: Monologue

A **monologue** is a speech in which one person tells about himself or herself. Choose either the lady or the spider. Write a monologue that presents the thoughts of the character that you chose.

- What adjectives will you use to describe the feelings of the lady or the spider?

_____

_____

- Explain what the lady thinks about spiders in general, or explain what the spider thinks about humans in general.

_____

_____

_____

- How did the meeting of the lady and the spider affect the rest of the lady's or the spider's day?

_____

_____

Atlases

About Atlases

An **atlas** is a book of maps. The maps show cities, mountains, rivers, and roads. Some atlases also have facts or short articles about the places on the maps. Atlas maps usually have the following:

- a *compass rose* that shows north, south, east, and west
- a *scale bar* that shows how many miles or kilometers are in one inch on the map
- a *legend* or key that explains the symbols and colors on the map
- *labels* that have the names and locations of places
- an *inset map* that shows where a location can be found on the globe

Reading Skill

An **assertion** is a statement, such as "The weather is cold today" or "I like all kinds of animals." A reasonable assertion about a text is supported by examples. Look at this example:

Atlas Entry	Travel Brochure
Provides facts	Provides generalizations
Compass rose, scale bar, and **key** can be used to support generalizations	Generalizations may be supported by accurate facts
Accurate research tool	May be useful for preliminary research

A **generalization** is a broad assertion based on many examples. In the following texts, look for assertions and generalizations the writers make and how those assertions are supported. Then, think about an assertion you can make, based on your reading.

The purpose of the atlas entry is to give facts about a place. The purpose of a travel brochure is to convince people to visit a place. Understanding the purpose of an informational text can help you decide whether the information in the text is true.

The Caribbean

The Caribbean Sea is enclosed by an arc of many hundreds of islands, islets, and offshore reefs that reach from Florida, in the US, round to Venezuela in South America. From 1492, Spain, France, Britain, and the Netherlands claimed the islands as colonies.

LAND HEIGHT
- 6,560–13,120ft
- 3,280–6,560ft
- 1,640–3,280ft
- 820–1,640ft
- 330–820ft
- 0–330ft

SEA DEPTH
- 0–820ft
- 820–1,640ft
- 1,640–3,280ft
- 3,280–6,560ft
- 6,560–9,840ft
- 9,840–13,120ft
- Below 13,120ft

CITIES AND TOWNS
- Over 500,000 people
- 100,000–500,000
- 50,000–100,000
- Less than 50,000

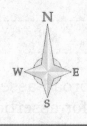

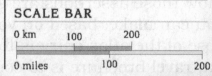

SCALE BAR

0 km   100   200

0 miles   100   200

NORTH
AMERICA

The Caribbean

The assertions in
this paragraph
are supported by
the information
in this map.

THE LANDSCAPE

The islands are formed from two main mountain chains: the Greater Antilles, which
are part of a chain running from west to east, and the Lesser Antilles, which run from
north to south. The mountains are now almost submerged below the Atlantic Ocean and
Caribbean Sea. Only the higher peaks reach above sea level to form islands.

The Bahamas
The Bahamas are
low-lying islands
formed from limestone
rock. Their coastlines
are fringed by
coral reefs,
lagoons, and
mangrove swamps.
Some of the bigger
islands are covered
with forests.

Hispaniola
Two countries, Haiti and the Dominican Republic,
occupy the island of Hispaniola. The land is mostly
mountainous, broken by fertile valleys.

Cuba
Cuba is the largest island in the Antilles.
Its landscape is made up of wide, fertile
plains, with rugged hills and mountains in
the southeast.

The Lesser Antilles
Most of these small volcanic islands have mountainous
interiors. Barbados and Antigua are flatter, with some
higher volcanic areas. Monserrat was evacuated in
1997 following volcanic eruptions on the island.

FARMING AND LAND USE

Agriculture is an important source of income, with more than half of all produce
exported. Many islands have fertile, well-watered land and large areas set aside for commercial crops such as sugar cane, tobacco, and coffee. Some islands rely heavily
on a single crop. In Dominica, bananas provide more than half the country's
income. Cuba is one of the world's biggest sugar producers.

Havana

San Juan

Kingston   Port-au-
Prince

FARMING AND LAND USE

Cattle	Bananas		Cropland
Fishing	Coffee		Forest
Pigs	Sugarcane		Pasture
Poultry	Tobacco	•	Major conurbation
Shellfish			

How do we decide what is true?
If you wanted to know the truth
about daily life in a particular place,
what information might you want that an
atlas would not provide? Explain.

Thinking About the Atlas

1. Which Caribbean islands are not mountainous?

_____

2. Compare the "Landscape" map with the "Farming and Land Use" map. Which map contains more details? Describe the types of details the map shows.

_____

TALK ABOUT IT Reading Skill

3. What assertion does the writer of the travel brochure makes about the size of Cuba in relation to other island in the Antilles?

_____

4. Look closely at the atlas. Make an assertion about the city of Santo Domingo.

_____

WRITE ABOUT IT Timed Writing: Description **(20 minutes)**

Find the city of Havana, Cuba, on the Farming and Land Use map. Write a description of the island of Cuba. Use the facts presented in the atlas to make generalizations. Answer these questions to help you write your generalizations.

• What kinds of food are grown in Cuba?

_____

• What kinds of animals are raised in Cuba?

_____

• What are the waters surrounding the island used for?

_____

The Wounded Wolf

A **short story** is a type of fiction. It has a plot, characters, a setting, and a theme. **Plot** is the action in the story. All plots have these features:

- a **conflict**, or struggle
- a series of events linked by cause and effect
- a high point of conflict called the **climax**
- a **resolution**, through which the conflict is resolved

Conflict

A problem between two opposing forces

Internal

- Takes place inside a character
- Character struggles to make decision, take action, or overcome problem
- Example: A character cannot decide whether to save money or buy something he or she wants.

External

- Takes place outside a character
- Character struggles with an outside force such as another character or nature
- Example: A character gets caught outside in a snowstorm.

Characters are the people or animals who take part in the action of the story.

- **Characterization**: An author uses characterization to create and develop a character.

- **Character's traits**: A character's traits, or qualities, help readers understand why the character acts in a certain way. Traits can include stubbornness and dependability.
- **Character's motives:** A character's motives are the reasons why he or she does something. Motives can include what a character thinks, feels, or wants.

Setting is the time and place of the story's action. Details can include the year, the time of day, and the weather.

The setting can serve as the background for the plot. It helps set the story's mood.

- Realistic details are included in stories that take place in recent times.
- Real and made-up details are usually included in stories that take place in the past.

Theme

A message about life

Stated

- Directly said by author
- Example: The author says that the characters will have to make a decision that will change their lives.

Implied

- Shown through what the characters do and say
- Example: The characters talk about how they are handling a tough situation.

The Wounded Wolf

Jean Craighead George

Summary Roko the wolf is hurt while fighting for food. Hungry animals that prey on dying animals follow him. Roko finds shelter under a rock. The hungry animals wait nearby. The lead wolf from Roko's pack finds Roko. All of the animals wait to see whether Roko will get better or die under the rock.

Note-taking Guide

Many animals watch Roko after he is injured. Use this chart to record what the animals do.

Ravens	White Fox	Snowy Owl	Grizzly Bear	Kiglo
Pick Roko's open wound				

The Wounded Wolf

Jean Craighead George

Activate Prior Knowledge

What have you heard or read about wolves? Give two details below.

_____

_____

Short Story

The **setting** of a story is the time and place in which the action happens. Circle the words in the first paragraph that give details about the setting.

Short Story

An **external conflict** is a struggle between a character and something outside that character. What is Roko's conflict at the start of the story?

_____

_____

_____

A wounded wolf climbs Toklat Ridge,[1] a massive spine of rock and ice. As he limps, dawn strikes the ridge and lights it up with sparks and stars. Roko, the wounded wolf, blinks in the ice fire, then stops to rest and watch his pack run the thawing Arctic valley.

They plunge and turn. They fight the mighty caribou that struck young Roko with his hoof and wounded him. He jumped between the beast and Kiglo, leader of the Toklat pack. Young Roko spun and fell. Hooves, paws, and teeth roared over him. And then his pack and the beast were gone.

Gravely injured, Roko pulls himself toward the shelter rock. Weakness overcomes him. He stops. He and his pack are thin and hungry. This is the season of starvation. The winter's harvest has been taken. The produce of spring has not begun.

Young Roko glances down the valley. He droops his head and stiffens his tail to signal to his pack that he is badly hurt. Winds wail. A frigid blast picks up long shawls of snow and drapes them between young Roko and his pack. And so his message is not read.

A raven scouting Toklat Ridge sees Roko's signal. "Kong, kong, kong," he bells—death is coming to the ridge; there will be flesh and bone for all. His voice rolls out across the valley. It penetrates the rocky cracks where the Toklat ravens rest. One by one they hear and spread their wings. They beat their way to Toklat Ridge. They alight upon the snow and walk behind the wounded wolf.

"Kong," they toll with keen excitement, for the raven clan is hungry, too. "Kong, kong"—there will be flesh and bone for all.

Vocabulary Development
toll (tol) v. to announce

1. **Toklat Ridge** the top of a mountain located in Alaska's Denali National Park and Preserve.

Roko snarls and hurries toward the shelter rock. A cloud of snow envelops him. He limps in blinding whiteness now.

A ghostly presence flits around. "Hahahahahahaha," the white fox states—death is coming to the Ridge. Roko smells the fox tagging at his heels.

The cloud whirls off. Two golden eyes look up at Roko. The snowy owl has heard the ravens and joined the deathwatch.

Roko limps along. The ravens walk. The white fox leaps. The snowy owl flies and hops along the rim of Toklat Ridge. Roko stops. Below the ledge out on the flats the musk-ox herd is circling. They form a ring and all face out, a fort of heads and horns and fur that sweeps down to their hooves. Their circle means to Roko that an enemy is present. He squints and smells the wind. It carries scents of thawing ice, broken grass—and earth. The grizzly bear is up! He has awakened from his winter's sleep. A craving need for flesh will drive him.

Roko sees the shelter rock. He strains to reach it. He stumbles. The ravens move in closer. The white fox boldly walks beside him. "Hahaha," he yaps. The snowy owl flies ahead, alights, and waits.

The grizzly hears the eager fox and rises on his flat hind feet. He twists his powerful neck and head. His great paws dangle at his chest. He sees the animal procession and hears the ravens' knell of death. Dropping to all fours, he joins the march up Toklat Ridge.

Roko stops; his breath comes hard. A raven alights upon his back and picks the open wound. Roko snaps. The raven flies and circles back. The white fox nips at Roko's toes. The snowy owl inches closer. The grizzly bear, still dulled by sleep, stumbles onto Toklat Ridge.

Only yards from the shelter rock, Roko falls.

Instantly the ravens mob him. They scream and peck and stab at his eyes. The white fox leaps upon his wound. The snowy owl sits and waits.

© Pearson Education

Vocabulary Development

knell (nel) *n.* mournful sound, like a slowly ringing bell, usually indicating a death

---

Short Story

The **conflict** is growing in the story. Read the bracketed paragraph. What is the **internal conflict** that Roko faces?

_____

_____

_____

Short Story

Characterization is the way in which the author develops characters. Read the underlined sentences. Then, write a brief description of the white fox.

_____

_____

Reading Check

How does the musk-ox herd tell Roko that an enemy is present? Circle the answer in the text.

Short Story

The **theme** of a story can be found by noticing how a character deals with a situation. How does Roko react to the ravens, fox, and owl?

_____

_____

Stop to Reflect

What do you think Roko's chances of survival are at this point? Explain.

_____

_____

Short Story

The description of the **setting** in the story helps set a mood. Read the first bracketed paragraph. How would you describe the mood in this paragraph?

_____

_____

Short Story

The **climax** is the high point of a story, when the end of the story becomes clear. Read the second bracketed paragraph. What is becoming clear about Roko?

_____

_____

Young Roko struggles to his feet. He bites the ravens. Snaps the fox. And lunges at the <u>stoic</u> owl. He turns and warns the grizzly bear. Then he bursts into a run and falls against the shelter rock. The wounded wolf wedges down between the rock and barren ground. Now protected on three sides, he turns and faces all his foes.

The ravens step a few feet closer. The fox slides toward him on his belly. The snowy owl blinks and waits, and on the ridge rim roars the hungry grizzly bear.

Roko growls.

The sun comes up. Far across the Toklat Valley, Roko hears his pack's "hunt's end" song. The music wails and sobs, wilder than the bleating wind. The hunt song ends. Next comes the roll call. Each member of the Toklat pack barks to say that he is home and well.

"Kiglo here," Roko hears his leader bark. There is a pause. It is young Roko's turn. He cannot lift his head to answer. The pack is silent. The leader starts the count once more. "Kiglo here."—A pause. Roko cannot answer.

The wounded wolf whimpers softly. A mindful raven hears. "Kong, kong, kong," he tolls—this is the end. His booming sounds across the valley. The wolf pack hears the raven's message that something is dying. They know it is Roko, who has not answered roll call.

The hours pass. The wind slams snow on Toklat Ridge. Massive clouds blot out the sun. In their gloom Roko sees the deathwatch move in closer. Suddenly he hears the musk-oxen thundering into their circle. The ice cracks as the grizzly leaves. The ravens burst into the air. The white fox runs. The snowy owl flaps to the top of the shelter rock. And Kiglo rounds the knoll.

In his mouth he carries meat. He drops it close to Roko's head and wags his tail excitedly. Roko licks Kiglo's chin to honor him. Then Kiglo puts his mouth around Roko's nose. This gesture says "I am your leader." And by mouthing Roko, he binds him and all the wolves together.

Vocabulary Development

stoic (STO ik) _adj._ calm and unaffected by hardship

The wounded wolf wags his tail. Kiglo trots away.

Already Roko's wound feels better. He gulps the food and feels his strength return. He shatters bone, flesh, and gristle and shakes the scraps out on the snow. The hungry ravens swoop upon them. The white fox snatches up a bone. The snowy owl gulps down flesh and fur. And Roko wags his tail and watches.

For days Kiglo brings young Roko food. He <u>gnashes</u>, gorges, and shatters bits upon the snow.

A purple sandpiper winging north sees ravens, owl, and fox. And he drops in upon the feast. The long-tailed jaeger gull flies down and joins the crowd on Toklat Ridge. Roko wags his tail.

One dawn he moves his wounded leg. He stretches it and pulls himself into the sunlight. He walks—he romps. He runs in circles. He leaps and plays with chunks of ice. Suddenly he stops. The "hunt's end" song rings out. Next comes the roll call.

"Kiglo here."

"Roko here," he barks out strongly.

The pack is silent.

"Kiglo here," the leader repeats.

"Roko here."

Across the distance comes the sound of whoops and yips and barks and howls. They fill the dawn with celebration. And Roko prances down the Ridge.

Reader's Response: Do you admire the wolves in this story? Why or why not?

_____

_____

_____

Short Story

The **plot** of a short story has a **resolution**. The resolution is the part of the story in which the conflict is resolved. How is Roko's conflict resolved?

_____

_____

_____

Short Story 📖

The **setting** in a story can change along with the plot. Read the bracketed paragraph. Circle words that describe how the setting has changed.

How does this change match the change in the plot?

_____

_____

_____

Reading Check

What does Kiglo bring to Roko? Underline the answer.

Vocabulary Development

gnashes (NASH iz) *v.* bites with grinding teeth

Short Stories

1. **Analyze:** What action does Roko take to save himself?

   _____

   _____

2. **Infer:** What does Kiglo's behavior show about how wolves take care of pack members?

   _____

   _____

3. **Short Story:** What is the main **conflict** in "The Wounded Wolf"? Explain.

   _____

   _____

4. Fill in the chart below with details about the **setting** of the story. In the first column, identify details that help you picture the setting. Then, tell what those details mean to the struggle for survival. Finally, explain in the third column why the setting is important to the story.

What It Says	What It Means	Why It Is Important

Plan for a Multimedia Presentation

- Jean Craighead George has written many books about animals and people surviving in the wild. She has also written a series on wolves. *Julie of the Wolves*, *Julie*, and *Julie's Wolf Pack* came out of the author's trip to Denali National Park in Alaska.

- Search the Internet for words and phrases such as "Jean Craighead George" or "Jean Craighead George books." Search the author's Web site for information about her writing: www.jeancraigheadgeorge.com/

  What I learned:

  _____

  _____

  _____

- Search the library and the Internet for photographs of the author. You might even find photographs or drawings of her subjects.

- Search through Jean Craighead George's books to find the two or three that you like the most. Write a summary for each book by including the most important information. Add this information to your report for your presentation.

- Watch the video interview with Jean Craighead George, and review your source material. Use this information to answer the following questions.

1. What did you learn about Craighead George's life that is interesting?

   _____

2. How has the author's interest in the natural world influenced her books?

   _____

The Tail • Dragon, Dragon

Reading Skill

When you **make inferences**, you make logical assumptions about something that is not directly stated. To make inferences, **use details** the text provides.

   Example: Arnie *ran* to the mailbox to see whether Jim's letter had *finally* arrived.

- You can infer from the word *finally* that Arnie has been waiting to hear from Jim.

- You can infer from *ran* that Arnie is eager to get the letter.

Literary Analysis

Characterization is the way in which writers develop characters and reveal their traits, or qualities.

- With **direct characterization**, writers make straightforward statements about a character.

- With **indirect characterization**, writers present a character's thoughts, words, and actions and reveal what others say and think about the character. These details help you understand a character's traits, or qualities.

   As you read, use this graphic organizer to note details that reveal what each character is like.

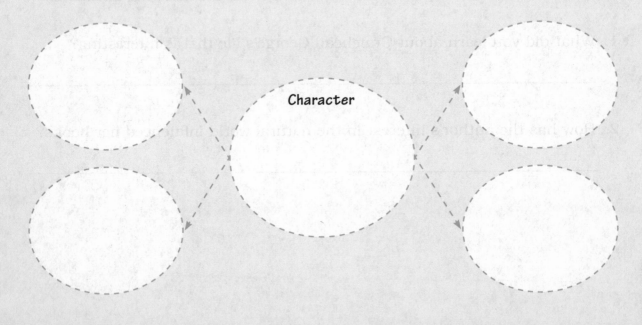

Character

The Tail
Joyce Hansen

Summary Tasha is upset. She has to babysit all summer for her seven-year-old brother, Junior. Their mother gives rules for Tasha and Junior to follow. Junior plays a trick on his sister. The trick teaches Tasha how important it is to obey her mother's rules.

Writing About the Big Question

Is Conflict Always Bad? In "The Tail," a 13-year old girl is upset when her mother tells her that she has to babysit her brother all summer. Complete this sentence:

Arguments between children and their parents can start when

_____

Note-taking Guide

Fill in this chart with details about the events in "The Tail." List one unexpected thing that happens to each character in the story.

Tasha	Junior	Naomi	Mother	Dog
She has to babysit for her brother all summer.				

Activate Prior Knowledge

Describe how you feel when you are told to do something that you do not want to do.

_____

_____

_____

Literary Analysis 🔍

Writers use **direct characterization** to tell about a character. Writers **use indirect characterization** to show what a character thinks, says, and does. Which type of characterization does the writer use in the first bracketed paragraph? How do you know?

_____

_____

_____

Reading Skill

Readers **make inferences,** or their best guesses, by using **details** in the story. Read the second bracketed paragraph. How does Tasha feel about babysitting for her brother?

_____

_____

_____

The Tail
Joyce Hansen

It began as the worst summer of my life. The evening before the first day of summer vacation, my mother broke the bad news to me. I was in the kitchen washing dishes and dreaming about the wonderful things my friends and I would be doing for two whole months—practicing for the annual double-dutch[1] contest, which we would definitely win; going to the roller skating rink, the swimming pool, the beach; and sleeping as late in the morning as I wanted to.

"Tasha," my ma broke into my happy thoughts, "your father and I decided that you're old enough now to take on certain responsibilities."

My heart came to a sudden halt. "Responsibilities?"

"Yes. You do know what that word means, don't you?"

I nodded, watching her dice an onion into small, perfect pieces.

"You're thirteen going on fourteen and your father and I decided that you're old enough to watch Junior this summer, because I'm going to start working again."

"Oh, no!" I broke the dish with a crash. "Not that, Mama." Junior is my seven-year-old brother and has been following me like a tail ever since he learned how to walk. And to make matters worse, there are no kids Junior's age on our block. Everyone is either older or younger than he is.

I'd rather be in school than minding Junior all day. I could've cried.

"Natasha! There won't be a dish left in this house. You're not going to spend all summer ripping and roaring. You'll baby-sit Junior."

"But, Ma," I said, "it'll be miserable. That's not fair. All summer with Junior. I won't be able to play with my friends."

She wiped her hands on her apron. "Life ain't always fair."

I knew she'd say that.

---

1. **double-dutch** a jump-rope game in which two ropes are used at the same time.

"You'll still be able to play with your friends," she continued, "but Junior comes first. He is your responsibility. We're a family and we all have to help out."

Mama went to work that next morning. Junior and I both stood by the door as she gave her last-minute instructions. Junior held her hand and stared up at her with an innocent look in his bright brown eyes, which everyone thought were so cute. Dimples decorated his round cheeks as he smiled and nodded at me every time Ma gave me an order. I knew he was just waiting for her to leave so he could torment me.

"Tasha, I'm depending on you. Don't leave the block."

"Yes, Ma."

"No company."

"Not even Naomi? She's my best friend."

"No company when your father and I are not home."

"Yes, Ma."

"Don't let Junior hike in the park."

"Yes, Ma."

"Make yourself and Junior a sandwich for lunch."

"Yes, Ma."

"I'll be calling you at twelve, so you'd better be in here fixing lunch. I don't want you all eating junk food all day long."

"Yes, Ma."

"Don't ignore Junior."

"Yes, Ma."

"Clean the breakfast dishes."

"Yes, Ma."

"Don't open the door to strangers."

"Yes, Ma."

Then she turned to Junior. "Now you, young man. You are to listen to your sister."

"Yes, Mommy," he sang out.

"Don't give her a hard time. Show me what a big boy you can be."

"Mommy, I'll do whatever Tasha say."

She kissed us both good-bye and left. I wanted to cry. A whole summer with Junior.

Junior turned to me and raised his right hand. "This is a vow of obedience." He looked up at the ceiling. "I promise to do whatever Tasha says."

© Pearson Education

Literary Analysis

Read the bracketed paragraph. Who is being described? Is this **direct** or **indirect** **characterization**? Explain.

_____

_____

_____

_____

Reading Skill

Tasha's mother gives Tasha instructions before leaving for work. What **inference** can you make about her mother from this detail?

_____

_____

_____

_____

Reading Check

Who is Tasha's best friend? Circle the answer in the text.

Reading Skill

What can you **infer** about Junior from his actions in the bracketed passage?

_____

_____

_____

_____

Stop to Reflect

Do you think Tasha is right to be so upset? Explain.

_____

_____

_____

Reading Check

What is the first thing that Tasha orders Junior to do? Circle the answer.

"What do you know about vows?" I asked.

"I saw it on television. A man—"

"Shut up, Junior. I don't feel like hearing about some television show. It's too early in the morning."

I went into the kitchen to start cleaning, when the downstairs bell rang. "Answer the intercom,[2] Junior. If it's Naomi, tell her to wait for me on the stoop," I called out. I knew that it was Naomi, ready to start our big, fun summer. After a few minutes the bell rang again.

"Junior!" I yelled. "Answer the intercom."

The bell rang again and I ran into the living room. Junior was sitting on the couch, looking at cartoons. "What's wrong with you? Why won't you answer the bell?"

He looked at me as if I were crazy. "You told me to shut up. I told you I'd do everything you say."

I pulled my hair. "See, you're bugging me already. Do something to help around here."

I pressed the intercom on the wall. "That you, Naomi?"

"Yeah."

"I'll be down in a minute. Wait for me out front."

"Okay."

I quickly washed the dishes. I couldn't believe how messed up my plans were. Suddenly there was a loud blast from the living room. I was so startled that I dropped a plate and it smashed to smithereens. Ma will kill me, I thought as I ran to the living room. It sounded like whole pieces of furniture were being sucked into the vacuum cleaner.

"Junior," I screamed over the racket, "you have it on too high."

He couldn't even hear me. I turned it off myself.

"What's wrong?"

"Ma vacuumed the living room last night. It doesn't need cleaning."

"You told me to do something to help," he whined.

I finished the dishes in a hurry so that I could leave the apartment before Junior bugged out again.

I was so anxious to get outside that we ran down the four flights of stairs instead of waiting for the elevator. Junior clutched some comic books and his

2. **intercom** n. a communication system used in apartment buildings.

checkers game. He put his Mets baseball cap on backward as usual. Naomi sat on the stoop and Junior plopped right next to her like they were the best of friends.

"Hi, cutey." She smiled at him, turning his cap to the front of his head the way it was supposed to be.

"What are we going to do today, Naomi?" he asked.

"Junior, you're not going to be in our faces all day," I snapped at him.

"Mama said you have to watch me. So I have to be in your face."

"You're baby-sitting, Tasha?" Naomi asked.

"Yeah." I told her the whole story.

"Aw, that's not so bad. At least you don't have to stay in the house. Junior will be good. Right, cutey?"

He grinned as she pinched his cheeks.

"See, you think he's cute because you don't have no pesty little brother or sister to watch," I grumbled.

"You ready for double-dutch practice?" she asked. "Yvonne and Keisha are going to meet us in the playground."

"Mama said we have to stay on the block," Junior answered before I could even open my mouth.

"No one's talking to you, Junior." I pulled Naomi up off the stoop. "I promised my mother we'd stay on the block, but the playground is just across the street. I can see the block from there."

"It's still not the block," Junior mumbled as we raced across the street.

We always went over to the playground to jump rope. The playground was just by the entrance to the park. There was a lot of space for us to do our fancy steps. The park was like a big green mountain in the middle of Broadway.

I'd figure out a way to keep Junior from telling that we really didn't stay on the block. "Hey, Tasha, can I go inside the park and look for caves?" People said that if you went deep inside the park, there were caves that had been used centuries ago when Native Americans still lived in northern Manhattan.

"No, Ma said no hiking in the park."

"She said no leaving the block, too, and you left the block."

"Look how close we are to the block. I mean, we can even see it. You could get lost inside the park."

Reading Skill

Read the bracketed passage. What **inference** can you make about the difference in attitude between Tasha and Naomi?

_____

_____

What do you think causes this difference?

_____

_____

Literary Analysis

What **character** trait does Tasha show by deciding to go to the playground? Explain your response.

_____

_____

Reading Check

Who are Tasha and Naomi going to meet at the playground? Underline the sentence that tells you.

TAKE NOTES

Stop to Reflect

Tasha and Junior go to play across the street. They have disobeyed Ma's orders. What do you think may happen?

_____

_____

_____

Reading Skill

What can you **infer** are Tasha's feelings as the girls begin to jump? Underline details that support your answer.

_____

_____

Literary Analysis

Read the bracketed passage. What does this say about Tasha's **character**?

_____

_____

_____

Reading Check

What does Tasha promise Junior to keep him from telling Ma that they went to the park? Circle the answer.

_____

"I'm going to tell Ma you didn't stay on the block."

"Okay, me and Naomi will hike with you up to the Cloisters later." That's a museum that sits at the top of the park, overlooking the Hudson River. "Now read your comic books."

"Will you play checkers with me too?"

"You know I hate checkers. Leave me alone." I spotted Keisha and Yvonne walking into the playground. All of us wore shorts and sneakers.

Junior tagged behind me and Naomi as we went to meet them. "Remember you're supposed to be watching me," he said.

"How could I forget."

The playground was crowded. Swings were all taken and the older boys played stickball. Some little kids played in the sandboxes.

Keisha and Yvonne turned and Naomi and I jumped together, practicing a new routine. We were so good that some of the boys in the stickball game watched us. A few elderly people stopped to look at us too. We had an audience, so I really showed off—spinning and doing a lot of fancy footwork.

Suddenly Junior jumped in the ropes with us and people laughed and clapped.

"Junior!" I screamed. "Get out of here!"

"Remember, your job is to watch me." He grinned. My foot slipped and all three of us got tangled in the ropes and fell.

"Your feet are too big!" Junior yelled.

Everybody roared. I was too embarrassed. I tried to grab him, but he got away from me. "Get lost," I hollered after him as he ran toward the swings.

I tried to forget how stupid I must've looked and went back to the ropes. I don't know how long we'd been jumping when suddenly a little kid ran by us yelling, "There's a wild dog loose up there!" He pointed to the steps that led deep inside the park.

People had been saying for years that a pack of abandoned dogs who'd turned wild lived in the park, but no one ever really saw them.

We forgot about the kid and kept jumping. Then one of the boys our age who'd been playing stickball came over to us. "We're getting out of here," he said. "A big yellow dog with red eyes just bit a kid."

I took the rope from Yvonne. It was time for me and Naomi to turn. "That's ridiculous. Who ever heard of a yellow dog with red eyes?"

Naomi stopped turning. "Dogs look all kind of ways. Especially wild dogs. I'm leaving."

"Me too," Yvonne said.

Keisha was already gone. No one was in the swings or the sandboxes. I didn't even see the old men who usually sat on the benches. "Guess we'd better get out of here too," I said. Then I realized that I didn't see Junior anywhere.

"Junior!" I shouted.

"Maybe he went home," Naomi said.

We dashed across the street. Our block was empty. Yvonne ran ahead of us and didn't stop until she reached her stoop. When I got to my stoop I expected to see Junior there, but no Junior.

"Maybe he went upstairs," Naomi said.

"I have the key. He can't get in the house."

"Maybe he went to the candy store?"

"He doesn't have any money, I don't think. But let's look."

We ran around the corner to the candy store, but no Junior.

As we walked back to the block, I remembered something.

"Oh, no, Naomi, I told him to get lost. And that's just what he did."

"He's probably hiding from us somewhere. You know how he likes to tease." She looked around as we walked up our block. "He might be hiding and watching us right now looking for him." She peeped behind parked cars, in doorways, and even opened the lid of a trash can.

"Junior," I called. "Junior!"

No answer. Only the sounds of birds and cars, sirens and a distant radio. I looked at the empty stoop where Junior should have been sitting. A part of me was gone and I had to find it. And another part of me would be gone if my mother found out I'd lost Junior.

I ran back toward the playground and Naomi followed me. "He's got to be somewhere right around here," she panted.

Reading Skill

Make an **inference** about Tasha. How does she feel about Junior's disappearance?

_____

_____

_____

How can you tell?

_____

_____

Literary Analysis 🔍

Read the bracketed passage. Notice how Naomi acts and what she says. What are Naomi's feelings in this passage?

_____

Is this **direct** or **indirect characterization**? Explain.

_____

_____

Underline details that support your answer.

Stop to Reflect

Who was left on the swings and in the sandboxes after people began to talk about the wild dog? Underline the sentence that tells you.

Literary Analysis

Read the first bracketed passage. Underline the first action that Tasha takes.

_____

_____

What does this **indirect characterization** tell you about how she feels?

_____

_____

Literary Analysis

Read the second bracketed passage. Underline the instance of **indirect characterization** about Junior. What does this suggest about him?

_____

_____

Reading Check

What three things does Tasha promise to do if she finds Junior? Number the answers in the story.

I ran past the playground and into the park. "Tasha, you're not going in there, are you? The dog."

I didn't answer her and began climbing the stone steps that wound around and through the park. Naomi's eyes stretched all over her face and she grabbed my arm. "It's dangerous up here!"

I turned around. "If you're scared, don't come. Junior's my only baby brother. Dear God," I said out loud, "please let me find him. I will play any kind of game he wants. I'll never yell at him again. I promise never to be mean to him again in my life!"

Naomi breathed heavily behind me. "I don't think Junior would go this far by himself."

I stopped and caught my breath. The trees were thick and the city street sounds were far away now.

"I know Junior. He's somewhere up here making believe he's the king of this mountain. Hey, Junior," I called, "I was just kidding. Don't get lost." We heard a rustling in the bushes and grabbed each other. "Probably just a bird," I said, trying to sound brave.

As we climbed some more, I tried not to imagine a huge yellow dog with red eyes <u>gnawing</u> at my heels.

The steps turned a corner and ended. Naomi screamed and pointed up ahead. "What's that?"

I saw a big brown and gray monstrous thing with tentacles reaching toward the sky, jutting out of the curve in the path. I screamed and almost ran.

"What is that, Naomi?"

"I don't know."

"This is a park in the middle of Manhattan. It can't be a bear or anything." I screamed to the top of my lungs, "Junior!" Some birds flew out of a tree, but the thing never moved.

All Naomi could say was, "Dogs, Tasha."

I found a stick. "I'm going up. You wait here. If you hear growling and screaming, run and get some help." I couldn't believe how brave I was. Anyway, that thing, whatever it was, couldn't hurt me any more than my mother would if I didn't find Junior.

"You sure, Tasha?"

Vocabulary Development

gnawing (NAW ing) *v.* biting and cutting with the teeth

"No sense in both of us being <u>mauled</u>," I said.

I tipped lightly up the steps, holding the stick like a club. When I was a few feet away from the thing, I crumpled to the ground and laughed so hard that Naomi ran to me. "Naomi, look at what scared us."

She laughed too. "A dead tree trunk."

We both laughed until we cried. Then I saw one of Junior's comic books near a bush. I picked it up and started to cry. "See, he was here. And that animal probably tore him to pieces." Naomi patted my shaking shoulders.

Suddenly, there was an unbelievable growl. My legs turned to air as I flew down the steps. Naomi was ahead of me. Her two braids stuck out like propellers. My feet didn't even touch the ground. We screamed all the way down the steps. I tripped on the last step and was sprawled out on the ground. Two women passing by bent over me. "Child, are you hurt?" one of them asked.

Then I heard a familiar laugh above me and looked up into Junior's dimpled face. He laughed so hard, he held his stomach with one hand. His checkers game was in the other. A little tan, mangy³ dog stood next to him, wagging its tail.

I got up slowly. "Junior, I'm going to choke you."

He doubled over with squeals and chuckles. I wiped my filthy shorts with one hand and stretched out the other to snatch Junior's neck. The stupid little dog had the nerve to growl.

"Me and Thunder hid in the bushes. We followed you." He continued laughing. Then he turned to the dog. "Thunder, didn't Tasha look funny holding that stick like she was going to beat up the tree trunk?"

I put my hands around Junior's neck. "This is the end of the tail," I said.

Junior grinned. "You promised. 'I'll play any game he wants. I'll never yell at him again. I promise never to be mean to him again in my life.'"

TAKE NOTES

Reading Skill

What can you **infer** from Tasha's reaction when she finds Junior's comic book?

_____

_____

_____

Literary Analysis

What does Junior's reaction in the bracketed paragraph show about his character?

_____

_____

_____

_____

Is this **direct** or **indirect** **characterization**?

_____

Reading Check

What happened to Tasha as she was running down the steps? Underline the sentence that tells you.

Vocabulary Development

mauled (mawld) *v.* badly injured by being attacked

3. **mangy** (MAYN jee) *adj.* shabby and dirty.

Reading Skill

What can you **infer** about the dog from the bracketed paragraph?

_____

_____

Stop to Reflect

What do you think of the trick that Junior plays on Tasha? Does it seem fair? Why or why not?

_____

_____

_____

_____

Reading Check

What time is it when Tasha and Junior return home? Underline the sentence that tells you.

Naomi giggled. "That's what you said, Tasha." The mutt barked at me. Guess he called himself Junior's protector. I took my hands off Junior's neck.

Then Naomi had a laughing spasm. She pointed at the dog. "Is that what everyone was running from?"

"This is my trusted guard. People say he's wild. He just wants a friend."

"Thunder looks like he's already got a lot of friends living inside his fur," I said. We walked back to the block with the dog trotting right by Junior's side.

I checked my watch when we got to my building. "It's ten to twelve. I have to make lunch for Junior," I told Naomi. "But I'll be back out later."

The dog whined after Junior as we entered the building. "I'll be back soon, Thunder," he said, "after I beat my sister in five games of checkers."

Now he was going to blackmail me.

I heard Naomi giggling as Junior and I walked into the building. The phone rang just as we entered the apartment. I knew it was Ma.

"Everything okay, Tasha? Nothing happened?"

"No, Ma, everything is fine. Nothing happened at all."

Well, the summer didn't turn out to be so terrible after all. My parents got Thunder cleaned up and let Junior keep him for a pet. Me and my friends practiced for the double-dutch contest right in front of my building, so I didn't have to leave the block. After lunch when it was too hot to jump rope, I'd play a game of checkers with Junior or read him a story. He wasn't as pesty as he used to be, because now he had Thunder. We won the double-dutch contest. And Junior never told my parents that I'd lost him. I found out that you never miss a tail until you almost lose it.

Reader's Response: How do you think Junior felt about the way the summer turned out? Explain.

_____

_____

Vocabulary Development

spasm (SPAZ uhm) *n.* a short sudden burst

The Tail

1. **Analyze Cause and Effect:** What causes Junior to disappear?

   _____

2. **Interpret:** What does Tasha mean when she says, "I found out that you never miss a tail until you almost lose it"?

   _____

   _____

3. **Reading Skill:** Use this chart to list the details that led you to **make an inference** about Tasha. One example is provided. Give two more examples.

Details	Inference
Tasha tells Naomi, "If you're scared, don't come. Junior's my only baby brother."	Tasha is worried. She is determined to find Junior, with or without Naomi's help.

4. **Literary Analysis:** List two examples of **direct characterization** from the story.

   _____

   _____

Writing: Help-Wanted Advertisement

Write a **help-wanted ad** for a babysitter. Answer the following questions to help you organize information for your ad.

- What would you give a babysitter in return for his or her services?

  _____

- What kind of on-the-job training might you provide?

  _____

- What information is usually at the top of an ad?

  _____

- What information needs to be in large or bold print?

  _____

Research and Technology: Compare-and-Contrast Chart

Make a **compare-and-contrast chart** that describes games children can play outdoors. Fill in the chart with details about three games you have played outdoors.

Name of Game	Materials Needed to Play the Game	Room or Weather Needed to Play the Game	Imagination Needed to Play the Game

Dragon, Dragon
John Gardner

Summary A terrible dragon is frightening the people in a kingdom. The king offers a reward to whoever can kill the dragon. A poor cobbler's three sons have different ideas of how to fight the dragon. The father's advice to his sons becomes the key to success.

? Writing About the Big Question

Is Conflict Always Bad? In "Dragon, Dragon," a king sets out to stop a dragon from terrorizing his kingdom. Complete this sentence:

To defend his or her home, a person might _____.

Note-taking Guide

Use this chart to record what happens to each of the cobbler's sons.

	Does he follow his father's advice?	What happens to him?
Eldest son	No, he does not.	
Middle son		
Youngest son		

Dragon, Dragon

1. **Connect:** Why do the two elder sons doubt their father's advice about slaying the dragon?

   _____

   _____

2. **Analyze:** Why is the youngest son successful in killing the dragon?

   _____

   _____

3. **Reading Skill:** Use the chart below to list details that led you to **make an inference** about the youngest son. One example is provided. Give two more examples.

Details	Inference
He listens to his father's advice.	He trusts his father's wisdom.

4. **Literary Analysis:** List two examples of **direct characterization** from the story.

   _____

   _____

Writing: Help-Wanted Advertisement

Write a **help-wanted ad** for a dragon slayer. Answer the following questions to help you organize information for your ad.

- What would you give a dragon slayer in return for his or her services?

  _____

- What kind of on-the-job training might you provide?

  _____

- What information is usually at the top of an ad?

  _____

- What information needs to be in large or bold print?

  _____

Research and Technology: Compare-and-Contrast Chart

Fill out a **compare-and-contrast chart** for two dragon tales from different cultures. Label each circle with the culture you have chosen. In the overlapping parts of the circles, write characteristics of dragons that each culture shares. In the non-overlapping portions, write what is different about dragons in each culture.

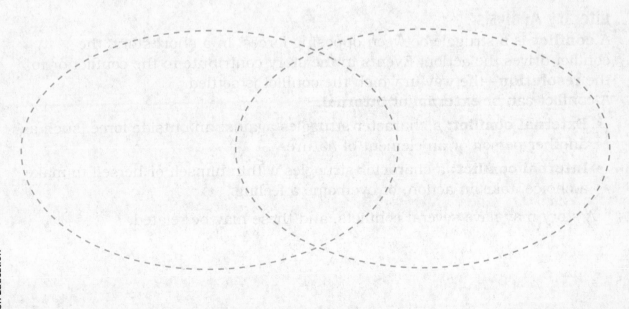

Zlateh the Goat • The Old Woman Who Lived With The Wolves

Reading Skill

An **inference** is a logical assumption about information not directly stated. It is based on information from the text and on your own thoughts. To make an inference, combine text clues with your **prior knowledge**, or what you already know. For example, from the sentence "Tina smiled when she saw the snow," you might infer that Tina is happy. This inference is based on your prior knowledge that people often smile when they are happy. Because the text states that Tina is smiling at the snow, you can infer that the snow is the reason she is happy.

To help make inferences as you read, use a chart like this one.

Details	Prior Knowledge	Inference

Literary Analysis

A **conflict** is a struggle between opposing forces. In a short story, the conflict drives the action. Events in the story contribute to the conflict or to the **resolution**—the way in which the conflict is settled.

A conflict can be **external** or **internal**.

- **External conflict:** a character struggles against an outside force, such as another person or an element of nature.

- **Internal conflict:** a character struggles within himself or herself to make a choice, take an action, or overcome a feeling.

A story may have several conflicts, and these may be related.

Zlateh the Goat
Isaac Bashevis Singer

Summary Reuven needs to sell the family goat, Zlateh. A blizzard hits as Reuven's son Aaron walks the goat to the butcher. The two find shelter in a haystack for three days. Zlateh eats hay. Aaron drinks the goat's milk. Aaron takes the goat back home, and she becomes part of the family.

 Writing About the Big Question

Is Conflict Always Bad? In "Zlateh the Goat," a winter snowstorm forces a boy to find a way to save his life and that of the family goat. Complete this sentence:

A shared struggle for survival (does/does not) bring friends closer

together because _____.

Note-taking Guide

Fill in this chart to help clarify Aaron's character.

Character's Name: Aaron	
What Character Says	**What Character Does**
He asks Zlateh what she thinks about their situation.	He tries to take the goat to the butcher. He finds shelter in a haystack. He keeps the air hole open.
What Character Thinks	**What Others Say About Character**

Zlateh the Goat

1. **Deduce:** Think about the danger Aaron and Zlateh face on the way to town. Why is this situation dangerous for them?

_____

_____

2. **Apply:** What is this story's message about friendship and trust?

_____

_____

3. **Reading Skill:** Aaron's mother and sisters cry over selling Zlateh. What **inference** can you make about their feelings for the goat?

_____

_____

4. **Literary Analysis:** For each conflict listed, tell whether it is **internal** or **external**. Explain how the conflict was resolved.

Conflict	What Kind?	Resolution
Reuven needs the money he could get for Zlateh, but he loves Zlateh.		
Aaron and Zlateh need food and shelter but are caught in a blizzard.		

Writing: Persuasive Speech

Write a short **persuasive speech** that Aaron might give to urge his father to keep Zlateh. A persuasive speech tries to convince an audience to believe or do something.

- List three reasons for keeping the goat that Reuven might agree with.

_____

_____

_____

- List three other choices that Aaron could offer in place of selling Zlateh.

_____

_____

_____

- Strengthen your speech by using only the strongest points. Which two or three arguments are most likely to convince Reuven? Circle those reasons.

Research and Technology: Chart

Use the following questions to help you gather information for your **chart**.

1. What were homes in the shtetl like? _____

   What were the homes made of? _____

2. What responsibilities might a twelve-year-old boy have had in a shtetl?

   _____

3. How did most people make a living in the shtetl?

   _____

The Old Woman Who Lived With The Wolves
Chief Luther Standing Bear

Summary Marpiyawin's puppy gets lost. She searches for him. A snowstorm forces her to hide in a cave. A pack of wolves helps her stay warm. The wolves lead her to her camp after the snowstorm. Marpiyawin gets a new name because of her friendship with the wolves.

 Writing About the Big Question

Is Conflict Always Bad? In "The Old Woman Who Lived With The Wolves," a young girl loses her way during a blizzard and must trust a pack of wolves for her survival. Complete this sentence:

Sometimes, when we persuade ourselves to trust instead of fear something,

it may help us _____.

Note-taking Guide

Use this chart to record details that show how the characters and animals treat one another in this story.

How Marpiyawin Treats the Wolves	How the Wolves Treat Marpiyawin During the Storm	How Marpiyawin's People Treat the Wolves
She trusts them.		

The Old Woman Who Lived With The Wolves

Chief Luther Standing Bear

The Sioux were a people who traveled about from place to place a great deal within the borders of their own country. They did not trespass upon the territory of their neighbor Indians, but liked to make their home first here and then there upon their own ground, just as they pleased. It was not like moving from one strange town to another, but wherever they settled it was home. Taking down and putting up the tipis was not hard for them to do.

The reasons for their moving were many. Perhaps the grass for their ponies ran short, or the water in the creek became low. Maybe the game had gone elsewhere, and maybe the people just moved the camp to a fresh green spot, for the Sioux loved pure water, pure air, and a clean place on which to put their tipis.

One day, long ago, a Sioux village was on the march. There were many people in the party, and many children. A great number of horses carried the tipis, and herds of racing and war horses were being taken care of by the young men. In this crowd was a young woman who carried with her a pet dog. The dog was young and playful, just past the puppy age. The young woman was very fond of her pet, as she had cared for it since it was a wee little thing with eyes still closed. She romped along with the pup, and the way seemed short because she played with it and with the young folks when not busy helping her mother with the packing and unpacking.

One evening Marpiyawin missed her dog. She looked and she called, but he was not to be found. Perhaps someone liked her playful pet and was keeping him concealed, but after a search she became satisfied that no one in camp was hiding him. Then she thought that perhaps he had lain down to sleep somewhere along the way and had been left behind. Then, lastly, she thought that the wolves had enticed him to join their pack. For

Activate Prior Knowledge

Share your feelings about a pet that you like. It could be your pet or someone else's.

_____

_____

_____

_____

Reading Skill

Readers make **inferences,** or intelligent guesses, by looking at the details in a text. Read the bracketed paragraphs. You can make the inference that the Sioux enjoy traveling. Explain how the details in these paragraphs support this inference.

_____

_____

_____

_____

Reading Check

What did the Sioux people love? Underline the answer.

Literary Analysis

A **conflict** is a struggle between opposing forces.

What conflict is developing in the underlined passage?

_____

_____

Is this an internal or external conflict?

_____

Stop to Reflect

Why do you think Marpiyawin is not afraid of getting lost?

_____

_____

Literary Analysis

How has the snow added to the **conflict** in this story?

_____

_____

Which type of conflict is this?

_____

Reading Check

Why does Marpiyawin leave her tribe? Circle the answer.

oftentimes the Sioux dogs were <u>coaxed</u> away and ran with the wolf-pack, always returning, however, in a few days or weeks to the village.

So Marpiyawin, thinking the matter over, decided that she would go back over the way her people had journeyed and that somewhere she would find her dog. She would then bring him back to camp with her. Without a word to anyone, she turned back, for she had no fear of becoming lost. Nothing could befall her, so why should she fear? As she walked back, she came to the foothills at the base of the mountains where her village people had spent the summer. As she slept that night, the first snowfall of the autumn came so silently that it did not awaken her. In the morning everything was white with snow, but it was not far to the place where the village had been in camp and so determined was she to find her dog that she decided to keep going. Marpiyawin now felt that her pet had gone back to the old camping-ground, as dogs often do, and was now there howling and crying to be found.

That afternoon the snow fell thicker and faster and Marpiyawin was forced to seek shelter in a cave, which was rather dark, but warm and comfortable. She was not hungry, for in her little rawhide[1] bag was still some wasna.[2] She was tired, however, so it was not long till she fell asleep, and while she slept she had a most wonderful vision. In her dream the wolves talked to her and she understood them, and when she talked to them they understood her too. They told her that she had lost her way, but that she should trust them and they would not see her suffer from cold or hunger. She replied that she would not worry, and when she awoke it was without fear, even though in the cave with her were the wolves sitting about in a friendly manner.

Vocabulary Development

coaxed (kohkst) *v.* persuaded by gentle urging

---

1. **rawhide** (RAW hyd) *n.* rough leather.
2. **wasna** (WAHS nuh) *n.* meat and berries pounded and pressed together in flat strips to make a nutritious food that is easy to carry.

The blizzard raged outside for many days, still she was contented, for she was neither cold nor hungry. For meat the wolves supplied her with tender rabbits and at night they kept her body warm with their shaggy coats of fur. As the days wore on, she and the wolves became fast friends.

But clear days finally came and the wolves offered to lead her back to her people, so they set out. They traversed many little valleys and crossed many creeks and streams; they walked up hills and down hills, and at last came to one from which she could look down upon the camp of her people. Here she must say "Good-bye" to her friends and companions—the wolves. This made her feel very sad, though she wanted to see her people again. Marpiyawin thanked all the wolves for their kindness to her and asked what she might do for them. All they asked was that, when the long winter months came and food was scarce, she bring to the top of the hill some nice fat meat for them to eat. This she gladly promised to do and went down the hill toward the camp of her people.

As Marpiyawin neared the village, she smelled a very unpleasant odor. At first it mystified her, then she realized it was the smell of human beings. At once the knowledge came to her that the smell of humans was very different from the smell of animals. This was why she now knew that animals so readily track human beings and why the odor of man is oftentimes so offensive to them. She had been with the wolves so long that she had lost the odor of her people and now was able to see that, while man often considers the animal offensive, so do animals find man offensive.

Marpiyawin came to the camp of her people and they were happy to see her, for they had considered her lost and thought she had been taken by an enemy tribe. But she pointed to the top of the hill in the distance, and there sat her friends, their forms black against the sky. In great surprise her people

Vocabulary Development

traversed (truh VERST) *v.* went across
offensive (uh FEN siv) *adj.* unpleasant

TAKE NOTES

Reading Skill

The underlined passage contains descriptions of different types of land. What **inference** can you make from these descriptions?

_____

_____

_____

_____

Literary Analysis

Reread the underlined passage. What **conflict** does Marpiyawin face in this passage?

_____

_____

Is this an **internal** or **external** **conflict**? Explain.

_____

_____

_____

Reading Check

What did the wolves ask Marpiyawin to do for them? Circle the answer.

Reading Skill

What do the people in the village ask the old woman about?

_____

_____

What do the wolves warn the people about?

_____

_____

What **inference** can you make about how the Sioux feel about the wolves?

_____

_____

Stop to Reflect

What types of warnings do people rely on today for bad weather in cities and in neighborhoods?

_____

_____

_____

Reading Check ✏

What did Marpiyawin's people think had happened to her while she was missing? Circle the answer.

looked, not knowing what to say. They thought she must have just escaped a great danger. So she explained to them that she had been lost and would have perished had not the wolves saved her life. She asked them to give her some of their fat meat that she might carry it to the top of the hill. Her people were so grateful and happy that a young man was sent about the camp telling of the safe return of Marpiyawin and collecting meat from each tipi. Marpiyawin took the meat, placed the bundle on her back, and went up the hill, while the village people looked on in wonder. When she reached the hilltop she spread the meat on the ground and the wolves ate it.

Ever after that, when the long winter months came and food was scarce and hard to find, Marpiyawin took meat to her friends the wolves. She never forgot their language and oftentimes in the winter their voices calling to her would be heard throughout the village. Then the people would ask the old woman what the wolves were saying. Their calls would be warnings that a blizzard was coming, or that the enemy was passing close, and to send out a scout or to let the old woman know that they were watching her with care.

And so Marpiyawin came to be known to the tribe as "The Old Woman Who Lived with the Wolves," or, in the Sioux language as, "Win yan wan si k'ma nitu ompi ti."

Reader's Response: Why do you think Marpiyawin is not afraid of the wolves?

_____

_____

_____

The Old Woman Who Lived With The Wolves

1. **Draw Conclusions:** Would Marpiyawin have survived without the wolves? Support your answer.

_____

_____

_____

2. **Generalize:** What does Marpiyawin's experience suggest about the way the Sioux view nature?

_____

_____

_____

3. **Reading Skill:** Think of a time when you lost something. Make an **inference** about how Marpiyawin feels as she sets out to find her dog.

_____

_____

_____

4. **Literary Analysis:** For each **conflict** listed in this chart, note whether it is **internal** or **external**. Then, explain how it was resolved.

Conflict	What Kind?	Resolution
Marpiyawin needs food and shelter, but she is lost.		
She is sad to leave the wolves but misses her people.		

Writing: Persuasive Speech

Write a short **persuasive speech** that Marpiyawin might give to urge her people to help the wolves. Answer the following questions to help you write your speech.

- What is the best reason for helping the wolves?

  _____

  _____

  _____

- What argument might people have for not helping the wolves? How could you respond to their arguments?

  _____

  _____

  _____

Research and Technology: Chart

Prepare a **chart** that shows the Sioux people's day-to-day life. Answer the following questions to help you find information for your chart.

- What kinds of books can you use to find information about Sioux settlements?

  _____

  _____

- What keywords can you use to find information on the Internet about Sioux girls?

  _____

  _____

Online Almanacs

About Online Almanacs

An **online almanac** gives facts about a variety of topics. It can help you learn new information. The information is organized into topics and subtopics. General topics include:

- history
- government
- countries
- biography
- sports
- entertainment

Interactive features in online almanacs help students learn more about a topic. They may include links to other parts of the almanac or search functions.

Online almanacs also include **text aids and text features.** Text aids and text features help readers understand and use the information given.

Text Aids	Text Features
<ul><li>Chapter titles</li><li>Main headings and subheadings</li><li>Highlighted vocabulary</li></ul>	<ul><li>Maps, graphs, and charts</li><li>Photographs, drawings, and diagrams with captions</li></ul>

Reading Skill

Text aids and text features organize details in a text. They also highlight important information. Here are some tips for using text aids and text features.

Tips for Using Text Aids and Text Features
<ul><li>Headings and subheadings tell you the main ideas of the chapters.</li><li>Maps, graphs, and charts help you understand the main ideas of the chapters.</li><li>Pictures and diagrams with captions give examples or make clear the main ideas of the chapters.</li></ul>

The main heading shows the general topic of the almanac entry.

THE SEVEN WONDERS OF THE WORLD

from **Infoplease**®

Since ancient times, numerous "seven wonders" lists have been created. The content of these lists tends to vary, and none is definitive. The seven wonders that are most widely agreed upon as being in the original list are **the Seven Wonders of the Ancient World**, which was compiled by ancient Greek historians and is thus confined to the most magnificent structures known to the ancient Greek world. Of all the Ancient Wonders, the pyramids alone survive.

The Pyramids of Egypt are three pyramids at Giza, outside modern Cairo. The largest pyramid, built by Khufu (Cheops), a king of the fourth dynasty, had an original estimated height of 482 ft (now approximately 450 ft). The base has sides 755 ft long. It contains 2,300,000 blocks; the average weight of each is 2.5 tons. Estimated date of completion is 2680 B.C.

The subheadings serve as a list of the Seven Wonders of the Ancient World.

The Hanging Gardens of Babylon were supposedly built by Nebuchadnezzar around 600 B.C. to please his queen, Amuhia. They are also associated with the mythical Assyrian queen Semiramis. Archeologists surmise that the gardens were laid out atop a vaulted building, with provisions for raising water. The terraces were said to rise from 75 to 300 ft.

The Statue of Zeus (Jupiter) at Olympia was made of gold and ivory by the Greek sculptor Phidias (5th century B.C.). Reputed to be 40 ft high, the statue has been lost without a trace, except for reproductions on coins.

The Temple of Artemis (Diana) at Ephesus was begun about 350 B.C., in honor of a non-Hellenic goddess who later became identified with the Greek goddess of the same name. The temple, with Ionic columns 60 ft high, was destroyed by invading Goths in A.D. 262.

The Mausoleum at Halicarnassus was erected by Queen Artemisia in memory of her husband, King Mausolus of Caria in Asia Minor, who died in 353 B.C. Some remains of the structure are in the British Museum. This shrine is the source of the modern word mausoleum.

The Colossus at Rhodes was a bronze statue of Helios (Apollo), about 105 ft high. The work of the sculptor Chares, who reputedly labored for 12 years before completing it in 280 B.C., it was destroyed during an earthquake in 224 B.C.

The Pharos (Lighthouse) of Alexandria was built by Sostratus of Cnidus during the 3rd century B.C. on the island of Pharos off the coast of Egypt. It was destroyed by an earthquake in the 13th century.

(Some lists include the Walls of Babylon in place of the second or seventh wonder.)

See also The Seven Wonders of the Modern World.

THE BIG ?

Is conflict always bad?
In researching this topic, would you expect all sources to agree on the Seven Wonders of the World? Why or why not?

Thinking About the Online Almanac

1. Describe the construction of the Colossus at Rhodes.

_____

2. What is the main topic of this almanac article?

_____

What text feature helped you find the answer?

_____

TALK ABOUT IT **Reading Skill**

3. Look at the subheadings in the almanac article. What do these headings identify?

_____

4. Look at the illustrations of the Hanging Gardens of Babylon. Is the statement "The gardens had no trees" true or false?

_____

WRITE ABOUT IT **Timed Writing: Explanation (20 minutes)**

Explain why each of the Seven Wonders of the World were considered to be amazing. Use facts from the Online Almanac to write your paragraph.

What details in the text aids and features support your answer?

_____

_____

How was the Pharos of Alexandria destroyed?

_____

The All-American Slurp • The Circuit

Reading Skill

A **conclusion** is a decision or an opinion that you reach on the basis of details in a literary work. To identify the details that will help you draw conclusions, **ask questions** such as *Why is this detail included in the story?* For example, if a boy falls off his bicycle and then says that he does not want to ride anymore, you might ask why he makes that decision. You could conclude that he is afraid.

Literary Analysis

The **theme**, or central idea of a story, is a thought about life that the story conveys. Sometimes the theme is directly stated. Other times you must figure it out by considering the events in the story, the characters' thoughts and feelings, and the story's title.

Fill in this chart with details from the story as you read. The details you record will help you find the theme of the story.

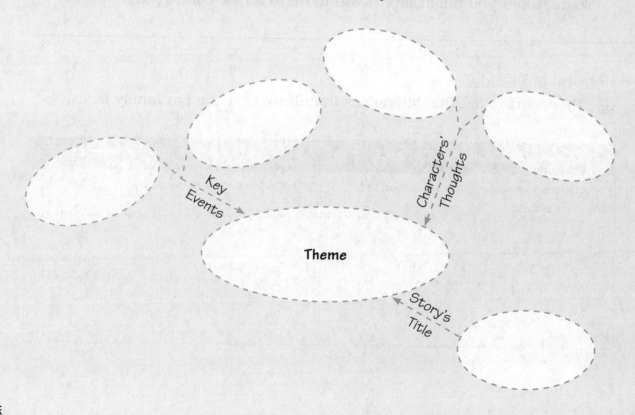

The All-American Slurp
Lensey Namioka

Summary The Lins have moved to the United States from China. People notice the Lins' Chinese habits. The family tries to act more American. One day they invite some American friends for dinner. The Lins find out that they are not as different as they think.

❓ Writing About the Big Question

Is Conflict Always Bad? In **"The All-American Slurp,"** the narrator feels conflicted when her family's Chinese customs differ from the American customs of her neighbors. Complete this sentence:

Some issues you might face if you move to a new country are

_____.

Note-taking Guide

Use this chart to list the differences in culture that the Lin family faces.

How things are done in China	How things are done in America
Vegetables are always boiled in water before they are served.	Vegetables can be served raw.

The All-American Slurp

1. **Infer:** What does each member of the Lin family's way of learning English show about that person?

_____

_____

2. **Compare and Contrast:** In what ways are the Gleasons's actions at the Lins's house similar to those of the Lins at the Gleasons's house?

_____

_____

3. **Reading Skill:** Use this chart to **draw conclusions** about the story.

Question	Details That Answer Question	Conclusion
Why do the Gleasons stare as the Lins pull celery strings?		
Why do people in the restaurant stare when the Lins slurp their soup?		
What makes the narrator uneasy when the Gleasons come to dinner?		

4. **Literary Analysis:** What **theme** about cultural differences does the story illustrate?

_____

Writing: Description

Write a **description** of a character from "The All-American Slurp." Answer the following questions to gather details for your description.

- What quality do you find most interesting about your character?

  _____

  _____

- How does the character get along with other characters?

  _____

  _____

- What challenges does this character face?

  _____

  _____

Use your answers to write your description.

Listening and Speaking: Interview

Prepare an **interview** with the narrator of the story. To help you to prepare for your interview, write a question and response for these topics.

Topics	Interviewer's Questions	Narrator's Responses
American food	How did you feel when Mrs. Gleason first offered you raw celery?	I was confused. We never eat raw vegetables in China.
American kids		
American dinner parties		
American manners		

Use notes from the chart to conduct your interview.

The Circuit

Francisco Jiménez

Summary Panchito and his family move often to pick crops in California. He is lucky to get to go to school. His teacher, Mr. Lema, offers to teach him to play the trumpet. Panchito rushes home to tell his family. He finds that his life is about to change again.

Writing About the Big Question

Is Conflict Always Bad? In **"The Circuit"** Panchito, the narrator, is upset that his family has to keep moving in order to find work on farms. Complete this sentence:

When a family has to move a lot, they face conflicts such as

_____.

Note-taking Guide

Use this chart to record what Panchito does during certain months.

June and July	August	September and October	November
He picks strawberries.			

The Circuit
Francisco Jiménez

Constant change makes life difficult for Panchito. Describe an unexpected change you have faced.

_____

_____

_____

_____

Literary Analysis

The **theme** of a story is its central idea. The bracketed passage gives clues to the theme of "The Circuit." Underline the words that might indicate this theme. Then write what the words mean.

_____

_____

_____

_____

Stop to Reflect

How does Panchito feel about moving again?

_____

_____

It was that time of year again. Ito, the strawberry sharecropper,[1] did not smile. It was natural. The peak of the strawberry season was over and the last few days the workers, most of them *braceros*,[2] were not picking as many boxes as they had during the months of June and July.

As the last days of August disappeared, so did the number of *braceros*. Sunday, only one—the best picker—came to work. I liked him. Sometimes we talked during our half-hour lunch break. That is how I found out he was from Jalisco, the same state in Mexico my family was from. That Sunday was the last time I saw him.

When the sun had tired and sunk behind the mountains, Ito signaled us that it was time to go home. *"Ya esora,"*[3] he yelled in his broken Spanish. Those were the words I waited for twelve hours a day, every day, seven days a week, week after week. And the thought of not hearing them again saddened me.

As we drove home Papá did not say a word. With both hands on the wheel, he stared at the dirt road. My older brother, Roberto, was also silent. He leaned his head back and closed his eyes. Once in a while he cleared from his throat the dust that blew in from outside.

Yes, it was that time of year. When I opened the front door to the shack, I stopped. Everything we owned was neatly packed in cardboard boxes. Suddenly I felt even more the weight of hours, days, weeks, and months of work. I sat down on a box. The thought of having to move to Fresno[4] and knowing what was in store for me there brought tears to my eyes.

That night I could not sleep. I lay in bed thinking about how much I hated this move.

A little before five o'clock in the morning, Papá woke everyone up. A few minutes later, the yelling

1. **sharecropper** (SHER krahp er) *n.* one who works for a share of a crop; tenant farmer.
2. **braceros** (brah SER ohs) *n.* migrant Mexican farm laborers who harvest crops.
3. **Ya esora** (yah es OH rah) Spanish for "It's time" (Ya es hora).
4. **Fresno** (FREZ noh) *n.* city in central California.

and screaming of my little brothers and sisters, for whom the move was a great adventure, broke the silence of dawn. Shortly, the barking of the dogs accompanied them.

While we packed the breakfast dishes, Papá went outside to start the "Carcanchita."[5] That was the name Papá gave his old '38 black Plymouth. He bought it in a used-car lot in Santa Rosa in the winter of 1949. Papá was very proud of his little jalopy. He had a right to be proud of it. He spent a lot of time looking at other cars before buying this one. When he finally chose the "Carcanchita," he checked it thoroughly before driving it out of the car lot. He examined every inch of the car. He listened to the motor, tilting his head from side to side like a parrot, trying to detect any noises that spelled car trouble. After being satisfied with the looks and sounds of the car, Papá then insisted on knowing who the original owner was. He never did find out from the car salesman, but he bought the car anyway. Papá figured the original owner must have been an important man because behind the rear seat of the car he found a blue necktie.

Papá parked the car out in front and left the motor running. "Listo,"[6] he yelled. Without saying a word, Roberto and I began to carry the boxes out to the car. Roberto carried the two big boxes and I carried the two smaller ones. Papá then threw the mattress on top of the car roof and tied it with ropes to the front and rear bumpers.

Everything was packed except Mamá's pot. It was an old large galvanized[7] pot she had picked up at an army surplus store in Santa Mar'a the year I was born. The pot had many dents and nicks, and the more dents and nicks it acquired the more Mamá liked it. "Mi olla,"[8] she used to say proudly.

I held the front door open as Mamá carefully carried out her pot by both handles, making sure not to spill the cooked beans. When she got to the car, Papá reached out to help her with it. Roberto opened the rear car door and Papá gently placed it on the

---

5. **Carcanchita** (kahr kahn CHEE tah) affectionate name for the car.
6. **Listo** (LEES toh) Spanish for "Ready."
7. **galvanized** (GAL vuh nyzd) *adj.* coated with zinc to prevent rusting.
8. **Mi olla** (mee OH yah) Spanish for "My pot."

Reading Skill

A **conclusion** is a decision you reach based on details in a story. Reread the first bracketed paragraph. What conclusion can you make about the importance of the car to Panchito's father?

_____

_____

_____

_____

Literary Analysis

The **theme** is often shown through events in a story. How is Mamá's pot described in the second bracketed paragraph?

_____

_____

How might the description connect with the story's theme?

_____

_____

Reading Check

Why did Papá believe that the original owner of his Plymouth must have been an important man? Circle the words that tell you.

Reading Skill

Reread the first bracketed passage. What **conclusion** can you make about the family from the description of the garage?

_____

_____

_____

Literary Analysis 🔍

Reread the second bracketed passage. How does the family make their new place a home?

_____

_____

_____

What does this tell you about the **theme** of this story?

_____

_____

_____

Reading Check

Why does Mamá, instead of Papá, speak to the foremen about getting work? Underline the words that tell you.

floor behind the front seat. All of us then climbed in. Papá sighed, wiped the sweat off his forehead with his sleeve, and said wearily: *"Es todo."*[9]

As we drove away, I felt a lump in my throat. I turned around and looked at our little shack for the last time.

At sunset we drove into a labor camp near Fresno. Since Papá did not speak English, Mamá asked the camp foreman if he needed any more workers. "We don't need no more," said the foreman, scratching his head. "Check with Sullivan down the road. Can't miss him. He lives in a big white house with a fence around it."

When we got there, Mamá walked up to the house. She went through a white gate, past a row of rose bushes, up the stairs to the front door. She rang the doorbell. The porch light went on and a tall husky man came out. They exchanged a few words. After the man went in, Mamá clasped her hands and hurried back to the car. "We have work! Mr. Sullivan said we can stay there the whole season," she said, gasping and pointing to an old garage near the stables.

The garage was worn out by the years. It had no windows. The walls, eaten by termites, strained to support the roof full of holes. The dirt floor, populated by earthworms, looked like a gray road map.

That night, by the light of a kerosene lamp, we unpacked and cleaned our new home. Roberto swept away the loose dirt, leaving the hard ground. Papá plugged the holes in the walls with old newspapers and tin can tops. Mamá fed my little brothers and sisters. Papá and Roberto then brought in the mattress and placed it on the far corner of the garage. "Mamá, you and the little ones sleep on the mattress. Roberto, Panchito, and I will sleep outside under the trees," Papá said.

Early next morning Mr. Sullivan showed us where his crop was, and after breakfast, Papá, Roberto, and I headed for the vineyard to pick.

Around nine o'clock the temperature had risen to almost one hundred degrees. I was completely soaked in sweat and my mouth felt as if I had been

---

9. **Es todo** (es TOH <u>thoh</u>) Spanish for "That's everything."

chewing on a handkerchief. I walked over to the end of the row, picked up the jug of water we had brought, and began drinking. "Don't drink too much; you'll get sick," Roberto shouted. No sooner had he said that than I felt sick to my stomach. I dropped to my knees and let the jug roll off my hands. I remained motionless with my eyes glued on the hot sandy ground. All I could hear was the <u>drone</u> of insects. Slowly I began to recover. I poured water over my face and neck and watched the dirty water run down my arms to the ground.

I still felt a little dizzy when we took a break to eat lunch. It was past two o'clock and we sat underneath a large walnut tree that was on the side of the road. While we ate, Papá jotted down the number of boxes we had picked. Roberto drew designs on the ground with a stick. Suddenly I noticed Papá's face turn pale as he looked down the road. "Here comes the school bus," he whispered loudly in alarm. <u>Instinctively</u>, Roberto and I ran and hid in the vineyards. We did not want to get in trouble for not going to school. The neatly dressed boys about my age got off. They carried books under their arms. After they crossed the street, the bus drove away. Roberto and I came out from hiding and joined Papá. *"Tienen que tener cuidado,"*[10] he warned us.

<u>After lunch we went back to work. The sun kept beating down. The buzzing insects, the wet sweat, and the hot dry dust made the afternoon seem to last forever.</u> Finally the mountains around the valley reached out and swallowed the sun. Within an hour it was too dark to continue picking. The vines blanketed the grapes, making it difficult to see the bunches. *"Vámonos,"*[11] said Papá, signaling to us that it was time to quit work. Papá then took out a pencil and

Vocabulary Development

drone (drohn) *n.* continuous humming sound
instinctively (in STINGK tiv lee) *adv.* done automatically, without thinking

10. **Tienen que tener cuidado** (tee EN en kay ten ER kwee <u>THAH</u> thoh) Spanish for "You have to be careful."
11. **Vámonos** (VAH moh nohs) Spanish for "Let's go."

TAKE NOTES

Reading Skill

What **conclusion** can you draw about Panchito and Roberto reacting "instinctively" to the approach of the school bus?

_____

_____

_____

Literary Analysis

A circuit is an unbroken path, like a circle—something that goes around and around without ever changing. How does the underlined passage connect with this **theme**?

_____

_____

_____

Reading Check

What happens when Panchito drinks too much water? Underline the passage that tells you.

Literary Analysis

The **theme** plays out in this story through many of Panchito's experiences. Underline the passage that tells how Panchito slowly grew used to the new work. What is the connection between Panchito's experience here and the **theme** of the story?

_____

_____

_____

_____

Stop to Reflect

Panchito thinks about starting school that year. What is unusual about Panchito's starting the sixth grade "for the first time that year"?

_____

_____

_____

Reading Skill

What **conclusion** can you draw about why Roberto must continue to work while Panchito goes to school?

_____

_____

_____

began to figure out how much we had earned our first day. He wrote down numbers, crossed some out, wrote down some more. "*Quince,*"[12] he murmured.

When we arrived home, we took a cold shower underneath a waterhose. We then sat down to eat dinner around some wooden crates that served as a table. Mamá had cooked a special meal for us. We had rice and tortillas with "*carne con chile,*"[13] my favorite dish.

The next morning I could hardly move. My body ached all over. I felt little control over my arms and legs. This feeling went on every morning for days until my muscles finally got used to the work.

It was Monday, the first week of November. The grape season was over and I could now go to school. I woke up early that morning and lay in bed, looking at the stars and <u>savoring</u> the thought of not going to work and of starting sixth grade for the first time that year. Since I could not sleep, I decided to get up and join Papá and Roberto at breakfast. I sat at the table across from Roberto, but I kept my head down. I did not want to look up and face him. I knew he was sad. He was not going to school today. He was not going tomorrow, or next week, or next month. He would not go until the cotton season was over, and that was sometime in February. I rubbed my hands together and watched the dry, acid stained skin fall to the floor in little rolls.

When Papá and Roberto left for work, I felt relief. I walked to the top of a small grade next to the shack and watched the "Carcanchita" disappear in the distance in a cloud of dust.

Two hours later, around eight o'clock, I stood by the side of the road waiting for school bus number twenty. When it arrived I climbed in. Everyone was busy either talking or yelling. I sat in an empty seat in the back.

Vocabulary Development
  savoring (SAY vuhr ing) *v.* enjoying; tasting with delight

---

12. **Quince** (KEEN say) Spanish for "Fifteen."
13. **carne con chile** (KAR nay kohn CHEE lay) dish of ground meat, hot peppers, beans, and tomatoes.

When the bus stopped in front of the school, I felt very nervous. I looked out the bus window and saw boys and girls carrying books under their arms. I put my hands in my pant pockets and walked to the principal's office. When I entered I heard a woman's voice say: "May I help you?" I was startled. I had not heard English for months. For a few seconds I remained speechless. I looked at the lady who waited for my answer. My first instinct was to answer her in Spanish, but I held back. Finally, after struggling for English words, I managed to tell her that I wanted to enroll in the sixth grade. After answering many questions, I was led to the classroom.

Mr. Lema, the sixth-grade teacher, greeted me and assigned me a desk. He then introduced me to the class. I was so nervous and scared at that moment when everyone's eyes were on me that I wished I were with Papá and Roberto picking cotton. After taking roll, Mr. Lema gave the class the assignment for the first hour. "The first thing we have to do this morning is finish reading the story we began yesterday," he said enthusiastically. He walked up to me, handed me an English book, and asked me to read. "We are on page 125," he said politely. When I heard this, I felt my blood rush to my head; I felt dizzy. "Would you like to read?" he asked hesitantly. I opened the book to page 125. My mouth was dry. My eyes began to water. I could not begin. "You can read later," Mr. Lema said understandingly.

For the rest of the reading period I kept getting angrier and angrier at myself. I should have read, I thought to myself.

During recess I went into the restroom and opened my English book to page 125. I began to read in a low voice, pretending I was in class. There were many words I did not know. I closed the book and headed back to the classroom.

Mr. Lema was sitting at his desk correcting papers. When I entered he looked up at me and smiled. I felt better. I walked up to him and asked if he could help me with the new words. "Gladly," he said.

The rest of the month I spent my lunch hours working on English with Mr. Lema, my best friend at school.

Literary Analysis

In the bracketed passage, Panchito knows exactly how to enroll in school. How does this fact relate to the circle **theme** of the story?

_____

_____

_____

Reading Skill

What **conclusion** can you draw on the basis of Panchito's reaction to Mr. Lema's question in the underlined text?

_____

_____

_____

What details lead you to this **conclusion**?

_____

_____

_____

Reading Check

What does Panchito do during recess? Underline the text that tells you.

What happens in school that makes Panchito excited? Underline the answer.

Literary Analysis

The **theme** of this story is a circuit or circle. How does Panchito's experience at the end of the story support the story's theme?

_____

_____

_____

_____

_____

One Friday during lunch hour Mr. Lema asked me to take a walk with him to the music room. "Do you like music?" he asked me as we entered the building.

"Yes, I like *corridos*," [14] I answered. He then picked up a trumpet, blew on it and handed it to me. The sound gave me goose bumps. I knew that sound. I had heard it in many corridos. "How would you like to learn how to play it?" he asked. He must have read my face because before I could answer, he added: "I'll teach you how to play it during our lunch hours."

That day I could hardly wait to get home to tell Papá and Mamá the great news. As I got off the bus, my little brothers and sisters ran up to meet me. They were yelling and screaming. I thought they were happy to see me, but when I opened the door to our shack, I saw that everything we owned was neatly packed in cardboard boxes.

Reader's Response: How do you think Panchito felt when he came back to the shack and found the packed boxes? Explain.

_____

_____

_____

_____

---

14. **corridos** (koh REE thohs) *n.* ballads.

The Circuit

1. **Respond:** What do you admire about Panchito? Why?

_____

_____

2. **Infer:** Why do you think Panchito calls Mr. Lema his "best friend at school"?

_____

_____

3. **Reading Skill:** Complete this chart to **draw conclusions** about the story.

Question	Details That Answer Question	Conclusion
Why does Panchito work so much?		
Why does Panchito not read aloud on the first day of school?		
Why are the family's belongings packed in boxes?		

4. **Literary Analysis:** How does the title relate to the story's **theme**?

_____

_____

Writing: Character Description

Write a **description** of a character from "The Circuit." Answer the following questions to gather details for your description.

- What quality do you find most interesting about your character?

  _____

  _____

- How does this character get along with other characters?

  _____

  _____

- What challenges does this character face?

  _____

  _____

Use your answers to write your description.

Listening and Speaking: Interview

With a partner, prepare for an **interview** about migrant worker life. On another sheet of paper, write a series of questions and answers to develop the interview. Use the following topics as guides.

1. Questions about the migrant worker's name, age, or family

2. Questions about where the worker works and what he or she does

3. Questions about the worker's education

The King of Mazy May • Aaron's Gift

Reading Skill

Drawing conclusions means making decisions or forming opinions about what has happened in a literary work. Base your conclusions on details in the text and on your own **prior knowledge**, or things you know from your own experience. For example, if a dog in a story wags its tail, you might conclude that the dog is friendly because you have seen this behavior in your own pet.

As you read, use this graphic organizer to record the conclusions you draw from the text. Check to see that your conclusions make sense. If they do not, think of new conclusions.

Details	
1.	2.

+

Prior Knowledge

Conclusion

Literary Analysis

The **setting** of a literary work is the time and place of the action. The time may be a historical era, the present or future, the season of the year, or the hour of the day. The place can be as general as outer space or as specific as a particular street. As you read, notice the impact of the setting on characters and events in a story.

The King of Mazy May
Jack London

Summary Walt and his father live in the far North, where people search for gold. Walt is left alone on their land one day. He watches as thieves prepare to steal a neighbor's property. Walt takes some of the thieves' sled dogs to warn the neighbor. His bravery earns him his nickname.

 ## Writing About the Big Question

Is Conflict Always Bad? In "The King of Mazy May" is a story about a boy named Walt who goes to great lengths to protect his friend's gold from thieves. Complete this sentence:

To defend a friend's property, a person could _____.

Note-taking Guide
Use this chart to record details from the story.

Why does Loren Hall go to Dawson?	Why does Walt go to Dawson?	Why do the men follow Walt?
Loren Hall goes to Dawson to register his claim.		

The King of Mazy May
Jack London

Walt Masters is not a very large boy, but there is manliness in his make-up, and he himself, although he does not know a great deal that most boys know, knows much that other boys do not know. He has never seen a train of cars nor an elevator in his life, and for that matter he has never once looked upon a cornfield, a plow, a cow, or even a chicken. He has never had a pair of shoes on his feet, nor gone to a picnic or a party, nor talked to a girl. But he has seen the sun at midnight, watched the ice jams on one of the mightiest of rivers, and played beneath the northern lights,[1] the one white child in thousands of square miles of frozen wilderness.

Walt has walked all the fourteen years of his life in suntanned, moose-hide moccasins, and he can go to the Indian camps and "talk big" with the men, and trade calico and beads with them for their precious furs. He can make bread without baking powder, yeast, or hops, shoot a moose at three hundred yards, and drive the wild wolf dogs fifty miles a day on the packed trail.

Last of all, he has a good heart, and is not afraid of the darkness and loneliness, of man or beast or thing. His father is a good man, strong and brave, and Walt is growing up like him.

Walt was born a thousand miles or so down the Yukon,[2] in a trading post below the Ramparts. After his mother died, his father and he came up on the river, step by step, from camp to camp, till now they are settled down on the Mazy May Creek in the Klondike country. Last year they and several others had spent much toil and time on the Mazy May, and endured great hardships; the creek, in turn, was just beginning to show up its richness and to reward them for their heavy labor. But with the news of their discoveries, strange men began to come and go through the short days and long nights, and many

---

1. **northern lights** glowing bands or streamers of light, sometimes appearing in the night sky of the Northern Hemisphere.

2. **Yukon** (YOO kahn) river flowing through the Yukon Territory of northwest Canada.

Activate Prior Knowledge

What do you already know about what it is like to live in a cold climate?

_____

_____

Reading Skill

Read the underlined passage. Drawing **conclusions** means making decisions or forming opinions about what has happened in a literary work. Think about where you can find a cornfield, plow, cow, and chicken. **Draw a conclusion** about where Walt has never been.

_____

_____

Literary Analysis

The **setting** of a story is the time and place of the action. Describe the setting of this story.

_____

_____

Reading Check

How old is Walt Masters? Circle the answer.

© Pearson Education

Reading Skill

Walt is able to look after himself while his father is away. **Draw a conclusion** about Walt based on this detail.

_____

_____

_____

Literary Analysis 🔍

Characters' actions depend on the **setting**. What travel choices were available during the time in which the story is set?

_____

_____

How did people find out about Loren's accident?

_____

_____

How does the time of the story affect travel and communications?

_____

_____

Reading Check

Why is Walt worried? Underline the answer in the text.

unjust things they did to the men who had worked so long upon the creek.

Si Hartman had gone away on a moose hunt, to return and find new stakes driven and his claim jumped.[3] George Lukens and his brother had lost their claims in a like manner, having delayed too long on the way to Dawson to record them. In short, it was the old story, and quite a number of the earnest, industrious prospectors had suffered similar losses.

But Walt Masters's father had recorded his claim at the start, so Walt had nothing to fear now that his father had gone on a short trip up the White River prospecting for quartz. Walt was well able to stay by himself in the cabin, cook his three meals a day, and look after things. Not only did he look after his father's claim, but he had agreed to keep an eye on the adjoining one of Loren Hall, who had started for Dawson to record it.

Loren Hall was an old man, and he had no dogs, so he had to travel very slowly. After he had been gone some time, word came up the river that he had broken through the ice at Rosebud Creek and frozen his feet so badly that he would not be able to travel for a couple of weeks. Then Walt Masters received the news that old Loren was nearly all right again, and about to move on afoot for Dawson as fast as a weakened man could.

Walt was worried, however; the claim was <u>liable</u> to be jumped at any moment because of this delay, and a fresh stampede had started in on the Mazy May. He did not like the looks of the newcomers, and one day, when five of them came by with crack dog teams and the lightest of camping outfits, he could see that they were prepared to make speed, and resolved to keep an eye on them. So he locked up the cabin and followed them, being at the same time careful to remain hidden.

He had not watched them long before he was sure that they were professional stampeders, bent on

Vocabulary Development

liable (LY uh buhl) *adj.* likely to do something or to happen

---

3. **claim jumped** A claim is a piece of land marked by a miner with stakes to show where the borders are. A claim that is jumped is stolen by someone else.

jumping all the claims in sight. Walt crept along the snow at the rim of the creek and saw them change many stakes, destroy old ones, and set up new ones.

In the afternoon, with Walt always trailing on their heels, they came back down the creek, unharnessed their dogs, and went into camp within two claims of his cabin. When he saw them make preparations to cook, he hurried home to get something to eat himself, and then hurried back. He crept so close that he could hear them talking quite plainly, and by pushing the underbrush aside he could catch occasional glimpses of them. They had finished eating and were smoking around the fire.

"The creek is all right, boys," a large, black-bearded man, evidently the leader, said, "and I think the best thing we can do is to pull out tonight. The dogs can follow the trail; besides, it's going to be moonlight. What say you?"

"But it's going to be beastly cold," objected one of the party. "It's forty below zero now."

"An' sure, can't ye keep warm by jumpin' off the sleds an' runnin' after the dogs?" cried an Irishman. "An' who wouldn't? The creek's as rich as a United States mint! Faith, it's an ilegant chanst to be gettin' a run fer yer money! An' if ye don't run, it's mebbe you'll not get the money at all, at all."

"That's it," said the leader. "If we can get to Dawson and record, we're rich men; and there's no telling who's been sneaking along in our tracks, watching us, and perhaps now off to give the alarm. The thing for us to do is to rest the dogs a bit, and then hit the trail as hard as we can. What do you say?"

Evidently the men had agreed with their leader, for Walt Masters could hear nothing but the rattle of the tin dishes which were being washed. Peering out cautiously, he could see the leader studying a piece of paper. Walt knew what it was at a glance—a list of all the unrecorded claims on Mazy May. Any man could get these lists by applying to the gold commissioner at Dawson.

"Thirty-two," the leader said, lifting his face to the men. "Thirty-two isn't recorded, and this is thirty-three. Come on; let's take a look at it. I saw somebody had been working on it when we came up this morning."

Reading Skill

Why does Walt keep watch on the men?

_____

_____

Read the bracketed passage. **Draw a conclusion** about Walt's feelings. What does Walt's behavior tell you about his attitude toward the men?

_____

_____

_____

Literary Analysis

Study the **setting** of this story. During what time of year does the story take place?

_____

Put a star next to two details that support your answer.

Reading Check

What can a sled driver do to keep warm, according to the Irishman? Underline the answer.

Reading Skill

Read the bracketed paragraph. What do the men find on Loren's claim?

_____

_____

Draw a conclusion about why the leader is interested in the unrecorded claim.

_____

_____

_____

Stop to Reflect

Walt decides to steal the thieves' dogs in order to stop the thieves from stealing Loren's claim. Do you agree with his decision? Explain.

_____

_____

_____

_____

Reading Check

How many miles is it to Dawson? Circle the answer.

Three of the men went with him, leaving one to remain in camp. Walt crept carefully after them till they came to Loren Hall's shaft. One of the men went down and built a fire on the bottom to thaw out the frozen gravel, while the others built another fire on the dump and melted water in a couple of gold pans. This they poured into a piece of canvas stretched between two logs, used by Loren Hall in which to wash his gold.

In a short time a couple of buckets of dirt were sent up by the man in the shaft, and Walt could see the others grouped anxiously about their leader as he proceeded to wash it. When this was finished, they stared at the broad streak of black sand and yellow gold grains on the bottom of the pan, and one of them called excitedly for the man who had remained in camp to come. Loren Hall had struck it rich and his claim was not yet recorded. It was plain that they were going to jump it.

Walt lay in the snow, thinking rapidly. He was only a boy, but in the face of the threatened injustice to old lame Loren Hall he felt that he must do something. He waited and watched, with his mind made up, till he saw the men begin to square up new stakes. Then he crawled away till out of hearing, and broke into a run for the camp of the stampeders. Walt's father had taken their own dogs with him prospecting, and the boy knew how impossible it was for him to undertake the seventy miles to Dawson without the aid of dogs.

Gaining the camp, he picked out, with an experienced eye, the easiest running sled and started to harness up the stampeders' dogs. There were three teams of six each, and from these he chose ten of the best. Realizing how necessary it was to have a good head dog, he strove to discover a leader amongst them; but he had little time in which to do it, for he could hear the voices of the returning men. By the time the team was in shape and everything ready, the claim-jumpers came into sight in an open place not more than a hundred yards from the trail, which ran down the bed of the creek. They cried out to Walt, but instead of giving heed to them he grabbed up one of their fur sleeping robes, which lay loosely in the snow, and leaped upon the sled.

© Pearson Education

"Mush! Hi! Mush on!" he cried to the animals, snapping the keen-lashed whip among them.

The dogs sprang against the yoke straps, and the sled jerked under way so suddenly as to almost throw him off. Then it curved into the creek, poising perilously on the runner. He was almost breathless with suspense, when it finally righted with a bound and sprang ahead again. The creek bank was high and he could not see the men, although he could hear their cries and knew they were running to cut him off. He did not dare to think what would happen if they caught him; he just clung to the sled, his heart beating wildly, and watched the snow rim of the bank above him.

Suddenly, over this snow rim came the flying body of the Irishman, who had leaped straight for the sled in a desperate attempt to capture it; but he was an instant too late. Striking on the very rear of it, he was thrown from his feet, backward, into the snow. Yet, with the quickness of a cat, he had clutched the end of the sled with one hand, turned over, and was dragging behind on his breast, swearing at the boy and threatening all kinds of terrible things if he did not stop the dogs; but Walt cracked him sharply across the knuckles with the butt of the dog whip till he let go.

It was eight miles from Walt's claim to the Yukon— eight very crooked miles, for the creek wound back and forth like a snake, "tying knots in itself," as George Lukens said. And because it was so crooked the dogs could not get up their best speed, while the sled ground heavily on its side against the curves, now to the right, now to the left.

Travelers who had come up and down the Mazy May on foot, with packs on their backs, had declined to go round all the bends, and instead had made shortcuts across the narrow necks of creek bottom. Two of his pursuers had gone back to harness the remaining dogs, but the others took advantage of these shortcuts, running on foot, and before he knew it they had almost overtaken him.

Vocabulary Development
declined (di KLYND) *v.* refused

TAKE NOTES

Literary Analysis

Read the first bracketed paragraph. What almost happens when Walt's sled curves into the creek? Underline the answer in the text. What conditions of the **setting** make it difficult for Walt to get to Dawson?

_____

_____

Reading Skill

Reread the second bracketed paragraph. What is Walt's heart doing?

_____

_____

Given your **prior knowledge**, what **conclusion** can you draw about the way Walt feels?

_____

_____

Reading Check

How far is it from Walt's claim to the Yukon? Underline the answer.

Literary Analysis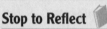

The landscape that is described in the bracketed paragraph helps Walt escape from the men. Describe the **setting**.

_____

_____

_____

Stop to Reflect

What does Walt do when he sees that the stampeders have given up the chase? Underline the answer in the text. Do you agree with Walt? Explain.

_____

_____

_____

Reading Check

Why is the trail "hard and glassy"? Underline the answer.

"Halt!" they cried after him. "Stop, or we'll shoot!"

But Walt only yelled the harder at the dogs, and dashed around the bend with a couple of revolver bullets singing after him. At the next bend they had drawn up closer still, and the bullets struck uncomfortably near him but at this point the Mazy May straightened out and ran for half a mile as the crow flies. Here the dogs stretched out in their long wolf swing, and the stampeders, quickly winded, slowed down and waited for their own sled to come up.

Looking over his shoulder, Walt reasoned that they had not given up the chase for good, and that they would soon be after him again. So he wrapped the fur robe about him to shut out the stinging air, and lay flat on the empty sled, encouraging the dogs, as he well knew how.

At last, twisting abruptly between two river islands, he came upon the mighty Yukon sweeping grandly to the north. He could not see from bank to bank, and in the quick-falling twilight it loomed a great white sea of frozen stillness. There was not a sound, save the breathing of the dogs, and the churn of the steel-shod sled.

No snow had fallen for several weeks, and the traffic had packed the main river trail till it was hard and glassy as glare ice. Over this the sled flew along, and the dogs kept the trail fairly well, although Walt quickly discovered that he had made a mistake in choosing the leader. As they were driven in single file, without reins, he had to guide them by his voice, and it was evident the head dog had never learned the meaning of "gee" and "haw."[4] He hugged the inside of the curves too closely, often forcing his comrades behind him into the soft snow, while several times he thus capsized[5] the sled.

There was no wind, but the speed at which he traveled created a bitter blast, and with the thermometer down to forty below, this bit through fur and flesh to the very bones. Aware that if he remained constantly upon the sled he would freeze to death, and knowing the practice of Arctic travelers,

---

4. **"gee" and "haw"** (jee) and (haw) commands used to tell an animal to turn to the right or the left.

5. **capsized** (KAP syzd) v. overturned.

Walt shortened up one of the lashing thongs, and whenever he felt chilled, seized hold of it, jumped off, and ran behind till warmth was restored. Then he would climb on and rest till the process had to be repeated.

Looking back he could see the sled of his pursuers, drawn by eight dogs, rising and falling over the ice hummocks like a boat in a seaway. The Irishman and the black-bearded leader were with it, taking turns in running and riding.

Night fell, and in the blackness of the first hour or so Walt toiled desperately with his dogs. On account of the poor lead dog, they were continually floundering off the beaten track into the soft snow, and the sled was as often riding on its side or top as it was in the proper way. This work and strain tried his strength sorely. Had he not been in such haste he could have avoided much of it, but he feared the stampeders would creep up in the darkness and overtake him. However, he could hear them yelling to their dogs, and knew from the sounds they were coming up very slowly.

When the moon rose he was off Sixty Mile, and Dawson was only fifty miles away. He was almost exhausted, and breathed a sigh of relief as he climbed on the sled again. Looking back, he saw his enemies had crawled up within four hundred yards. At this space they remained, a black speck of motion on the white river breast. Strive as they would, they could not shorten this distance, and strive as he would, he could not increase it.

Walt had now discovered the proper lead dog, and he knew he could easily run away from them if he could only change the bad leader for the good one. But this was impossible, for a moment's delay, at the speed they were running, would bring the men behind upon him.

When he was off the mouth of Rosebud Creek, just as he was topping a rise, the report of a gun and the ping of a bullet on the ice beside him told him that they were this time shooting at him with a rifle. And from then on, as he cleared the summit of each ice

Vocabulary Development
summit (sum it) *n.* highest part

Reading Skill

Read the bracketed paragraph. Why does Walt not fix the problem with the dogs?

_____

_____

What **conclusion** can you **draw** about how close Walt believes the men to be?

_____

_____

Literary Analysis

How has the **setting** changed by this point in the story?

_____

_____

Underline details that support your answer.

Reading Skill

Draw a conclusion about Walt's dogs. How would having the proper lead dog help Walt?

_____

_____

_____

The King of Mazy May **129**

Read the bracketed paragraphs. Why do the men stop shooting at Walt so often?

_____

_____

Whom do the men shoot? Underline the answer. What **conclusion** can you **draw** about what or whom the men hoped to shoot? Explain.

_____

_____

_____

Literary Analysis

Read the bracketed paragraphs. How has the **setting** changed?

_____

_____

Reading Check

What does Walt do when his enemies pull up beside him? Draw a box around the answer.

jam, he stretched flat on the leaping sled till the rifle shot from the rear warned him that he was safe till the next ice jam was reached.

Now it is very hard to lie on a moving sled, jumping and plunging and yawing[6] like a boat before the wind, and to shoot through the deceiving moonlight at an object four hundred yards away on another moving sled performing equally wild antics. So it is not to be wondered at that the black-bearded leader did not hit him.

After several hours of this, during which, perhaps, a score of bullets had struck about him, their ammunition began to give out and their fire slackened. They took greater care, and shot at him at the most favorable opportunities. He was also leaving them behind, the distance slowly increasing to six hundred yards.

Lifting clear on the crest of a great jam off Indian River, Walt Masters met with his first accident. A bullet sang past his ears, and struck the bad lead dog.

The poor brute plunged in a heap, with the rest of the team on top of him.

Like a flash Walt was by the leader. Cutting the traces with his hunting knife, he dragged the dying animal to one side and straightened out the team.

He glanced back. The other sled was coming up like an express train. With half the dogs still over their traces, he cried "Mush on!" and leaped upon the sled just as the pursuers dashed abreast[7] of him.

The Irishman was preparing to spring for him— they were so sure they had him that they did not shoot—when Walt turned fiercely upon them with his whip.

He struck at their faces, and men must save their faces with their hands. So there was no shooting just then. Before they could recover from the hot rain of blows, Walt reached out from his sled, catching their wheel dog by the forelegs in midspring, and throwing him heavily. This snarled the team, capsizing the sled and tangling his enemies up beautifully.

Away Walt flew, the runners of his sled fairly screaming as they bounded over the frozen surface.

6. **yawing** (YAW ing) _adj._ swinging from side to side.
7. **abreast** (uh BREST) _adv._ alongside.

And what had seemed an accident proved to be a blessing in disguise. The proper lead dog was now to the fore, and he stretched low and whined with joy as he jerked his comrades along.

By the time he reached Ainslie's Creek, seventeen miles from Dawson, Walt had left his pursuers, a tiny speck, far behind. At Monte Cristo Island he could no longer see them. And at Swede Creek, just as daylight was silvering the pines, he ran plump into the camp of old Loren Hall.

Almost as quick as it takes to tell it, Loren had his sleeping furs rolled up, and had joined Walt on the sled. They permitted the dogs to travel more slowly, as there was no sign of the chase in the rear, and just as they pulled up at the gold commissioner's office in Dawson, Walt, who had kept his eyes open to the last, fell asleep.

And because of what Walt Masters did on this night, the men of the Yukon have become proud of him, and speak of him now as the King of Mazy May.

Reader's Response: Would you enjoy Walt's way of life? Why or why not?

_____

_____

_____

Reading Skill

Read the bracketed paragraph. **Draw conclusions** about why Walt falls asleep when the sled pulls into Dawson.

_____

_____

_____

Stop to Reflect

Why would people call Walt "The King of Mazy May"?

_____

_____

Reading Check 🖉

Where is Loren Hall's camp? Circle the answer.

The King of Mazy May

1. **Compare and Contrast:** How are Walt's responsibilities different from those of other children his age?

_____

_____

_____

2. **Apply:** Suppose that you had lived during the time in which the story is set. Would you have been tempted to go to the Klondike in search of gold? Explain.

_____

_____

_____

3. **Reading Skill:** Given your **prior knowledge**, how do you think Walt feels when people call him the "King of Mazy May"?

_____

_____

4. **Literary Analysis:** Use this chart to list ways in which details of the **setting** affect events in the story.

	Details of Setting	Story Events
Time		
Place		

Writing: Personal Narrative

Write a short **personal narrative** about a time when you worked hard to meet a goal. Answer these questions to help you get started:

- What was the goal?

  _____

- What was the first thing that happened?

  _____

- What happened before you met your goal?

  _____

  _____

- What happened when you finally reached your goal?

  _____

  _____

Use your answers to write your narrative in the correct order.

Research and Technology: Presentation

Prepare a **presentation** on gold mining. Be sure to use reliable sources, such as encyclopedias or Web sites that are managed by schools. Use this chart to organize your research.

Source	Information Found	Reliable? Yes or No

Use your chart to prepare your presentation.

Aaron's Gift
Myron Levoy

Summary Ten-year-old Aaron fixes a hurt pigeon's wing. Aaron plans to give the bird to his grandmother. A gang of neighborhood boys tries to burn the pigeon. Aaron is beaten up while trying to save the bird. The bird flies away. Aaron is surprised that he has still given a gift to his grandmother.

Writing About the Big Question

Is Conflict Always Bad? In "Aaron's Gift," Aaron does not listen to his mother when she tells him to stay away from a gang of boys and, as a result, Aaron gets hurt. Complete this sentence:

Children might oppose their parents, but very often _____.

Note-taking Guide
Use this chart to record the most important events of the story.

Where does Aaron find the pigeon?	
How does Aaron help it?	
Who invites Aaron to join her club?	
What happens when the boys try to burn the pigeon?	
Why is his grandmother grateful?	

Aaron's Gift

1. **Compare and Contrast:** How are Carl and the boys like the Cossacks?

   _____

   _____

2. **Apply:** Aaron's grandmother thanks him for the gift of the bird's freedom. Name two other "gifts" that are not objects a person could buy, find, or make. Explain why they are important.

   _____

   _____

3. **Reading Skill:** Given your **prior knowledge**, why do you think Aaron's mother forbids him to play with Carl and the other boys?

   _____

   _____

4. **Literary Analysis:** Complete the chart to list ways in which details of the **setting** affect events in the story.

	Details of Setting	Story Events
Time		
Place		

Writing: Personal Narrative

Write a short **personal narrative** about a time when you worked hard to meet a goal. Answer these questions to help you get started:

- What was the goal?

_____

- What happened before you met your goal?

_____

_____

- What happened when you finally reached your goal?

_____

_____

Research and Technology: Presentation

Create a chart like the following on a separate sheet of paper. Then add information that you find about carrier pigeons. Use this information in your **presentation**.

What Carrier Pigeons Look Like	What Carrier Pigeons Eat	What Carrier Pigeons Can Do	How Carrier Pigeons are Trained

Compare-and-Contrast Articles

About Compare-and-Contrast Articles

A **compare-and-contrast article** is descriptive writing. This type of writing looks at what is alike and what is different about two or more subjects. There are two common ways of organizing these articles.

- **Block organization:** First, the writer gives all of the details of one subject. Then, the writer gives all of the details of the other subject.
- **Point-by-point organization:** First, the writer gives one detail about both subjects. Then, the writer gives another detail about both subjects.

Reading Skill

The best way to understand a compare-and-contrast article is by **identifying and analyzing the organization.**

Identifying: First, identify what kind of organization the writer uses. Then, use the organization to find the main points. This method will help you understand how the subjects are alike and different.

Analyzing: Study the information by breaking it into parts and groups. Ask yourself questions like the ones in the chart to evaluate the comparisons.

Questions for evaluating comparison-and-contrast organization
Are the same categories covered for each half of the comparison?
Are an approximately equal number of details supplied for each category?
Does the writer support compare-and-contrast statements with examples and facts?

Vocabulary Builder

Parts of Speech The word *so* can be a conjunction showing why something happens. It can also be an adverb that emphasizes the word the follows it. Find the word *so* in the paragraph that begins "The drifts were . . ." What part of speech does the word *so* have in this paragraph? Circle the answer below.

conjunction   adverb

Text Structure

The boldface word on this page is a heading. The headings tell you what the writer will compare in the next section of the article. What is the first thing the writer is going to compare?

_____

_____

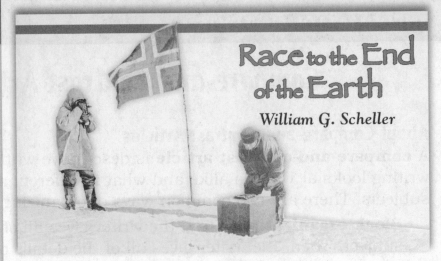

Race to the End of the Earth

William G. Scheller

Amundsen's team proving South Pole location

Two explorers competed against each other and a brutal environment to reach the South Pole.

The drifts were so deep and the snow was falling so heavily that the team of five Norwegian explorers could hardly see their sled dogs a few feet ahead of them. Behind rose a monstrous mountain barrier. The men had been the first to cross it. But now they and their dogs were stumbling toward a stark and desolate plateau continually blasted by blizzards. The landscape was broken only by the towering peaks of mountains that lay buried beneath a mile of ancient ice. Led by Roald Amundsen, the men were still 300 miles from their goal: the South Pole.

On that same day, a party of 14 British explorers was also struggling across a similarly terrifying landscape toward the same destination. But they were almost twice as far from success. Their commander was Capt. Robert Falcon Scott, a naval officer. Amundsen was Scott's rival.

Preparation Both expedition leaders had long been preparing for their race to the South Pole. Amundsen came from a family of hardy sailors, and he had decided at the age of 15 to become a polar explorer. He conditioned himself by taking long ski trips across the Norwegian countryside and by sleeping with his windows open in winter.

By the time of his South Pole attempt, Amundsen was an experienced explorer. He had sailed as a naval officer on an expedition in 1897 that charted sections of the Antarctic coast. Between 1903 and 1906 he commanded the ship that made the first voyage through the Northwest Passage, the icy route that threads its way through the Canadian islands separating the Atlantic and Pacific Oceans. During that long journey Amundsen learned how the native people of the Arctic dress and eat to survive in extreme cold. He also learned that the dogsled was the most efficient method of polar transportation. These lessons would serve him well at Earth's frozen southern end.

Robert Scott was an officer in the British Navy. He had decided that leading a daring expedition of discovery would be an immediate route to higher rank. He heard that Great Britain's Royal Geographical Society was organizing such an exploration, and he volunteered in 1899 to be its commander. Now he was in command again.

The two expedition leaders had different styles. Scott followed a British tradition of brave sacrifice. He felt that he and his men should be able to reach the South Pole with as little help as possible from sled dogs and special equipment. He did bring dogs to Antarctica, as well as 19 ponies and three gasoline-powered sledges, or sturdy sleds. But his plan was for his team to "man-haul," or carry, all of their own supplies along the final portion of the route.

Scott's ill-fated team

TAKE NOTES

Fluency Builder

The comma in the underlined sentence is used to set off words that describe the Northwest Passage. Circle two other sentences on this page that also use a comma to set off a description. Then, read the underlined sentence aloud.

Cultural Understanding

The Navy is the branch of the military that is organized for fighting a war at sea. The adjective that describes things relating to the Navy is *naval*.

Vocabulary Builder

Proper Nouns In English, a *proper noun* names a specific person, place, or thing. Proper nouns always begin with a capital letter. *Scott* is one proper noun in the last paragraph on this page. Circle the other proper nouns in the paragraph.

Roald Amundsen had spent much time in the far north, and he was a practical man. He'd seen how useful dogs were to Arctic inhabitants. He would be traveling in one of the most dangerous places on Earth, and he knew that sled dogs would be able to get his party all the way to the South Pole and make a safe return. Amundsen also placed great faith in skis, which he and his Norwegian team members had used since childhood. The British explorers had rarely used skis before this expedition and did not understand their great value.

The two leaders even had different ideas about diet. Scott's men would rely on canned meat. But Amundsen's plan made more sense. He and his men would eat plenty of fresh seal meat. Amundsen may not have fully understood the importance of vitamins, but fresh meat is a better source of vitamin C, which prevents scurvy, a painful and sometimes deadly disease.

The Race Is On! After making long sea voyages from Europe, Scott and Amundsen set up base camps in January on opposite edges of the Ross Ice Shelf. Each team spent the dark winter months making preparations to push on to the Pole when spring would arrive in Antarctica. Amundsen left base camp on October 20, 1911, with a party of four. Scott, accompanied by nine men, set off from his camp 11 days later. Four others had already gone ahead on the motorized sledges.

Scott's Final Diary Entry Things went wrong for Scott from the beginning. The sledges broke down and had to be abandoned. Scott and his men soon met up with the drivers, who were traveling on foot. Blizzards then struck and lasted several weeks into December. Scott's ponies were proving to be a poor choice for Antarctic travel as well. Their hooves sank deep into the snow, and their perspiration froze on their bodies, forming sheets of ice. (Dogs do not perspire; they pant.) On December 9, the men shot the last of the surviving weak and frozen ponies. Two days later Scott sent his remaining dogs back to base camp along with several members of the expedition. Over the next month, most of the men returned to the camp. Scott's plan from here on was for the five men remaining to man-haul supplies the rest of the way to the Pole and back.

For Scott and his men, the journey was long and brutal. To cover only ten miles each day, the team toiled like dogs—like the dogs they no longer had. Food and fuel were in short supply, so the men lacked the energy they needed for such a crushing task.

Roald Amundsen's careful planning and Arctic experience were paying off. Even so, there's no such thing as easy travel by land in Antarctica. To the men who had just crossed those terrible mountains, the Polar Plateau might have looked easy. But Amundsen's team still had to cross a long stretch they later named the "Devil's Ballroom." It was a thin crust of ice that concealed crevasses, or deep gaps, that could swallow men, sleds, and dogs. Stumbling into one crevasse, a team of dogs dangled by their harnesses until the men could pull them up to safety.

Reaching the Goal On skis, with the "ballroom" behind them and well-fed dogs pulling their supply sleds, Amundsen and his men swept across the ice. The going was smooth for them, and the weather was fine. The Norwegian's only worry was that they'd find Scott had gotten to the Pole first. On the afternoon of December 14, 1911, it was plain that no one was ahead of them. At three o'clock, Amundsen skied in front of the team's sleds, then stopped to look at his navigation instruments. There was no point further south. He was at the South Pole!

Vocabulary Builder

Multiple-meaning Words The adverb *here* usually means "in or to this place." It can also refer to a period of time that has already begun. Find the word *here* in the first paragraph on this page. To what does the adverb refer? Circle the answer below.

place   time

Vocabulary Builder

Possessive Nouns A *possessive noun* is formed by adding an apostrophe (') and the letter *s*, such as in the phrase *Roald Amundsen's careful planning*. Underline the other possessive nouns in the paragraph.

Comprehension Builder

Which explorer reached the South Pole?

_____

_____

Was your prediction correct?

_____

_____

Thinking About the
Compare-and-Contrast Article

1. Contrast the strategies used by each team.

   Scott: _____

   Amundsen: _____

2. Evaluate the organization of "Race to the End of the Earth." Does the writer balance the details? Describe an example.

   _____

   _____

TALK ABOUT IT Reading Skill

3. Describe a major difference between Scott and Amundsen.

   _____

4. Describe a similarity in the backgrounds of the two men.

   _____

WRITE ABOUT IT Timed Writing: Analysis (20 minutes)

Analyze the reasons why Amundsen reached the South Pole before Scott. Use this chart to organize details from the article.

	Amundsen	Scott
Preparation		
Dogs and special equipment		
Diet		

Zlata's Diary

Nonfiction writing is about real people, places, ideas, and experiences. The stories sometimes come from the author's life.

The **organization** of nonfiction writing is important. Essays and articles should be organized so that information is clear. This chart lists different types of organization.

Organization	Definition	Example
Chronological	• presents details in time order, from first to last or even from last to first	a vacation journal
Cause-and-effect	• shows relationships among events	essay about reasons why a neighborhood pool closed and the effect the pool's closing has on kids in the neighborhood
Comparison-and-contrast	• shows ways in which two or more subjects are similar and different	essay that compares how two schools are the same and different

How an author approaches a subject is important. The following list tells about the importance of the author in nonfiction writing.

- **Author's influence:** Everyone has a different background, culture, and personal beliefs. Authors are shaped by these experiences.
- **Author's style:** Every author has a different writing style. An author's style might be formal, friendly, or even funny.
- **Mood:** The mood is the overall feeling created by an essay or article. The mood of a piece of writing can depend on an author's influence and style.
- **Author's purpose:** Every author has a purpose, or reason, for writing. The purpose helps the writer decide which details to include. Some purposes are to entertain, to inform, or to persuade.

The following are some types of nonfiction writing:

Letters, journals, and diaries: personal thoughts and memories

Biographies and autobiographies: stories about a person's life

- **Biography:** story about a person's life written by another person

- **Autobiography:** story a person writes about his or her own life

Media accounts: newspaper and magazine articles, television or radio reports

Essays and articles: short works that focus on a certain subject

- **Historical writing:** gives facts and explanations about historic events

- **Persuasive writing:** persuades reader to adopt a point of view or take an action

- **Descriptive writing:** appeals to the five senses

- **Expository writing:** presents facts, discusses ideas, or explains a process

- **Narrative writing:** tells the story of real-life experiences

- **Visual writing:** uses text and images to share information

- **Reflective writing:** tells why an event is important to the author

Zlata's Diary
Zlata Filipović

Summary Zlata Filipović is a young girl in fifth grade in Sarajevo. She begins to keep a diary as a war is beginning in her country. Her diary becomes a journal of the war. She writes about the difficulties that her family, her friends, and her city face.

Note-taking Guide

Fill in this chart with details about Zlata.

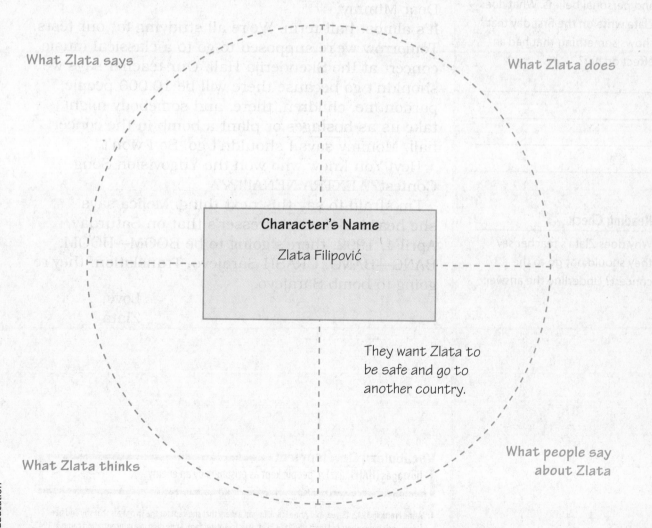

What Zlata says

What Zlata does

Character's Name

Zlata Filipović

They want Zlata to be safe and go to another country.

What Zlata thinks

What people say about Zlata

Zlata's Diary

Zlata Filipović

Monday, March 30, 1992

Hey, Diary! You know what I think? Since Anne Frank[1] called her diary Kitty, maybe I could give you a name too. What about:
ASFALTINA PIDZAMETA
SEFIKA HIKMETA
SEVALA MIMMY
or something else???
I'm thinking, thinking . . .
I've decided! I'm going to call you
MIMMY[2]
All right, then, let's start.

Nonfiction

The **author's influence** includes the author's background, culture, and personal beliefs. What does Zlata write on the first day that shows something that had an effect on her?

_____

_____

_____

_____

Dear Mimmy,
It's almost half-term. We're all studying for our tests. Tomorrow we're supposed to go to a classical music concert at the Skenderija Hall. Our teacher says we shouldn't go because there will be 10,000 people, pardon me, children, there, and somebody might take us as <u>hostages</u> or plant a bomb in the concert hall. Mommy says I shouldn't go. So I won't.
   Hey! You know who won the Yugovision Song Contest?![3] EXTRA NENA!!!???
   I'm afraid to say this next thing. Melica says she heard at the hairdresser's that on Saturday, April 4, 1992, there's going to be BOOM—BOOM, BANG—BANG, CRASH Sarajevo. Translation: they're going to bomb Sarajevo.

Love,
Zlata

Reading Check

Why does Zlata's teacher say they should not go to the concert? Underline the answer.

Vocabulary Development

hostages (HAHS tij iz) *n.* people kept as prisoners by an enemy

1. **Anne Frank** In 1942, 13-year-old Anne Frank began a diary that she kept for the two years that she and her family and some others hid from the Nazis in an attic in Amsterdam. Anne died in a concentration camp in 1945. Her father published parts of the diary in 1947, and it has since become a classic.
2. **Mimmy** (MEE mee)
3. **Yugovision Song Contest** competition to pick Yugoslavia's entry in the big Eurovision Song Contest.

Sunday, April 12, 1992

Dear Mimmy,
The new sections of town—Dobrinja, Mojmilo,
Vojnicko polje—are being badly <u>shelled</u>. Everything is
being destroyed, burned, the people are in shelters.
Here in the middle of town, where we live, it's different.
It's quiet. People go out. It was a nice warm spring
day today. We went out too. Vaso Miskin Street was
full of people, children. It looked like a peace march.
People came out to be together, they don't want war.
They want to live and enjoy themselves the way they
used to. That's only natural, isn't it? Who likes or
wants war, when it's the worst thing in the world?

I keep thinking about the march I joined today. It's
bigger and stronger than war. That's why it will win.
The people must be the ones to win, not the war,
because war has nothing to do with humanity. War
is something inhuman.

Zlata

Tuesday, April 14, 1992

Dear Mimmy,
People are leaving Sarajevo. The airport, train and
bus stations are packed. I saw sad pictures on TV
of people parting. Families, friends separating. Some
are leaving, others staying. It's so sad. Why? These
people and children aren't guilty of anything. Keka
and Braco[4] came early this morning. They're in the
kitchen with Mommy and Daddy, whispering. Keka
and Mommy are crying. I don't think they know what
to do—whether to stay or to go. Neither way is good.

Zlata

Saturday, May 2, 1992

Dear Mimmy,
<u>Today was truly, absolutely the worst day ever in
Sarajevo. The shooting started around noon. Mommy
and I moved into the hall. Daddy was in his office,
under our apartment, at the time. We told him on the</u>

© Pearson Education

Vocabulary Development
shelled (sheld) *v.* bombed

---

4. **Keka and Braco** nicknames of a husband and wife who are friends of Zlata's parents.

TAKE NOTES

Nonfiction

A diary can have different kinds
of **organization. Comparison-
and-contrast organization**
shows how two things are alike
and different. What two things
does Zlata **contrast** on April 12,
1992?

_____

_____

_____

Nonfiction

Diaries record someone's
thoughts. These thoughts can
show strong beliefs. What belief
does Zlata show in the bracketed
paragraph?

_____

_____

_____

_____

Nonfiction

Cause-and-effect organization
shows how one event leads to
another event. List a cause and
an effect from the underlined
passage.

_____

_____

_____

_____

Zlata's Diary 147

Nonfiction

The author controls the **mood** of a piece of writing by how he or she uses words. What mood does Zlata show with her choice of words in the underlined passage? Explain.

_____

_____

_____

_____

Nonfiction

The **author's purpose** is the reason an author writes. The purpose helps the author decide which details to include. What details does the author use early in the bracketed paragraph to show that the war is moving closer to home?

_____

_____

_____

_____

Reading Check

How did Zlata and her family learn that their President had been kidnapped? Circle the text that tells you.

intercom to run quickly to the downstairs lobby where we'd meet him. We brought Cicko[5] with us. The gunfire was getting worse, and we couldn't get over the wall to the Bobars',[6] so we ran down to our own cellar.

The cellar is ugly, dark, smelly. Mommy, who's terrified of mice, had two fears to cope with. The three of us were in the same corner as the other day. We listened to the pounding shells, the shooting, the thundering noise overhead. We even heard planes. At one moment I realized that this awful cellar was the only place that could save our lives. Suddenly, it started to look almost warm and nice. It was the only way we could defend ourselves against all this terrible shooting. We heard glass shattering in our street. Horrible. I put my fingers in my ears to block out the terrible sounds. I was worried about Cicko. We had left him behind in the lobby. Would he catch cold there? Would something hit him? I was terribly hungry and thirsty. We had left our half-cooked lunch in the kitchen.

When the shooting died down a bit, Daddy ran over to our apartment and brought us back some sandwiches. He said he could smell something burning and that the phones weren't working. He brought our TV set down to the cellar. That's when we learned that the main post office (near us) was on fire and that they had kidnapped our President. At around 8:00 we went back up to our apartment. Almost every window in our street was broken. Ours were all right, thank God. I saw the post office in flames. A terrible sight. The fire-fighters battled with the raging fire. Daddy took a few photos of the post office being devoured by the flames. He said they wouldn't come out because I had been fiddling with something on the camera. I was sorry. The whole apartment smelled of the burning fire. God, and I used to pass by there every day. It had just been

Vocabulary Development

intercom (IN ter kahm) *n.* communication system that allows people to speak to one another from different parts of a building

5. **Cicko** (CHEEK oh) Zlata's canary.
6. **Bobars'** (BOH brz) next-door neighbors.

done up. It was huge and beautiful, and now it was being swallowed up by the flames. It was disappearing. That's what this neighborhood of mine looks like, my Mimmy. I wonder what it's like in other parts of town? I heard on the radio that it was awful around the Eternal Flame[7]. The place is knee-deep in glass. We're worried about Grandma and Granddad. They live there. Tomorrow, if we can go out, we'll see how they are. A terrible day. This has been the worst, most awful day in my eleven-year-old life. I hope it will be the only one. Mommy and Daddy are very edgy. I have to go to bed.

Ciao![8]

Zlata

Tuesday, May 5, 1992

Dear Mimmy,
The shooting seems to be dying down. I guess they've caused enough misery, although I don't know why. It has something to do with politics. <u>I just hope the "kids" come to some agreement.</u> Oh, if only they would, so we could live and breathe as human beings again. The things that have happened here these past few days are terrible. I want it to stop forever. PEACE! PEACE!

I didn't tell you, Mimmy, that we've rearranged things in the apartment. My room and Mommy and Daddy's are too dangerous to be in. They face the hills, which is where they're shooting from. If only you knew how scared I am to go near the windows and into those rooms. So, we turned a safe corner of the sitting room into a "bedroom." We sleep on mattresses on the floor. It's strange and awful. But, it's safer that way. We've turned everything around for safety. We put Cicko in the kitchen. He's safe there, although once the shooting starts there's nowhere safe except the cellar. I suppose all this will stop and we'll all go back to our usual places.

Ciao!

Zlata

7. **Eternal Flame** Sarajevo landmark that honors those who died resisting the Nazi occupation during World War II.

8. **Ciao!** (chow) *interj.* hello or goodbye.

TAKE NOTES

Nonfiction

Every author has a different writing style. An **author's style** might be formal or informal, friendly or funny. Is Zlata's writing style formal or informal? Explain.

_____

_____

_____

Stop to Reflect

To whom do you think Zlata is referring when she says "kids" in the underlined sentence?

_____

_____

Why might she use quotation marks around the word *kids*?

_____

_____

Nonfiction

Read the second bracketed paragraph. What is the **author's purpose**? Explain.

_____

_____

_____

Chronological organization is writing details in the order in which they happen. Underline the first clue in the May 7 entry that shows this way of writing.

Nonfiction

What is Zlata's **mood** on this page?

_____

_____

_____

_____

_____

Stop to Reflect

Read the bracketed paragraph. Zlata reflects on the suffering in her life. How do you think writing a diary helps Zlata cope with the war?

_____

_____

_____

_____

Reading Check

Underline the sentence that tells what "it" is that the war is taking from Zlata.

Thursday, May 7, 1992

Dear Mimmy,
I was almost positive the war would stop, but today . . . Today a shell fell on the park in front of my house, the park where I used to play and sit with my girlfriends. A lot of people were hurt. From what I hear Jaca, Jaca's mother, Selma, Nina, our neighbor Dado and who knows how many other people who happened to be there were wounded. Dado, Jaca and her mother have come home from the hospital, Selma lost a kidney but I don't know how she is, because she's still in the hospital. AND NINA IS DEAD. A piece of shrapnel lodged in her brain and she died. She was such a sweet, nice little girl. We went to kindergarten together, and we used to play together in the park. Is it possible I'll never see Nina again? Nina, an innocent eleven-year-old little girl—the victim of a stupid war. I feel sad. I cry and wonder why? She didn't do anything. A disgusting war has destroyed a young child's life. Nina, I'll always remember you as a wonderful little girl.

Love, Mimmy,
Zlata

Monday, June 29, 1992

Dear Mimmy,
BOREDOM!!! SHOOTING!!! SHELLING!!! PEOPLE BEING KILLED!!! DESPAIR!!! HUNGER!!! MISERY!!! FEAR!!!

That's my life! The life of an innocent eleven-year-old schoolgirl!! A schoolgirl without a school, without the fun and excitement of school. A child without games, without friends, without the sun, without birds, without nature, without fruit, without chocolate or sweets, with just a little powdered milk. In short, a child without a childhood. A wartime child. I now realize that I am really living through a war, I am witnessing an ugly, disgusting war. I and thousands of other children in this town that is being destroyed, that is crying, weeping, seeking help, but getting none. God, will this ever stop, will I ever be a schoolgirl again, will I ever enjoy my childhood again? I once heard that childhood is the most wonderful time of your life. And it is. I loved it, and now an ugly war is taking it all away from me. Why? I feel sad. I feel like crying. I am crying.

Your Zlata

Thursday, October 29, 1992

Dear Mimmy,
Mommy and Auntie Ivanka (from her office) have received grants to specialize in Holland. They have letters of guarantee[9], and there's even one for me. But Mommy can't decide. If she accepts, she leaves behind Daddy, her parents, her brother. I think it's a hard decision to make. One minute I think—no, I'm against it. But then I remember the war, winter, hunger, my stolen childhood and I feel like going. Then I think of Daddy, Grandma and Granddad, and I don't want to go. It's hard to know what to do. I'm really on edge, Mimmy, I can't write anymore.

Your Zlata

Monday, November 2, 1992

Dear Mimmy,
Mommy thought it over, talked to Daddy, Grandma and Granddad, and to me, and she's decided to go. The reason for her decision is—ME. What's happening in Sarajevo is already too much for me, and the coming winter will make it even harder. All right. But . . . well, I suppose it's better for me to go. I really can't stand it here anymore. I talked to Auntie Ivanka today and she told me that this war is hardest on the children, and that the children should be got out of the city. Daddy will manage, maybe he'll even get to come with us.

Ciao!
Zlata

Thursday, December 3, 1992

Dear Mimmy,
Today is my birthday. My first wartime birthday. Twelve years old. Congratulations. Happy birthday to me!
  The day started off with kisses and congratulations. First Mommy and Daddy, then everyone else. Mommy and Daddy gave me three Chinese vanity cases—with flowers on them!
  As usual there was no electricity. Auntie Melica came with her family (Kenan, Naida, Nihad) and gave me a book. And Braco Lajtner came, of course. The whole neighborhood got together in the evening. I

9. **letters of guarantee** letters from people or companies promising to help individuals who wanted to leave the country during the war.

 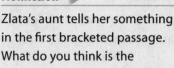

Nonfiction

Zlata's aunt tells her something in the first bracketed passage. What do you think is the **author's purpose** for writing this in her diary?

_____

_____

_____

Nonfiction

How is the second bracketed passage **organized**?

_____

_____

Underline the words that support your answer.

Reading Check 🖉

To which country might Zlata and her family travel? Circle the answer in the text.

Read the July entry. How does Zlata's **mood** change?

_____

_____

_____

What is she doing that she has not done in a long time?

_____

_____

Nonfiction

Diaries contain reflections as well as personal thoughts. Read the bracketed passage. What does Zlata say that shows she understands what the war has done to her family?

_____

_____

_____

Reading Check

What one thing does Zlata say is missing from her birthday celebration? Circle the answer in the text.

got chocolate, vitamins, a heart-shaped soap (small, orange), a key chain with a picture of Maja and Bojana, a pendant made of a stone from Cyprus, a ring (silver) and earrings (bingo!).

The table was nicely laid, with little rolls, fish and rice salad, cream cheese (with Feta), canned corned beef, a pie, and, of course—a birthday cake. Not how it used to be, but there's a war on. Luckily there was no shooting, so we could celebrate.

It was nice, but something was missing. It's called peace!

Your Zlata

Tuesday, July 27, 1993

Dear Mimmy,

Journalists, reporters, TV and radio crews from all over the world (even Japan). They're interested in you, Mimmy, and ask me about you, but also about me. It's exciting. Nice. Unusual for a wartime child.

My days have changed a little. They're more interesting now. It takes my mind off things. When I go to bed at night I think about the day behind me. Nice, as though it weren't wartime, and with such thoughts I happily fall asleep.

But in the morning, when the wheels of the water carts wake me up, I realize that there's a war on, that mine is a wartime life. SHOOTING, NO ELECTRICITY, NO WATER, NO GAS, NO FOOD. Almost no life.

Zlata

Thursday, October 7, 1993

Dear Mimmy,

Things are the way they used to be, lately. There's no shooting (thank God), I go to school, read, play the piano . . .

Winter is approaching, but we have nothing to heat with.

I look at the calendar and it seems as though this year of 1993 will again be marked by war. God, we've lost two years listening to gunfire, battling with electricity, water, food, and waiting for peace.

I look at Mommy and Daddy. In two years they've aged ten. And me? I haven't aged, but I've grown, although I honestly don't know how. I don't eat fruit or vegetables, I don't drink juices, I don't eat meat . . . I am a child of rice, peas and spaghetti. There I am talking about food again. I often catch myself dreaming about chicken, a good cutlet, pizza, lasagna . . . Oh, enough of that.

Zlata

Tuesday, October 12, 1993

Dear Mimmy,
I don't remember whether I told you that last summer I sent a letter through school to a pen-pal in America. It was a letter for an American girl or boy.

Today I got an answer. A boy wrote to me. His name is Brandon, he's twelve like me, and lives in Harrisburg, Pennsylvania. It really made me happy.

I don't know who invented the mail and letters, but thank you whoever you are. I now have a friend in America, and Brandon has a friend in Sarajevo. This is my first letter from across the Atlantic. And in it is a reply envelope, and a lovely pencil.

A Canadian TV crew and journalist from *The Sunday Times* (Janine) came to our gym class today. They brought me two chocolate bars. What a treat. It's been a long time since I've had sweets.

Love,
Zlata

December 1993

Dear Mimmy,
PARIS. There's electricity, there's water, there's gas. There's, there's . . . life, Mimmy. Yes, life; bright lights, traffic, people, food . . . Don't think I've gone nuts, Mimmy. Hey, listen to me, Paris!? No, I'm not crazy, I'm not kidding, it really is Paris and (can you believe it?) me in it. Me, my Mommy and my Daddy. At last. You're 100% sure I'm crazy, but I'm serious, I'm telling you, dear Mimmy, that I have arrived in Paris. I've come to be with you. You're mine again now and together we're moving into the light. The darkness has played out its part. The darkness is behind us; now we're bathed in light lit by good people. Remember that—good people. Bulb by bulb, not candles, but bulb by bulb, and me bathing in the lights of Paris. Yes, Paris. Incredible. You don't understand. You know, I don't think I understand either. I feel as though I must be crazy, dreaming, as though it's a fairy tale, but it's all TRUE.

Nonfiction

How has the **mood** at the beginning of the December entry changed compared to the beginning of the diary?

_____

_____

_____

Nonfiction

Reflective writing is about an event in a writer's life. The writer gives insight into important events. What does Zlata reflect on in the last diary entry?

_____

_____

_____

Reading Check

What does the Canadian TV crew bring Zlata? Circle the answer in the text.

Nonfiction

1. **Infer:** How did the difficulties during the war change Zlata's life?

_____

_____

_____

_____

2. **Analyze Cause and Effect:** Why did Zlata have mixed feelings about leaving Sarajevo?

_____

_____

_____

_____

3. **Infer:** Writing in a diary is like writing to yourself. Does Mimmy have the same personality as Zlata? Support your answer.

_____

_____

_____

_____

4. Fill in the chart below with examples of **nonfiction** writing in the diary.

Examples of Nonfiction Writing	
Narration	
Description	

Biographical Sketch

- Search the Internet for information about Zlata in Paris. Use words and phrases such as "Zlata Filipović Paris." Look for Web sites that tell specifically about Paris. Look for an e-mail address so that you can write directly to Zlata. You might ask her questions for information that you have not been able to find in your research.

What I learned: _____

_____

_____

- Search the library for books about and by Zlata. Look for information about what it was like for Zlata to live in another country while her own was at war. Look for details about what she was able to do in Paris that she was not able to do in Bosnia.

What I learned: _____

_____

_____

_____

- Watch the video interview with Zlata Filipović. Review your source material. Use this information to answer the following questions.

1. What do you think is important about what Zlata Filipović has done?

_____

_____

_____

2. How has the author's interest in journalism influenced her work?

_____

_____

_____

Water • Hard as Nails

Reading Skill

An **author's purpose** is the main reason the author writes a work. An author can have more than one purpose. For example, in an article about trees, the author's purpose might be to inform readers about fir trees and to persuade readers that fir trees should be protected.

Learn to recognize details that indicate the author's purpose.

• Facts and statistics are used to inform or persuade.

• Stories about experiences are used to entertain.

• Opinions and thoughts are used to reflect on an experience.

Use this chart to help you determine an author's purpose.

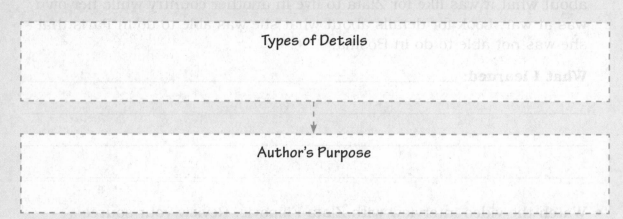

Types of Details

Author's Purpose

Literary Analysis

In a **narrative essay**, the author tells the true story of real events that happened to real people. An **autobiographical narrative** tells about an event or a time in the author's own life. The author may therefore include his or her own thoughts, feelings, and reactions.

Authors also include specific details to achieve a purpose. For example, authors may share lessons they have learned from mistakes they have made.

Water
Helen Keller

Summary Helen Keller was blind and deaf. Her new teacher, Anne Sullivan, tried to teach Helen how to communicate. Helen did not understand. The teacher ran water over Helen's hand one day. Miss Sullivan then spelled "w-a-t-e-r" in Helen's other hand. Helen connected the word to the thing she felt. Helen wanted to learn more words.

 Writing About the Big Question

What is important to know? In "Water," Helen Keller's teacher helps her to begin to communicate using words. Complete this sentence:

One important purpose of communicating clearly with others is

_____.

Note-taking Guide
Use this chart to record details from the story.

What did Miss Sullivan give Helen when shw first arrived?	Miss Sullivan gave Helen a doll.
Why did Helen break the doll?	
How did Miss Sullivan teach Helen the word *water*?	
How did Helen feel after she learned her first word?	

Water

Helen Keller

Activate Prior Knowledge

Think of a time when you felt upset because you could not understand something. Describe how you felt when you finally understood it.

_____

_____

_____

_____

Literary Analysis

A **narrative essay** is a true story about real events. What details in the first paragraph indicate that this is a narrative essay?

_____

_____

_____

_____

Reading Check

What was the first word that Miss Sullivan tried to teach Helen? Circle the answer.

The morning after my teacher came she led me into her room and gave me a doll. The little blind children at the Perkins Institution had sent it and Laura Bridgman had dressed it; but I did not know this until afterward. When I had played with it a little while, Miss Sullivan slowly spelled into my hand the word "d-o-l-l." I was at once interested in this finger play and tried to <u>imitate</u> it. When I finally succeeded in making the letters correctly I was flushed with childish pleasure and pride. Running downstairs to my mother I held up my hand and made the letters for *doll.* I did not know that I was spelling a word or even that words existed; I was simply making my fingers go in monkey-like imitation. In the days that followed I learned to spell in this uncomprehending way a great many words, among them *pin, hat, cup* and a few verbs like *sit, stand* and *walk.* But my teacher had been with me several weeks before I understood that everything has a name.

One day, while I was playing with my new doll, Miss Sullivan put my big rag doll into my lap also, spelled "d-o-l-l" and tried to make me understand that "d-o-l-l" applied to both. Earlier in the day we had had a tussle over the words "m-u-g" and "w-a-t-e-r." Miss Sullivan had tried to impress it upon me that "m-u-g" is *mug* and that "w-a-t-e-r" is *water*, but I <u>persisted</u> in confounding the two. In despair she had dropped the subject for the time, only to renew it at the first opportunity. I became impatient at her repeated attempts and, seizing the new doll, I dashed it upon the floor. I was keenly delighted when I felt the fragments of the broken doll at my feet. Neither sorrow nor regret followed my passionate outburst. I had not loved the doll. In the still, dark world in

Vocabulary Development

imitate (IM uh tayt) *v.* copy; mimic

persisted (per SIST id) *v.* refused to give up

which I lived there was no strong <u>sentiment</u> or tenderness. I felt my teacher sweep the fragments to one side of the hearth,[1] and I had a sense of satisfaction that the cause of my discomfort was removed. She brought me my hat, and I knew I was going out into the warm sunshine. This thought, if a wordless sensation may be called a thought, made me hop and skip with pleasure.

We walked down the path to the well-house, attracted by the fragrance of the honeysuckle with which it was covered. Some one was drawing water and my teacher placed my hand under the spout. As the cool stream gushed over one hand she spelled into the other the word *water*, first slowly, then rapidly. I stood still, my whole attention fixed upon the motions of her fingers. Suddenly I felt a misty consciousness as of something forgotten-a thrill of returning thought; and somehow the mystery of language was revealed to me. I knew then that "w-a-t-e-r" meant the wonderful cool something that was flowing over my hand. That living word awakened my soul, gave it light, hope, joy, set it free! There were barriers still, it is true, but barriers that could in time be swept away.

I left the well-house eager to learn. Everything had a name, and each name gave birth to a new thought. As we returned to the house every object which I touched seemed to quiver with life. That was because I saw everything with the strange, new sight that had come to me. On entering the door I remembered the doll I had broken. I felt my way to the hearth and picked up the pieces. I tried vainly to put them together. Then my eyes filled with tears; for I realized what I had done, and for the first time I felt repentance and sorrow.

I learned a great many new words that day. I do not remember what they all were; but I do know that

© Pearson Education

Vocabulary Development
sentiment (SEN tuh muhnt) *n.* a gentle feeling

---

1. **hearth** (hahrth) *n.* the stone or brick floor of a fireplace, sometimes extending into the room.

Reading Skill

An **author's purpose** may be to instruct, to entertain, to persuade, or to express ideas. Based on the details in the first bracketed paragraph, what do you think is Helen Keller's purpose for writing? Explain.

_____

_____

_____

_____

Stop to Reflect

Why does Helen's discovery of words change her attitude about everything?

_____

_____

_____

_____

Reading Check

What attracted Helen and Anne Sullivan to the well-house? Circle the answer.

© Pearson Education

mother, father, sister, teacher were among them—words that were to make the world blossom for me, "like Aaron's rod, with flowers." It would have been difficult to find a happier child than I was as I lay in my crib at the close of that eventful day and lived over the joys it had brought me, and for the first time longed for a new day to come.

Reader's Response: Before she learned to communicate, Helen Keller shows impatience and anger by smashing her doll. Should she be excused for such behavior? Explain.

_____

_____

_____

Reading Skill

Underline the words in the bracketed paragraph that show Helen Keller's feelings. What is Helen's **purpose** in sharing these feelings?

_____

_____

_____

Reading Check

What do words do for Helen? Circle the text that tells you.

Water

1. **Draw Conclusions:** Helen Keller learned the word *water*. What will Keller want to do when she wakes up the next day?

_____

_____

2. **Evaluate:** What do you think is the most valuable part of being able to communicate?

_____

_____

_____

3. **Reading Skill:** What are two **purposes** Keller may have had for writing this narrative essay?

_____

_____

4. **Literary Analysis:** Complete this chart to figure out why Keller includes particular events in her **autobiographical narrative**.

Event From Narrative	Author's Thoughts and Feelings	Why Is It Included?
Helen breaks her doll.		
Helen connects the word *w-a-t-e-r* with water from the pump.		

Writing: Letter

Write a **letter** to the director of the school for the blind as Anne Sullivan. Use the following questions to write notes for your letter:

- How do you think Sullivan felt about Helen Keller before she learned words?

  _____

  _____

- How did Sullivan teach Keller what *w-a-t-e-r* means?

  _____

  _____

- How do you think Sullivan feels about what happened?

  _____

  _____

Research and Technology: Project

Use the following chart to record information about careers, duties, and training from your source. Complete the chart on another sheet of paper.

Which source did you use? _____

Career	Duties	Training

Hard as Nails
Russell Baker

Summary Russell Baker is hired on his twelfth birthday to deliver newspapers in Baltimore. His boss, Mr. Deems, makes him work hard. Deems gives the newsboys a tour of the newsroom of the *Baltimore News-Post*. Russell dreams of having an important job at the newspaper. Later Russell remembers Deems as "hard as nails."

 Writing About the Big Question

What is important to know? In "Hard as Nails," Russell Baker must learn skills in order to do a job well. Complete this sentence:

Before you start a new job, you should have knowledge about

_____.

Note-taking Guide
Use this chart to record important details from the story.

Who makes Russell get a job?	Russell's mother
Where does he deliver papers?	
What does Mr. Deems do to make Russell sell more papers?	
How does Russell feel when he visits the newsroom?	
Why does Russell think Mr. Deems quit?	

Hard as Nails

1. **Respond:** Would you like to work for Deems? Explain your reasons.

_____

_____

_____

2. **Evaluate:** Does Deems treat the newsboys fairly or unfairly? Explain.

_____

_____

3. **Reading Skill:** What are two **purposes** Baker may have had for writing this narrative essay?

_____

_____

4. **Literary Analysis:** Authors sometimes include specific details to explain why a person does something. Complete this chart to think about why Baker includes particular events in his **autobiographical narrative**.

Event From Narrative	Author's Thoughts and Feelings	Why Is It Included?
Baker and his family move to Baltimore.		
Baker goes to the banquet.		

Writing: Letter

Imagine that you are Russell Baker. Write a **letter** to Deems. Follow these steps:

- List one of Deems's actions toward Russell and the newsboys.

  _____

  _____

- Describe how Russell felt about Deems at the time.

  _____

  _____

- Tell what Russell learned from Deems's action.

  _____

  _____

Use your notes to write a letter to Deems.

Research and Technology: Project

Prepare a **project** about a job in print journalism. Complete this chart for the job that you choose to research.

Job:			
What This Person Does	Training or Education Needed	Salary	Source(s) of Information

The Shutout • Jackie Robinson: Justice at Last

Reading Skill

An **author's purpose** is his or her reason for writing. To understand an author's specific purpose, **ask questions**.

- What kinds of details am I given?
- How are the details presented?
- Why does the author present these details in this way?

The chart shows the answers to these questions for two different works about building a doghouse. The answers reveal that the works have different purposes. Fill in the empty space with details from the story as you read.

What Kinds of Details?		
Directions for building a doghouse	Author tries to build a doghouse	

How Presented?		
Numbered steps	Exaggerated stories	

Why?		
To make the directions easy to follow	To make the situation funny	

Purpose		
To inform	To entertain	

Literary Analysis

An **essay** is a short piece of nonfiction about a specific subject. An **expository essay** provides information, discusses ideas and opinions, and explains how to do or make something.

Jackie Robinson: Justice at Last

Geoffrey C. Ward and Ken Burns

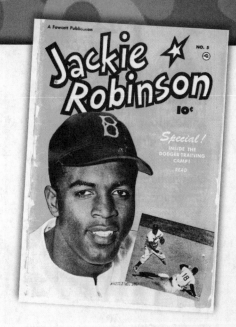

Summary Branch Rickey owned the Dodgers baseball team. He wanted African Americans to play major league baseball. He asked Jackie Robinson to become the first black player on his team. Robinson faced many obstacles and challenges. He became a role model.

Writing About the Big Question

What is important to know? In "Jackie Robinson: Justice at Last," Jackie Robinson knew how to be strong and brave, even when people were cruel to him. Complete this sentence:

If people are unfair to you, it's important to limit your reactions,

such as _____ because _____.

Note-taking Guide

Use the chart to recall the most important details of the story.

Who was Branch Rickey?	He was the owner of the Dodgers.
Why does he want Jackie Robinson on his team?	
What problems did Robinson have during his first season?	
Why was it important that Robinson not fight back?	

Jackie Robinson: Justice at Last
Geoffrey C. Ward and Ken Burns

Activate Prior Knowledge

Think about a person whose courage led to new opportunities for other people. Describe the person, and list his or her accomplishments.

_____

_____

_____

Reading Skill

The **author's purpose** is his or her main reason for writing. According to what you read in the bracketed passage, what is the authors' purpose for writing this essay?

_____

_____

Stop to Reflect

Would you have accepted a place on the team if you had been Jackie Robinson? Explain.

_____

_____

Reading Check

What baseball team were Robinson and Rickey associated with? Underline the answer in the text.

It was 1945, and World War II had ended. Americans of all races had died for their country. Yet black men were still not allowed in the major leagues. The national pastime was loved by all America, but the major leagues were for white men only.

Branch Rickey of the Brooklyn Dodgers thought that was wrong. He was the only team owner who believed blacks and whites should play together. Baseball, he felt, would become even more thrilling, and fans of all colors would swarm to his ballpark.

Rickey decided his team would be the first to integrate. There were plenty of brilliant Negro league players, but he knew the first black major leaguer would need much more than athletic ability.

Many fans and players were prejudiced—they didn't want the races to play together. Rickey knew the first black player would be cursed and booed. Pitchers would throw at him; runners would spike him. Even his own teammates might try to pick a fight.

But somehow this man had to rise above that. No matter what happened, he must never lose his temper. No matter what was said to him, he must never answer back. If he had even one fight, people might say integration wouldn't work.

When Rickey met Jackie Robinson, he thought he'd found the right man. Robinson was 28 years old, and a superb athlete. In his first season in the Negro leagues, he hit .387. But just as importantly, he had great intelligence and sensitivity. Robinson was college-educated, and knew what joining the majors would mean for blacks. The grandson of a slave, he was proud of his race and wanted others to feel the same.

In the past, Robinson had always stood up for his rights. But now Rickey told him he would have to stop. The Dodgers needed "a man that will take abuse."

Vocabulary Development

integrate (IN tuh grayt) *v.* remove all barriers and allow access to all

At first Robinson thought Rickey wanted someone who was afraid to defend himself. But as they talked, he realized that in this case a truly brave man would have to avoid fighting. He thought for a while, then promised Rickey he would not fight back.

Robinson signed with the Dodgers and went to play in the minors in 1946. Rickey was right—fans insulted him, and so did players. But he performed brilliantly and avoided fights. Then, in 1947, he came to the majors.

Many Dodgers were angry. Some signed a <u>petition</u> demanding to be traded. But Robinson and Rickey were determined to make their experiment work.

On April 15—Opening Day—26,623 fans came out to Ebbets Field. More than half of them were black—Robinson was already their hero. Now he was making history just by being on the field.

The afternoon was cold and wet, but no one left the ballpark. The Dodgers beat the Boston Braves, 5–3. Robinson went hitless, but the hometown fans didn't seem to care—they cheered his every move.

Robinson's first season was difficult. Fans threatened to kill him; players tried to hurt him. The St. Louis Cardinals said they would strike if he took the field. And because of laws separating the races in certain states, he often couldn't eat or sleep in the same places as his teammates.

Yet through it all, he kept his promise to Rickey. No matter who insulted him, he never <u>retaliated</u>.

Robinson's dignity paid off. Thousands of fans jammed stadiums to see him play. The Dodgers set attendance records in a number of cities.

Slowly his teammates accepted him, realizing that he was the spark that made them a winning team. No one was more daring on the base paths or better with the glove. At the plate, he had great bat control—he could hit the ball anywhere. That season, he was named baseball's first Rookie of the Year.

TAKE NOTES

Literary Analysis

An **expository essay** is a short piece of nonfiction about a specific subject. What situation do the writers explain in the essay?

_____

_____

_____

Reading Skill

Details can help you determine the **authors' purpose** for writing. Underline at least one important detail in the bracketed passage. Why do the authors present this detail?

_____

_____

_____

Reading Check

What was the final score in Jackie Robinson's first game with the Dodgers? Circle the answer.

Vocabulary Development

petition (puh TISH uhn) *n.* a document that people sign to express demands

retaliated (ri TAL ee ayt id) *v.* punished in return for an injury or a wrong done

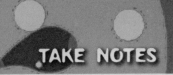

How does the final sentence help you understand the **authors' purpose** in writing this essay?

_____

_____

_____

Jackie Robinson went on to a glorious career. But he did more than play the game well—his bravery taught Americans a lesson. Branch Rickey opened a door, and Jackie Robinson stepped through it, making sure it could never be closed again. Something wonderful happened to baseball—and America—the day Jackie Robinson joined the Dodgers.

Reader's Response: Do you think it was difficult for Jackie Robinson to hold his temper? Explain.

_____

_____

_____

_____

_____

Jackie Robinson: Justice at Last

1. **Respond:** Fill out this chart. Write questions you have about the essay in the first column. Write an answer to each question in the second column, using details from the essay. Explain in the third column how the answers affect your understanding of the essay.

Questions	Answers	Has Understanding Changed? Explain:

2. **Speculate:** Robinson's teammates eventually accepted him as a member of their team. Why did everyone else eventually accept Robinson and the integration of baseball?

_____

_____

3. **Reading Skill:** What is the **purpose** of the essay?

_____

_____

4. **Literary Analysis:** What is the focus of this **expository essay**?

_____

_____

_____

Writing: Persuasive Letter

Write a **persuasive letter** to a friend, encouraging him or her to read "Jackie Robinson: Justice at Last." Answer the following questions:

• What is the main idea of the essay?

_____

• What specific details from the essay will persuade your friend to read it?

_____

• Why do you want your friend to read the essay?

_____

Use your answers to write your persuasive letter.

Listening and Speaking: Give Directions

You will **give directions** to younger students. Use the lines below to gather information for your instructional presentation on baseball. Use another sheet of paper if necessary.

• **Skills to present:** _____

_____

• **Key terms:** _____

_____

• **Steps in order:** _____

_____

_____

_____

_____

The Shutout

Patricia C. McKissack and Fredrick McKissack, Jr.

Summary This essay describes baseball's early history. At first, African Americans played on teams of black and white players. Baseball became a business after the Civil War. African American players were "shut out" from playing on major league teams until after World War II. They formed their own teams as a result.

 Writing About the Big Question

What is important to know? "The Shutout" describes ways that African American baseball players solved the problem of being prevented from playing in the major leagues. Complete this sentence:

Knowing different ways to solve problems is important because _____

_____.

Note-taking Guide

Fill in the dates on the chart to create a timeline of the history of baseball.

Event	Baseball started becoming popular.	The National Association of Base Ball Players was formed.	South Carolina seceded from the Union.	The National Association of Base Ball Players voted not to admit teams with African American members.
Date				

The Shutout

1. **Respond:** What questions do you have about the essay? Write your questions in the first column of the chart below. Then, look for details in the essay that answer your questions. Write an answer to each question in the second column. Explain in the third column how the answers affect your understanding of the essay.

Questions	Answers	Has Understanding Changed? Explain:

2. **Cause and Effect:** What effect did the exclusion of African Americans have on the history of baseball?

_____

_____

_____

3. **Reading Skill:** What is the general **purpose** of the essay?

_____

_____

_____

4. **Literary Analysis:** What is the focus of this **expository essay**?

_____

_____

_____

Writing: Persuasive Letter

Write a **persuasive letter** to a friend, encouraging him or her to read "The Shutout." Focus on the following questions:

• What is the main idea of the essay?

_____

• What specific details from the essay will persuade your friend to read it?

_____

• Why do you want your friend to read the essay?

_____

_____

Use your notes to write the persuasive letter.

Listening and Speaking: Give Directions

Prepare a presentation for younger students that **gives directions** on how to perform certain baseball moves. Take notes in this chart.

Steps to Follow:			
Swing a Bat	Steal a Base	Set Up a Double Play	Bunt

Persuasive Speeches

About Persuasive Speeches

A **persuasive speech** is a public presentation that argues for or against a particular position. A good persuasive speech can change people's minds about an issue. Examples of persuasive speeches include campaign speeches and sermons. Persuasive speeches usually have the following characteristics:

- an issue with two sides (For example, the death penalty is an issue with two sides. Some people are for it, and other people are against it.)
- a clear statement of the speaker's purpose, or reason
- a clear statement of the speaker's position, or opinion
- clear organization of the text
- facts, statistics, and examples to support the position
- powerful language meant to persuade

Reading Skill

You should always **evaluate evidence in an author's conclusion**. Look for a clear statement of the author's argument. Pay attention to facts and other information that support the argument.

Use the checklist below to evaluate the following speech.

Checklist for Evaluating an Author's Argument

❏ Does the author present a clear argument?

❏ Is the argument supported by evidence?

❏ Is the evidence believable?

❏ Does the author use sound reasoning to develop the argument?

❏ Do I agree with the message? Why or why not?

Build Understanding

Knowing these words will help you read this speech.

desecration (des uh KRAY shuhn) *n.* the act of insulting something holy
heinous (HAY nus) *adj.* very wicked or evil

Cultural Understanding

Many people consider baseball the American national pastime. The game has been played since the middle of the 1800s. Some famous players include Babe Ruth and Lou Gehrig.

Comprehension Builder

What type of bat might replace the wooden baseball bat? Write the answer on the lines below.

_____

_____

_____

Preserving a Great American Symbol

Richard Durbin

Congressman Richard Durbin gave the following humorous speech in the House of Representatives on July 26, 1989. While most speeches to Congress are serious, Durbin's is humorous yet persuasive and "drives home" the point that wooden baseball bats should not be replaced with metal ones.

Mr. Speaker, I rise to condemn the desecration of a great American symbol. No, I am not referring to flagburning; I am referring to the baseball bat.

Several experts tell us that the wooden baseball bat is doomed to extinction, that major league baseball players will soon be standing at home plate with aluminum bats in their hands.

Fluency Builder

A colon is often used to introduce items in a list. The text before the colon explains the list that is to follow. Read aloud the bracketed paragraph. What are the items after the colon describing? Circle the answer in the text.

Vocabulary Builder

To and Too Read the second bracketed passage. In the first paragraph, Durbin says that wooden bats may be considered *too expensive*. The adverb *too* means "more than is needed, wanted, or possible."
In the second paragraph, he asks others to *not try to sell*. The word *to* introduces an infinitive phrase. *Too* and *to* can both be pronounced *TOO*. Sometimes, *to* is pronounced *TUH*.

Comprehension Builder

Why does the speaker wish to keep wooden baseball bats? Summarize his reasons on the lines below.

_____

_____

_____

_____

Baseball fans have been forced to endure countless indignities by those who just cannot leave well enough alone: designated hitters,[1] plastic grass, uniforms that look like pajamas, chicken clowns dancing on the base lines, and, of course, the most heinous sacrilege, lights in Wrigley Field.[2]

Are we willing to hear the crack of a bat replaced by the dinky ping? Are we ready to see the Louisville Slugger replaced by the aluminum ping dinger? Is nothing sacred?

Please do not tell me that wooden bats are too expensive, when players who cannot hit their weight are being paid more money than the President of the United States.

Please do not try to sell me on the notion that these metal clubs will make better hitters.

What will be next? Teflon baseballs? Radar-enhanced gloves? I ask you.

I do not want to hear about saving trees. Any tree in America would gladly give its life for the glory of a day at home plate.

I do not know if it will take a constitutional amendment to keep our baseball traditions alive, but if we forsake the great Americana of broken-bat singles and pine tar,[3] we will have certainly lost our way as a nation.

1. **designated hitters** players who bat in place of the pitcher and do not play a defensive position. The position was created in 1973 in the American League. Some fans argue that it has changed the game for the worse.

2. **Wrigley Field** historic baseball field in Chicago. It did not have lights for night games until 1988. Some fans regretted the change.

3. **broken-bat singles . . . pine tar** When a batter breaks a wooden bat while hitting the ball and makes it to first base, it is a notable event in a baseball game. Pine tar is a substance used to improve the batter's grip on a wooden bat.

Thinking About the Persuasive Speech

1. Identify the author's purpose in delivering this speech.

_____

_____

2. How does the author's use of humorous images and language appeal to his audience's emotions?

_____

_____

_____

TALK ABOUT IT **Reading Skill**

3. Does the sentence "Metal bats should not replace wooden ones" state the position of the author in this speech?

_____

_____

_____

4. Does the statement "Baseball players make too much money" support the author's argument? Explain.

_____

_____

WRITE ABOUT IT **Timed Writing: Response (20 minutes)**

Respond to the speech "Preserving a Great American Symbol."

• Do you agree or disagree with Durbin's argument?

_____

• List at least two details from the speech that support your argument.

_____

_____

Turkeys • Langston Terrace

Reading Skill

The **main idea** is the most important point in a literary work. Sometimes the main idea is stated directly. Other times, you must figure it out by **identifying key details** in the text.

- Key details often reveal what a work is about.
- They are sometimes repeated throughout a literary work.
- They are related to other details in a work.

Use the graphic organizer below to record key details in the extra space as you read. Then, use those details to determine the main idea.

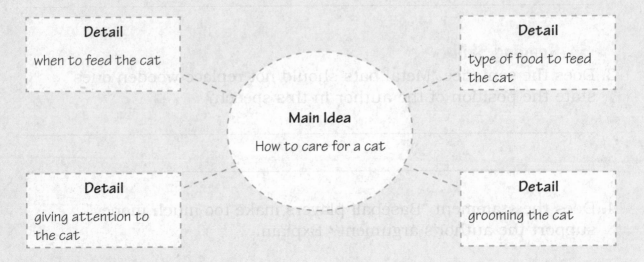

Detail

when to feed the cat

Detail

type of food to feed the cat

Main Idea

How to care for a cat

Detail

giving attention to the cat

Detail

grooming the cat

Literary Analysis

An **author's influences** are the cultural and historical factors that affect his or her writing. These factors may include the time and place of an author's birth, the author's cultural background, or world events that happened during the author's lifetime. For example, the gold rush of 1849 might have influenced the ideas of an author who grew up in California in the 1850s. As you read, look for details that indicate an author's influences.

Turkeys
Bailey White

Summary Bailey White's mother was a friend to local ornithologists, or people who study birds. The ornithologists found a wild turkey nest that was not watched over by a mother turkey. The ornithologists needed to keep the turkey eggs warm. Bailey's illness helped the ornithologists save the turkey eggs.

Writing About the Big Question

What is important to know? In "Turkeys," a girl helps save wild turkeys from disappearing, or becoming extinct. Complete these sentences:

People who work to save animals from extinction must **examine**

_____. The **knowledge** they gain from their

studies can be used to _____.

Note-taking Guide

Use the chart to record important details from the story.

Who is the narrator?	The narrator is Bailey White when she was a child.
What are the ornithologists studying?	
Why is the narrator surprised when she wakes up?	
How do the ornithologists save the turkey eggs?	

Turkeys
Bailey White

Activate Prior Knowledge

Have you or has someone you know ever helped a wild animal? What did you or the other person do?

_____

_____

Literary Analysis

An **author's influences** are factors that affect his or her writing. Influences include where and when an author was born and what happened in the world during the author's lifetime. Underline a detail that shows one of the author's influences.

Reading Skill

Key details can reveal the **main idea** of a selection. Reread the bracketed passage. How do these details support the main idea that pure-strain wild turkeys are becoming rare?

_____

_____

_____

Reading Check

What illness did the narrator have? Circle the answer.

Something about my mother attracts ornithologists.[1] It all started years ago when a couple of them discovered she had a rare species of woodpecker coming to her bird feeder. They came in the house and sat around the window, exclaiming and taking pictures with big fancy cameras. But long after the red cockaded woodpeckers had gone to roost, the ornithologists were still there. There always seemed to be three or four of them wandering around our place and staying for supper.

In those days, during the 1950's, the big concern of ornithologists in our area was the wild turkey. They were rare, and the pure-strain wild turkeys had begun to interbreed with farmers' domestic stock. The species was being degraded. It was extinction by <u>dilution</u>, and to the ornithologists it was just as tragic as the more dramatic demise of the passenger pigeon or the Carolina parakeet.

One ornithologist had devised a formula to compute the ratio of domestic to pure-strain wild turkey in an individual bird by comparing the angle of flight at takeoff and the rate of acceleration. And in those sad days, the turkeys were flying low and slow.

It was during that time, the spring when I was six years old, that I caught the measles. I had a high fever, and my mother was worried about me. She kept the house quiet and dark and crept around silently, trying different <u>methods</u> of cooling me down.

Even the ornithologists stayed away—but not out of fear of the measles or respect for a household with sickness. The fact was, they had discovered a wild turkey nest. According to the formula, the hen was pure-strain wild—not a taint of the sluggish domestic

Vocabulary Development

dilution (di LOO shuhn) *n.* process of weakening by mixing with something else

methods (METH uhdz) *n.* ways of doing something

1. **ornithologists** (awr nuh THAH luh jists) *n.* people who study birds.

bird in her blood—and the ornithologists were camping in the woods, protecting her nest from predators and taking pictures.

One night our phone rang. It was one of the ornithologists. "Does your little girl still have measles?" he asked.

"Yes," said my mother. "She's very sick. Her temperature is 102."

"I'll be right over," said the ornithologist.

In five minutes a whole carload of them arrived. They marched solemnly into the house, carrying a cardboard box. "A hundred and two, did you say? Where is she?" they asked my mother.

They crept into my room and set the box down on the bed. I was barely conscious, and when I opened my eyes, their worried faces hovering over me seemed to float out of the darkness like giant, glowing eggs. They snatched the covers off me and felt me all over. They consulted in whispers.

"Feels just right, I'd say."

"A hundred two—can't miss if we tuck them up close and she lies still."

I closed my eyes then, and after a while the ornithologists drifted away, their pale faces bobbing up and down on the black wave of fever.

The next morning I was better. For the first time in days I could think. The memory of the ornithologists with their whispered voices was like a dream from another life. But when I pulled down the covers, there staring up at me with googly eyes and wide mouths were sixteen fuzzy baby turkeys, and the cracked chips and caps of sixteen brown speckled eggs.

I was a <u>sensible</u> child. I gently stretched myself out. The eggshells crackled, and the turkey babies fluttered and cheeped and snuggled against me. I laid my aching head back on the pillow and closed my eyes. "The ornithologists," I whispered. "The ornithologists have been here."

It seems the turkey hen had been so disturbed by the elaborate protective measures that had been undertaken on her behalf that she had abandoned

---

Literary Analysis

Explain how the place where Bailey White grew up **influenced** this essay.

_____

_____

_____

_____

Reading Skill

What **key detail** do you learn here that is important to the ornithologists' plan?

_____

_____

_____

Reading Check

What was the narrator's temperature? Circle the answer.

Vocabulary Development

sensible (SEN suh buhl) *adj.* wise; intelligent

How do you think this experience has **influenced** Bailey White's feelings about wild turkeys?

_____

_____

_____

Stop to Reflect

How do you think White might feel when she sees the wild turkeys living in the woods today?

_____

_____

_____

Reading Check

What did the turkeys do when the narrator went outside for the first time? Underline the answer.

her nest on the night the eggs were due to hatch. It was a cold night. The ornithologists, not having an incubator on hand, used their heads and came up with the next best thing.

The baby turkeys and I gained our strength together. When I was finally able to get out of bed and feebly creep around the house, the turkeys peeped and cheeped around my ankles, scrambling to keep up with me and tripping over their own big spraddle-toed feet. When I went outside for the first time, the turkeys tumbled after me down the steps and scratched around in the yard while I sat in the sun.

Finally, in late summer, the day came when they were ready to fly for the first time as adult birds. The ornithologists gathered. I ran down the hill, and the turkeys ran too. Then, one by one, they took off. They flew high and fast. The ornithologists made Vs with their thumbs and forefingers, measuring angles. They consulted their stopwatches and paced off distances. They scribbled in their tiny notebooks. Finally they looked at each other. They sighed. They smiled. They jumped up and down and hugged each other. "One hundred percent pure wild turkey!" they said.

Nearly forty years have passed since then. Now there's a vaccine for measles. And the woods where I live are full of pure wild turkeys. I like to think they are all descendants of those sixteen birds I saved from the <u>vigilance</u> of the ornithologists.

Reader's Response: What can people do to protect birds such as wild turkeys from extinction?

_____

_____

_____

_____

Vocabulary Development
vigilance (VIJ uh luhns) *n.* watchfulness

Turkeys

1. **Evaluate:** Why is the author's fever important to the ornithologists?

   _____

   _____

2. **Interpret:** How do you think White feels when she watches the turkeys take off? Explain.

   _____

   _____

   _____

3. **Reading Skill:** In your own words, state the **main idea** of this essay.

   _____

   _____

   _____

4. **Literary Analysis:** In this chart, list cultural and historical factors that may have **influenced** White's writing of "Turkeys."

Time and Place	Cultural Background	World Events

Writing: Journal Entry

Write a **journal entry** as if you were Bailey White as a child. Focus on the following questions:

- Which event will you write about? Describe what happened.

_____

_____

- What did White say about the event in the essay? Explain why this event was important to White.

_____

_____

_____

Use your notes to write the journal entry.

Research and Technology: Presentation

Prepare a **presentation** on conservation. First, choose the conservation topic you will research. Focus on the following questions as you research your topic:

- What topic do you want to focus on?

_____

- Why is this topic important?

_____

_____

- What message do you want to bring to your audience?

_____

_____

Langston Terrace
Eloise Greenfield

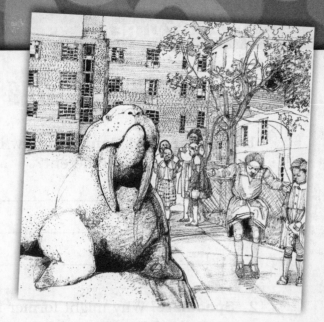

Summary Eloise Greenfield and her family move to a new house in Langston Terrace. Langston Terrace is a new, low-rent housing project in Washington, D.C. The people who live there start music, sports, and poetry programs. Eloise and her friends have pleasant memories of Langston Terrace.

 Writing About the Big Question

What is important to know? In "Langston Terrace" the narrator and her family move to a new neighborhood. Complete this sentence:

Knowledge you might like to have about your future neighborhood

includes _____

_____ .

Note-taking Guide

Use this chart to record important details from the story.

What is Langston Terrace?	A low-rent housing project
Where is it?	
How does Eloise's family get a house there?	
Why does Eloise have good memories of Langston Terrace?	

Langston Terrace

1. **Compare and Contrast:** How is the family's new home similar to the old home? How is it different?

_____

_____

_____

2. **Speculate:** Why might former residents of Langston Terrace want to have a reunion? Explain.

_____

_____

_____

3. **Reading Skill:** In your own words, state the **main idea** of this essay.

_____

_____

4. **Literary Analysis:** In the chart below, list cultural and historical factors that may have **influenced** Greenfield's writing of "Langston Terrace."

Time and Place	Cultural Background	World Events

Writing: Journal Entry

Write a **journal entry** as if you were a young Eloise Greenfield. Choose an event from the essay. Focus on these questions:

- What do you remember about this event?

_____

_____

_____

- Why does this event stand out in your mind?

_____

_____

Use your notes to write the journal entry.

Research and Technology: Presentation

Your group will decide which community it will research for the **presentation**. Then, you may wish to assign a task to each group member. For example, some students can research while others make maps. Use the chart below to gather information.

Community History	Community Features

La Leña Buena • from The Pigman & Me

Reading Skill

The **main idea** is the most important point in a literary work. Individual paragraphs or sections may also have a central idea that supports the main idea of the work. To determine the main idea, **distinguish between important and unimportant details**. Important details are small pieces of information that tell more about the main idea. They are also called *supporting details*.

- Ask yourself questions such as these about details in a literary work: *Why did the author include this detail? Does this detail help readers understand the main idea of the work?*

- Keep in mind that not all details support the main idea.

Use this chart to list details as you read. Decide whether the details are important. Then, use the important details to write the main idea.

Detail	Important?
Tio Abrán earns a living making charcoal from wood.	Yes
Main Idea:	

Literary Analysis

Mood is the overall feeling a literary work produces in a reader. For example, the mood of a work may be happy, sad, scary, or hopeful. To create a particular mood, writers carefully choose words and create word pictures that appeal to the reader's senses.

Some literary works present a single mood throughout a selection. In other works, the mood changes within the piece.

La Leña Buena
John Phillip Santos

Summary The narrator tells the story of his great-grandfather's brother, Tío Abrán. Tío Abrán made a successful living from wood in Mexico. He could tell the best way to use the wood from different trees. Tío Abrán had to deal with Mexican revolutionaries before coming to America.

Writing About the Big Question

What is important to know? In "La Leña Buena," the author explains that his uncle was an expert at making a very special kind of charcoal. Complete this sentence:

One way to distinquish an expert from someone who has basic

knowledge about a topic is _____.

Note-taking Guide

Use this chart to record three important details from "La Leña Buena."

Important Detail	Important Detail	Important Detail
1. Tío Abrán knows a lot about wood.	2.	3.

La Leña Buena

John Phillip Santos

La Leña Buena

Activate Prior Knowledge

Think about something you do very well. How would it feel if other people made it difficult for you to do this activity?

_____

_____

Literary Analysis

Mood is the overall feeling a literary work produces in a reader. Read the bracketed paragraph. What mood, or feeling, is created in this paragraph?

_____

_____

Reading Skill

Important details are small pieces of information that tell more about the **main idea**. List two important details that support the main idea that trees are important in Tío Abrán's life.

_____

_____

_____

Reading Check

Why did Tío Abrán and his family leave Mexico? Underline the sentence that tells you.

Good wood is like a jewel, Tío Abrán, my great-grandfather Jacobo's twin brother, used to say. Huisache burns fast, in twisting yellow flames, <u>engulfing</u> the log in a cocoon of fire. It burns brightly, so it is sought after for Easter bonfires. But it does not burn hot, so it's poor wood for home fires. On a cold morning in the sierra, you can burn a whole tree by noon. Mesquite, and even better, cedar—these are noble, hard woods. They burn hot and long. Their smoke is <u>fragrant</u>. And if you know how to do it, they make exquisite charcoal.

"La leña buena es como una joya."

Good wood is like a jewel. And old Tío Abrán knew wood the way a jeweler knows stones, and in northern Coahuila, from Múzquiz to Rosita, his charcoal was highly regarded for its sweet, long-burning fire.

Abrán was one of the last of the Garcias to come north. Somewhere around 1920, he finally had to come across the border with his family. He was weary of the treacheries[1] along the roads that had become a part of life in the sierra towns since the beginning of the revolution ten years earlier. Most of the land near town had been deforested and the only wood he could find around Palaú was huisache. To find any of the few pastures left with arbors of mesquite trees, he had to take the unpaved mountain road west from Múzquiz, along a route where many of the militantes[2] had their camps. Out by the old Villa las Rusias, in a valley far off the road, there were mesquite trees in every direction as far as you could see. He made an arrangement with the owner of the villa to give him a cut from the sale of charcoal

---

Vocabulary Development

engulfing (in GUHLF ing) _v._ swallowing up; overwhelming
fragrant (FRAY gruhnt) _adj._ having a pleasant odor

---

1. **treacheries** (TRECH uhr eez) _n._ acts of betrayal.

2. **militantes** (mee lee TAN tays) _n._ Spanish for "militants"—people who fight or are willing to fight.

he made from the mesquite. But many times, the revolucionarios <u>confiscated</u> his day's load of wood, leaving him to return home, humiliated, with an empty wagon.

Aside from Tía Pepa and Tío Anacleto, who had returned to Mexico by then, he had been the last of the Garcias left in Mexico, and he had left reluctantly. On the day he arrived in San Antonio with his family, he had told his brother Abuelo Jacobo, "If there was still any mesquite that was easy to get to, we would've stayed."

Reader's Response: How would you feel about leaving your home to help your family? Explain.

_____

_____

_____

_____

© Pearson Education

Vocabulary Development
confiscated (KAHN fuhs kayt id) *v.* seized, usually by governmental authority

Reading Skill

Unimportant details are small pieces of information that do not tell more about the **main idea**. List an unimportant detail you find in the bracketed paragraph.

_____

_____

Literary Analysis

What **mood** is created by the last paragraph?

_____

Circle words that help create this mood.

Stop to Reflect

Do you think Tío Abrán's decision to leave Mexico was a wise one for his family? Why or why not?

_____

_____

_____

_____

La Leña Buena

1. **Interpret:** What role do trees play in Tío Abrán's decision to stay and then to leave Mexico?

_____

_____

2. **Infer:** Tío Abrán says, "If there was still any mesquite that was easy to get to, we would've stayed." What does this remark tell you about his feelings toward Mexico?

_____

_____

3. **Reading Skill:** What is the **main idea** of this essay?

_____

_____

4. **Literary Analysis:** Complete this chart to analyze which words and images create the **mood** in "La Leña Buena."

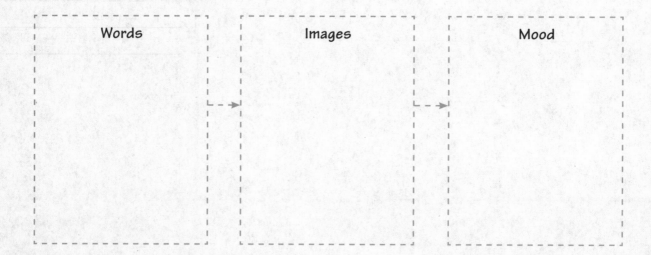

Words	Images	Mood

Writing: Problem-and-Solution Essay

Write a **problem-and-solution essay** to help immigrants adjust
to life in the United States. A problem-and-solution essay includes
possible solutions to a problem. Use the following chart to help you
brainstorm ideas for your essay.

1. Describe the problem.	
2. Describe the solution.	
3. Why will this solution work?	

Listening and Speaking: Informal Discussion

Use the following chart to write notes during your **informal
discussion**. Then, use your notes to summarize the discussion.

If Relatives Live . . .	Pros	Cons
Nearby		
Far away		

from The Pigman & Me
Paul Zindel

Summary Paul Zindel is the new kid at school. He does not know the rules yet. He accidentally gives John Quinn a black eye. John wants to fight Paul. Paul asks Nonno Frankie for advice about fighting. Paul tries to follow the advice during the fight. The fight does not end the way he expected.

? Writing About the Big Question

What is important to know? In *The Pigman & Me*, a boy gets into trouble because he doesn't know the rules in gym class at his new school. Complete this sentence:

The purpose of having rules at school is _____

_____.

Note-taking Guide
Use this chart to record important events from the story.

What does Richard Cahill forget to tell Paul?	What does Paul do to John Quinn?	What does Nonno Frankie teach Paul?	Who saves Paul at the end?
Richard forgets to tell Paul that he can only have a paddle for fifteen minutes.			

from The Pigman & Me

1. **Infer:** Paul pretends to be hurt when he falls during the fight. Why does Paul act as though he is hurt?

_____

_____

2. **Compare and Contrast:** Explain the difference between John's attitude and the attitude of the other students after Paul falls down.

_____

_____

3. **Reading Skill:** What is the **main idea** of this selection?

_____

_____

4. **Reading Skill:** What are two **important details** that support the main idea?

_____

_____

_____

5. **Literary Analysis:** Authors use words and images to create a **mood**. Complete the chart to analyze which words and images create the mood of this selection.

Words	Images	Mood

Writing: Problem-and-Solution Essay

Write a **problem-and-solution essay** to help new students adjust to one feature of life at your school. Think about written and unwritten rules at your school. Use this chart to list three problems and solutions that new students might face at your school. Choose the best problem and solution as the topic of your essay.

Problem			
Solution			

Listening and Speaking: Informal Discussion

Take part in an **informal discussion** about what a new student should or should not do. Answer the questions in the chart. List facts you use to back up your opinions.

	My Ideas
What could a new student do to make friends quickly?	
What should a new student not do if he or she wants to fit in?	
What can other students do to welcome new students?	

Advertisements

About Advertisements

An **advertisement** is a paid message. It may take the form of a picture, set of words, or a short movie. Advertisements are found in newspapers, magazines, Web sites, television, and radio. Companies use advertising to persuade customers to buy particular products or services. Sometimes, advertisers use propaganda techniques and faulty reasoning to sell their products.

- **Propaganda** is information that is one-sided or misleading. For example, an advertisement that reads "Everyone agrees that Muncheez is the best snack" uses propaganda.

- **Faulty reasoning** is an argument that is not logical. It is supported either by details that do not relate to the argument or by connections that are not based on facts. For example, the statement "People who eat Muncheez are very popular" makes a false connection between eating Muncheez and popularity.

Reading Skill

It is important to recognize propaganda techniques and faulty reasoning. This knowledge can help you avoid drawing faulty conclusions. Appeals that use these techniques are not based on facts. Using facts can help you make good decisions.

Study this chart. It shows examples of propaganda techniques and faulty reasoning.

Propaganda Technique	Explanation	Example
Broad generalizations	Sweeping claims that cannot be proved	"There's nothing like it in the world!"
Hidden messages	Pictures or words that convey an idea without stating it directly	A photo of an Olympic runner, suggesting you'll be a winner if you buy a certain brand of sneakers
Loaded language	Words that appeal to our emotions	"It's a miracle product!"
Bandwagon appeals	Implying that "everyone else" uses a certain product	"Thousands of allergy sufferers use Sneeze-Free."
Faulty reasoning	Using unrelated or unconnected details as support	More people have cats than dogs, so cats must be easier to take care of.

A Season of Fun for Everyone!

The hidden message in this picture is that wearing these shoes will provide family fun and recreation.

Jump into these sports shoes that let your feet enjoy life—and notice the difference they make in your day! No sissy footing here when there's hiking, picnicking or gardening to do. In many styles the Ball-Band scientific Arch-Gard* cradles your feet so leg muscles keep fresh when you're on the go.

And how those soles grip and help surefootedness—how the rubber treads wear, and wear. Yes—for dad, mother, sister and brother—Ball-Band casual style and down-to-earth comfort is great for the outdoors when you want to forget your feet.

Naturally—Ball-Band for youngsters, too. These shoes give every active toe a chance for normal use and development. So make foot health the style—your family's style this summer. Nothing could be smarter to wear than Ball-Band. See the complete line at your favorite shoe store.

Broad generalizations claim that these shoes are good for everyone.

For every foot of the Family—Every step of the way

PREMIER . . . an Arch-Gard shoe in black or brown for father and son.

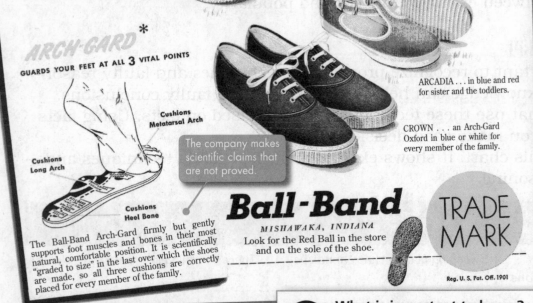

ARCADIA . . . in blue and red for sister and the toddlers.

CROWN . . . an Arch-Gard Oxford in blue or white for every member of the family.

ARCH-GARD *
GUARDS YOUR FEET AT ALL **3** VITAL POINTS

Cushions Metatarsal Arch

Cushions Long Arch

Cushions Heel Bone

The company makes scientific claims that are not proved.

The Ball-Band Arch-Gard firmly but gently supports foot muscles and bones in their most natural, comfortable position. It is scientifically "graded to size" in the last over which the shoes are made, so all three cushions are correctly placed for every member of the family.

Ball-Band
MISHAWAKA, INDIANA
Look for the Red Ball in the store and on the sole of the shoe.

TRADE MARK
Reg. U. S. Pat. Off. 1901

What is important to know?
What research should a shopper do before purchasing Ball-Band shoes?

Thinking About the Advertisements

1. What is the purpose of this advertisement?

_____

_____

2. What features of the advertisement support its purpose?

_____

_____

Reading Skill

3. Identify one example of faulty reasoning in this advertisement.

_____

_____

4. What broad generalization does the text in this advertisement make?

_____

_____

WRITE ABOUT IT ▷ **Timed Writing: Explanation (20 minutes)**

Describe a consumer who might be interested in buying Ball-Band shoes.

• What is the age group, gender, and concerns of this person?

_____

_____

• What features in the ad might attract this consumer?

_____

_____

_____

Oranges • Ode to Family Photographs

Poets use imaginative language for different reasons:

- to help the reader see an image
- to tell stories
- to share feelings
- to describe experiences

Poets use **sound devices** to make their writing sound musical. These devices enhance a poem's mood and meaning. This chart contains the most common sound devices.

Sound	Definition	Example
Rhyme	Repeating sounds at the ends of words	pool, rule, fool
Rhythm	Best created by pattern of stressed and unstressed syllables	Thĕ cát sắt ón thĕ mát.
Repetition	Use of any part of language (sound, word, and so on) more than one time	The tired dog watched. The tired cat slept.
Onomatopoeia	Use of words that imitate sounds	crash, bang, hiss, splat
Alliteration	Repeating consonant sounds in the beginnings of words	lovely, lonely nights

Figurative language is writing or speech that is not meant to be taken literally. The many types of figurative language are called **figures of speech**. Writers use these figures of speech to present ideas in an imaginative way.

Figurative Language	Definition	Example
Metaphor	Describes one thing as if it were another	The snow was a white blanket over the town.
Simile	Uses *like* or *as* to compare two unlike things	She is as slow as a turtle.
Personification	Gives human qualities to something that is not human	The ocean crashed angrily during the storm.

Sensory language is writing that appeals to one or more of the reader's senses. The five senses are sight, sound, smell, taste, and touch. Sensory language creates word pictures, or **images**. Images help the reader fully experience a poem.

Here are some different forms of poetry:

- **Narrative:** A narrative poem tells a story in verse. Verse is an ordered arrangement of lines. A narrative poem has a plot and characters as a short story does.
- **Lyric:** Lyric poetry expresses a single speaker's thoughts and feelings. This kind of poetry often has highly musical verse.
- **Concrete:** Concrete poems are shaped to look like the subject of the poem. The poet arranges the poem's lines to create a picture on the page.
- **Haiku:** Haiku is a three-line Japanese poem in verse form. The first and third lines each have five syllables. The second line has seven syllables.
- **Limerick:** A limerick is a rhyming, humorous poem that has five lines. Limericks also have a specific rhythm pattern and rhyme scheme.

Oranges • Ode to Family Photographs
Gary Soto

Summaries The speaker in "Oranges" is a twelve-year-old boy who shares his experience of visiting a store with a young girl. "Ode to Family Photographs" is about the photographs the poet's mother took of him and his family.

Note-taking Guide

Use this chart to record details about the characters and their actions in the poems.

	Characters	Actions
Oranges	the speaker a girl a saleslady	
Ode to Family Photographs		

Oranges
Gary Soto

The first time I walked
With a girl, I was twelve,
Cold, and weighted down
With two oranges in my jacket.
5 December. Frost cracking
Beneath my steps, my breath
Before me, then gone,
As I walked toward
Her house, the one whose
10 Porch light burned yellow
Night and day, in any weather.
A dog barked at me, until
She came out pulling
At her gloves, face bright
15 With rouge. I smiled,
Touched her shoulder, and led
Her down the street, across
A used car lot and a line
Of newly planted trees,
20 Until we were breathing
Before a drugstore. We
Entered, the tiny bell
Bringing a saleslady
Down a narrow aisle of goods.
25 I turned to the candies
Tiered like bleachers,
And asked what she wanted
Light in her eyes, a smile
Starting at the corners
30 Of her mouth. I fingered
A nickel in my pocket,
And when she lifted a chocolate
That cost a dime,
I didn't say anything.

Vocabulary Development

rouge (roozh) *n.* red makeup for coloring cheeks
tiered (tEErd) *v.* layered

Activate Prior Knowledge

Which experience from your childhood would you like to write about? Briefly describe it.

_____

_____

_____

_____

Poetry

Sensory language creates word pictures of sight, sound, smell, taste, and touch. Read the underlined sentence. For which two senses does the poet create word pictures? Circle the details that support your answer.

_____

_____

Poetry

A **simile** uses *like* or *as* to show how two different things are alike. Underline the simile on this page.

What is compared in this simile?

_____

_____

_____

Poetry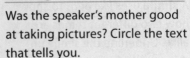

Narrative poetry tells a story in verse. Read the bracketed passage. Describe what happens in this part of "Oranges."

_____

_____

_____

_____

Poetry

Lyric poetry shows the thoughts of a single speaker. What are some of the speaker's thoughts and feelings in the second poem?

_____

_____

_____

_____

Reading Check

Was the speaker's mother good at taking pictures? Circle the text that tells you.

35 I took the nickel from
    My pocket, then an orange,
    And set them quietly on
    The counter. When I looked up,
    The lady's eyes met mine,
40 And held them, knowing
    Very well what it was all
    About.
            Outside,
    A few cars hissing past,
45 Fog hanging like old
    Coats between the trees.
    I took my girl's hand
    In mine for two blocks,
    Then released it to let
50 Her unwrap the chocolate.
    I peeled my orange
    That was so bright against
    The gray of December
    That, from some distance,
55 Someone might have thought
    I was making a fire in my hands.

Ode to Family Photographs
Gary Soto

This is the pond, and these are my feet.
This is the rooster, and this is more of
        my feet.

Mamá was never good at pictures.

This is a statue of a famous general who
        lost an arm
5   And this is me with my head cut off.

This is a trash can chained to a gate,
This is my father with his eyes half-closed.

This is a photograph of my sister
And a giraffe looking over her
        shoulder.

10   This is our car's front bumper.
     This is a bird with a pretzel in its
        beak.
     This is my brother Pedro standing
        on one leg on a rock,
     With a smear of chocolate on his
        face.

*   Mamá sneezed when she looked*
15 *Behind the camera: the snapshots*
       are blurry,
*   The angles dizzy as a spin on a*
       merry-go-round.

     But we had fun when Mamá picked
       up the camera.
     How can I tell?
     Each of us laughing hard.
20 Can you see? I have candy in my
       mouth.

Reader's Response: What do you find unusual or interesting about the subjects that the poet has written about in these poems?

_____

_____

_____

_____

Poetry

Lyric poetry is normally very musical. Is this poem musical? Explain.

_____

_____

_____

_____

Stop to Reflect

Think about all of the pictures the speaker describes. What do you think his family was like?

_____

_____

_____

_____

Reading Check ✏

Why are the photographs blurry? Underline the text that tells you.

Poetry

1. **Speculate:** The saleslady in "Oranges" knows that the boy cannot afford the piece of chocolate. How would the girl react if she knew what the saleslady knows?

   _____

2. **Draw Conclusions:** According to "Ode to Family Photographs," what are the speaker's feelings toward his mother?

   _____

3. **Poetry:** Analyze the **sensory language** in the poems by completing the chart. Use the first column to identify images that use sensory language. Use the second column to explain what the language means. Use the third column to explain why the image is important to the poem.

What It Says	What It Means	Why It Is Important

4. **Poetry:** What do the two poems have in common?

   _____

Poster

Design a **poster** about three poems by Gary Soto. Use the following prompts to take notes for your poster.

- Search the Internet for information about Gary Soto by using word searches with the following words: "Gary Soto" and "Gary Soto poetry." Read what fans have to say about his poetry and why they like it.

  What I learned:

  _____

  _____

  _____

- Gary Soto has written ten collections of poetry. One of his books of poetry is called *Neighborhood Odes*. Read his poems to learn how he describes living in a Chicano neighborhood and his life as a young boy.

  What I learned:

  _____

  _____

  _____

- Watch the video interview with Gary Soto. Review your source material. Use this information to answer the following questions.

1. How does the poet use the world around him to write poetry?

  _____

  _____

  _____

2. How has the poet's work changed or developed over the years?

  _____

  _____

  _____

Poetry Collection 1 • Poetry Collection 2

Reading Skill

Context clues are found in the text surrounding an unfamiliar word. They may be words with the same meaning, or descriptions or explanations. To use context clues, **ask questions**.

- *What kind of word is it?*
- *What word can I use in place of the unfamiliar word?*
- *Does the new sentence make sense?*

The chart helps you find the meaning of stride in this sentence:

Example: He lengthened his *stride* to catch up with his friend.

Use this chart to find the meaning of a new word from one of the poems.

Literary Analysis

Rhythm and **rhyme** add a musical quality to poems.

- **Rhythm:** the sound pattern created by stressed and unstressed syllables.

    Example: JACK and JILL went UP the HILL
    (4 stressed/3 unstressed)

- **Rhyme:** the repetition of sounds at the ends of words, such as *delight* and *excite*. After a rhyme pattern, or *scheme*, has been established, you come to expect rhymes.

Unfamiliar Word
stride

↓

Question
What kind of word?

↓

Answer
It names a way you move to catch up.

↓

"step"

Poetry Collection 1

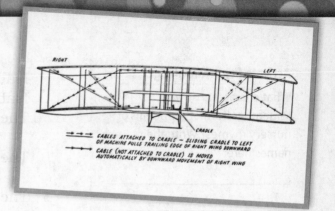

CABLES ATTACHED TO CRADLE – SLIDING CRADLE TO LEFT
OF MACHINE PULLS TRAILING EDGE OF RIGHT WING DOWNWARD

CABLE (NOT ATTACHED TO CRADLE) IS MOVED
AUTOMATICALLY BY DOWNWARD MOVEMENT OF RIGHT WING

Summaries Brave Isabel defeats a bear, a witch, a giant, and a doctor in "Adventures of Isabel." "Ankylosaurus" describes a tough dinosaur. How the Wright brothers built the first airplane is described in "Wilbur Wright and Orville Wright."

 Writing About the Big Question

Do we need words to communicate well? In "The Adventures of Isabel," Isabel communicates with action rather than words. The Wright brothers, on the other hand, use words to comfort and encourage each other. Complete this sentence:

Verbal and nonverbal communication styles are effective in different kinds

of situations because _____

_____.

Note-taking Guide

Use this chart to record information about characters' actions in each poem.

Characters	Actions
Isabel	eats a bear turns a witch into milk
Ankylosaurus	
The Wright brothers	

Activate Prior Knowledge

What characters do you remember from other poems or nursery rhymes? Write their names here.

_____

_____

_____

Reading Skill

Context clues are found in the text near an unfamiliar word. What clue might help you guess the meaning of *ravenous*?

_____

_____

Literary Analysis

Rhyme is the repetition of sounds at the ends of words. What two-word rhymes are used in lines 9 and 10?

_____

_____

Reading Check

What did the bear say to Isabel? Circle the text that tells you.

Adventures of Isabel
Ogden Nash

Isabel met an enormous bear,
Isabel, Isabel, didn't care;
The bear was hungry, the bear was
    ravenous,
The bear's big mouth was cruel and
    cavernous.
5 The bear said, Isabel, glad to meet you,
How do, Isabel, now I'll eat you!
Isabel, Isabel, didn't worry,
Isabel didn't scream or scurry.
She washed her hands and she
    straightened her hair up,
10 Then Isabel quietly ate the bear up.

Once in a night as black as pitch
Isabel met a wicked old witch.
The witch's face was cross and wrinkled,
The witch's gums with teeth were
    sprinkled.
15 Ho ho, Isabel! the old witch crowed,
I'll turn you into an ugly toad!
Isabel, Isabel, didn't worry,
Isabel didn't scream or scurry,
She showed no rage and she showed
    no rancor,
20 But she turned the witch into milk and
    drank her.

Isabel met a hideous giant,
Isabel continued self-reliant.
The giant was hairy, the giant was horrid,
He had one eye in the middle of his
    forehead.
25 Good morning Isabel, the giant said,
I'll grind your bones to make my bread.
Isabel, Isabel, didn't worry,
Isabel didn't scream or scurry.

Vocabulary Development
ravenous (RAV uh nuhs) *adj.* greedily hungry
rancor (RANG ker) *n.* bitter hate or ill will

She nibbled the zwieback that she always
    fed off,
30 And when it was gone, she cut the giant's
    head off.

Isabel met a troublesome doctor,
He punched and he poked till he really
    shocked her.
The doctor's talk was of coughs and chills
And the doctor's satchel bulged with pills.
35 The doctor said unto Isabel,
Swallow this, it will make you well.
Isabel, Isabel, didn't worry,
Isabel didn't scream or scurry.
She took those pills from the pill concocter,
40 And Isabel calmly cured the doctor.

Ankylosaurus
Jack Prelutsky

Clankity Clankity Clankity Clank!
Ankylosaurus was built like a tank,
its hide was a fortress as sturdy as steel,
it tended to be an <u>inedible</u> meal.

5 It was armored in front, it was armored
    behind,
there wasn't a thing on its minuscule mind,
it waddled about on its four stubby legs,
nibbling on plants with a mouthful of pegs.

Ankylosaurus was best left alone,
10 its tail was a cudgel of gristle and bone,
Clankity Clankity Clankity Clank!
Ankylosaurus was built like a tank.

© Pearson Education

Vocabulary Development

inedible (in ED uh buhl) *adj.* not fit to be eaten

Reading Skill

What **context clues** help you
understand that a *satchel* is
something that holds things?

_____

_____

Literary Analysis

What is the pattern of **rhymes** at
the ends of lines in the bracketed
stanza? Place an A next to the
first set of lines that rhyme. Place
a B next to the second set, and
so on.

Stop to Reflect

Do you find the description
of Ankylosaurus amusing or
frightening? Why?

_____

_____

_____

Reading Check

Why would Ankylosaurus make a
bad dinner for another dinosaur?
Circle the text that tells you.

Reading Skill

How are *W* and *O* used in this poem? What words would you use in their place? Look at the **context clues** in the poem.

_____

_____

_____

_____

Literary Analysis

Underline two words that **rhyme** with *another*.

Stop to Reflect

Which poem did you find the most humorous? Why?

_____

_____

_____

_____

Reading Check

What did the Wright brothers build first? Circle the text that tells you.

Wilbur Wright and Orville Wright
Rosemary and Stephen Vincent Benét

Said Orville Wright to Wilbur Wright,
"These birds are very trying.
I'm sick of hearing them cheep-cheep
About the fun of flying.
5 A bird has feathers, it is true.
That much I freely grant.
But, must that stop us, W?"
Said Wilbur Wright, "It shan't."

And so they built a glider, first,
10 And then they built another.
—There never were two brothers more
Devoted to each other.
They ran a dusty little shop
For bicycle-repairing,
15 And bought each other soda-pop
and praised each other's daring.

They glided here, they glided there,
They sometimes skinned their noses.
—For learning how to rule the air
20 Was not a bed of roses
But each would murmur, afterward,
While patching up his bro,
"Are we discouraged, W?"
"Of course we are not, O!"

25 And finally, at Kitty Hawk
In Nineteen-Three (let's cheer it!)
The first real airplane really flew
With Orville there to steer it!
—And kingdoms may forget their kings
30 And dogs forget their bites,
But, not till Man forgets his wings,
Will men forget the Wrights.

Poetry Collection 1

1. **Assess:** Is Isabel someone you would want to have as a friend? Explain.

   _____

   _____

2. **Evaluate:** Do you think the Wright brothers earned their fame? Why or why not?

   _____

   _____

   _____

3. **Reading Skill:** For the following line of poetry, write a **question** that you would ask to help you understand the underlined word. Then, explain how the italicized **context clues** help you figure out the meaning of the word. *nibbling on plants with a mouthful of* <u>pegs</u>

   _____

   _____

   _____

4. **Literary Analysis:** Complete this chart to give examples of **rhyming** words each poet uses. One example is given.

Poem	Rhyming Words		
Ankylosaurus	clank/tank		
Wilbur Wright and Orville Wright			
Adventures of Isabel			

Writing: Letter to an Author

Write a **letter to an author** of one of the poems in the collection. Answer the following questions:

- How do you feel about the poem?

  _____

  _____

- Why do you like or dislike the poem? Use details from the poem to support your answer.

  _____

  _____

  Use your answers to write notes for your letter.

Research and Technology: Booklet

Make a **booklet** that contains a variety of poems and stories about dinosaurs. Complete the following tasks for each poem and story as you research:

- Describe the poem or story in one sentence.

  _____

- Explain how the story or poem is like "Ankylosaurus."

  _____

  _____

- Explain how the story or poem is different from "Ankylosaurus."

  _____

  _____

  Use your notes to help create your booklet.

Poetry Collection 2

Summaries "A Dream Within a Dream" describes how someone feels after having lost a love. The speaker in "Life Doesn't Frighten Me" describes all of the things she is not afraid of. A walrus and a carpenter invite some oysters on a walk in "The Walrus and the Carpenter."

? Writing About the Big Question

Do we need words to communicate well? In "The Walrus and the Carpenter," the main characters fail to communicate their intentions to the young oysters. In "Life Doesn't Frighten Me," a girl insists that many scary things aren't scary at all. Complete this sentence:

Sometimes people do not use **language** to share their real thoughts and

feelings because _____

_____.

Note-taking Guide

Use this chart to record information about the characters' actions in each poem.

Characters	Actions
The speaker of "A Dream Within a Dream"	
The speaker of "Life Doesn't Frighten Me"	says boo, makes fun, smiles
The Walrus and the Carpenter	

Poetry Collection 2

1. **Respond:** Which speaker would you like to meet? Why?

_____

_____

_____

2. **Infer:** Why does the speaker of "Life Doesn't Frighten Me" smile at frightening things?

_____

_____

_____

3. **Reading Skill:** For the following line of poetry, write a **question** that you would ask to help you understand the underlined word. Then explain how the italicized **context clues** help you figure out the meaning of the word.

   I go _boo_ / Make them <u>shoo</u> / I _make fun_ / Way they _run_

   _____

   _____

4. **Literary Analysis:** Complete this chart to give examples of **rhyming** words each poet uses. One example is given.

Poem	Rhyming Words	
Life Doesn't Frighten Me	wall/hall/all	
A Dream Within a Dream		
The Walrus and the Carpenter		

Writing: Letter to an Author

Write a **letter to an author** of one of the poems in the collection. Answer the following questions:

- How do you feel about the poem?

  _____

- Why do you like or dislike the poem? Use details from the poem to support your answer.

  _____

  _____

  _____

Use your answers to write notes for your letter.

Research and Technology: Booklet

You will need to gather poems and stories written by Lewis Carroll to include in your **booklet**. Use the following chart to list each poem or story and the annotation that compares it to "The Walrus and the Carpenter."

Poem or Story Title	Annotation

Poetry Collection 3 • Poetry Collection 4

Reading Skill

Context is the situation in which a word or expression is used. Details in the surrounding text give you clues to the word's meaning. Some words have more than one meaning. **Reread and read ahead** to find context clues that clarify the meanings of words with multiple meanings. These examples show how context clarifies the meaning of *hide*.

- **Example:** The children tried to <u>hide</u> the broken vase.
  The elephant's gray <u>hide</u> was tough and leathery.

Literary Analysis

Figurative language is language that is not meant to be taken literally. Authors use figurative language to state ideas in fresh ways. They may use one or more of the following types of figurative language:

- **Similes** compare two unlike things using *like* or *as*.
- **Metaphors** compare two unlike things by stating that one thing is another.
- **Personification** compares an object or animal to a human by giving the object or animal human characteristics.

See the example of figurative language in the chart. Use this chart to unlock the meaning of f igurative language as you read.

> **Figurative Language**
> a day as soft as silk
>
> ↓
>
> **Type**
> simile
>
> ↓
>
> **What the Language Does**
> compares weather to soft fabric to show that the weather is gentle

Poetry Collection 3

Summaries The speaker in "Simile: Willow and Ginkgo" compares the delicate willow tree and the sturdy ginkgo tree to show different kinds of beauty. "Fame Is a Bee" describes how fame is similar to a bee. The speaker in "April Rain Song" uses powerful images to make the rain seem alive.

 Writing About the Big Question

Do we need words to communicate well? In Poetry Collection 3, you will notice that poets describe common things in uncommon ways. Complete this sentence:

Poets make **connections** between common and uncommon things in order

to _____.

Note-taking Guide

Use this chart to record important details that describe the subject of each poem.

Poem Title	Descriptions
Simile: Willow and Ginkgo	
Fame Is a Bee	Bee: is like a bee, has a song, has a sting, has a wing
April Rain Song	

Activate Prior Knowledge

Think about a time when you tried to explain to someone how happy or sad you felt. How did you describe how you felt?

_____

_____

_____

_____

Literary Analysis

Figurative language is a way writers use language to compare things. What two kinds of **figurative** language tell how the ginkgo grows?

_____

_____

_____

Underline the language in the text.

Reading Check

The willow and ginkgo are compared to types of drawings. Circle the two types of drawings described.

Simile: Willow and Ginkgo
Eve Merriam

The willow is like an etching,[1]
Fine-lined against the sky.
The ginkgo is like a crude sketch,
Hardly worthy to be signed.

5   The willow's music is like a <u>soprano</u>,
Delicate and thin.
The ginkgo's tune is like a <u>chorus</u>
With everyone joining in.

The willow is sleek as a velvet-nosed calf;
10   The ginkgo is leathery as an old bull.
The willow's branches are like silken thread;
The ginkgo's like stubby rough wool.

The willow is like a nymph[2] with streaming
      hair;
Wherever it grows, there is green and gold
      and fair.
15   The willow dips to the water,
Protected and precious, like the king's favorite
      daughter.

The ginkgo forces its way through gray
      concrete;
Like a city child, it grows up in the street.
Thrust against the metal sky,
20   Somehow it survives and even <u>thrives</u>.

My eyes feast upon the willow,
But my heart goes to the ginkgo.

Vocabulary Development

soprano (suh PRAN oh) *n.* a singer with a very high voice

chorus (KAWR us) *n.* the sound produced by many voices singing or speaking at the same time

thrives (thryvz) *v.* grows well

1. **etching** (ECH ing) *n.* print of a drawing made on metal, glass, or wood.

2. **nymph** (nimf) *n.* spirit of nature, thought of as a beautiful maiden.

Fame Is a Bee
Emily Dickinson

Fame is a bee.
It has a song—
It has a sting—
Ah, too, it has a wing.

April Rain Song
Langston Hughes

Let the rain kiss you.
Let the rain beat upon your head with silver
    liquid drops.
Let the rain sing you a lullaby.

5 The rain makes still pools on the sidewalk.
The rain makes running pools in the gutter.
The rain plays a little sleep-song on our roof
    at night—

And I love the rain.

Reader's Response: Do you like the way these poets use **figurative language** to show something unusual about their subjects? How does figurative language make their subjects more interesting? Explain.

_____

_____

_____

_____

Literary Analysis

What type of **figurative language** is used to compare fame to a bee?

_____

_____

Reading Skill

Context clues are words that help you figure out the meaning of words you do not understand. Read the bracketed stanza. What does _running_ mean?

_____

What **context** clues help you know the meaning of running?

_____

_____

Stop to Reflect

How might "April Rain Song" be different if it were about the rain that comes with a hurricane?

_____

_____

Describe another thing to which fame can be compared.

_____

_____

Poetry Collection 3

1. **Compare and Contrast:** Merriam compares the willow and ginkgo trees to drawings, singers, animals, fabrics, and humans. What overall impression do you get of each tree?

_____

_____

2. **Interpret:** Fill out the chart below with ideas from "Fame Is a Bee." Note good and bad things about fame in the first and second columns. Reread the poem. Tell how your ideas about fame have changed in the third column.

Good Things about Fame	Bad Things About Fame	Final Response to Poem
attracts attention		

3. **Reading Skill:** In "April Rain Song," what is the meaning of *beat*? What **context clues** help you decide?

_____

_____

4. **Literary Analysis:** Find an example of **personification** in one of the poems. Explain how your choice is an example of this type of **figurative language**.

_____

_____

Writing: Poem

Write a **poem** with figurative language. Use similes, metaphors, or personification to make your topic clear to your readers.

- Make a list of people and animals you have positive feelings about.

  _____

  _____

- Choose a subject from your list. _____

- What do you like about your subject? _____

  _____

- What other things share these good qualities? _____

  _____

Listening and Speaking: Poetry Reading

Answer the following questions to prepare for your **poetry reading**.

- Name of poem: _____

- After which words should I pause in the poem? _____

  _____

- Which words should be stressed? _____

  _____

- Which words should I read slowly? _____

  _____

Poetry Collection 4

Summaries The speaker in "Abuelito Who" compares the fun, happy man her grandfather was with the sick, weak man he has become. "The World Is Not a Pleasant Place to Be" reminds readers of the importance of friends. "Child on Top of a Greenhouse" describes the exciting and interesting world a child sees from the roof of a greenhouse.

Writing About the Big Question

Do we need words to communicate well? Poetry Collection 4 includes poems that convey the speaker's feelings about loved ones. You can let people know you care about them by using words or by your actions towards them. Complete this sentence:

You can reveal your love of friends by _____

_____.

Note-taking Guide

Use this chart to record important details that describe the people in each poem.

Poem Title	Person	Descriptions
Abuelito Who	Abuelito	dough and feathers, sad, sick, tired, hiding, blankets and spoons and big brown shoes, rain on the roof
The World Is Not a Pleasant Place to Be		
Child on Top of a Greenhouse		

Poetry Collection 4

1. **Interpret:** Why does the speaker of "Abuelito Who" feel as if Abuelito is "hiding underneath the bed"?

   _____

   _____

2. **Interpret:** Complete the chart below with ideas from "The World Is Not a Pleasant Place to Be." Note good things about friends in the first column. Describe life without friends in the second column. Reread the poem. Tell how your ideas about friends have changed in the third column.

Good Things About Friends	Life Without Friends	Final Response to Poem

3. **Reading Skill:** In "The World Is Not a Pleasant Place to Be," what is the meaning of *flow*? What **context clues** help you figure out the meaning?

   _____

   _____

4. **Literary Analysis:** Find an example of a **metaphor** in the poems in this collection. Explain your choice.

   _____

   _____

Writing: Poem

Write a **poem** with figurative language. Use similes, metaphors, or personification to make your topic clear to your readers.

- Make a list of things in nature and things in your community that you have positive feelings about.

  _____

  _____

- Choose a subject from your list. _____

- What do you like about your subject? _____

  _____

- What other things share these good qualities? _____

  _____

Listening and Speaking: Poetry Reading

Prepare for a **poetry reading**. First, choose a poem to read. Then, complete this chart to help plan your reading.

Title of Poem:		
Feelings in poem:	Words that show these feelings:	Voice changes and expressions that show these feelings:
_____	_____	_____
_____	_____	_____
_____	_____	_____
_____	_____	_____
_____	_____	_____
_____	_____	_____

Instruction Manuals

About Instruction Manuals

An **instruction manual** gives step-by-step directions for finishing a task. The text can explain the following:

- how to put something together
- how to do something
- how to use something

Most instruction manuals have these features:

- a description of something that the reader can do by following the directions
- a list of the materials the reader needs
- a series of steps explained in an order that makes sense

Reading Skill

In an instruction manual, the steps for a task often appear as a numbered or bulleted list. This format enables you to **follow multiple-step instructions.** Following instructions allows you to correctly perform a task. To follow the instructions,

- read each step carefully
- look at the illustrations or diagrams
- complete the steps in order

You can restate the steps in own words. This is one way to make sure that you understand the instructions. Study the graphic organizer below to learn more about following multiple-step instructions.

Checklist for Following Multi-Step Instructions

❑ Read all the requirements and instructions completely before starting to follow them.

❑ Look for clues such as bold type or capital letters that point out specific sections or important information.

❑ Use illustrations and other visual aids to see the process demonstrated.

❑ Follow each step in the exact order given.

❑ Do not skip any steps.

ORIGAMI

APATOSAURUS/DIMETRODON by Rachel Katz

Begin with a 9 inch by 12 inch piece of construction paper or an 8½ inch by 11 inch sheet of copy paper.

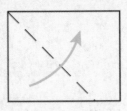 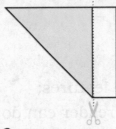  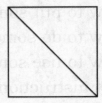

1 Place the rectangle sideways. Valley fold the left-hand side up to meet the top, thereby making a triangle.

2 Cut along the side of the triangle.

3 Save the rectangular piece of paper for the dinosaur's legs.

4 Open out the triangle into a square. Turn the square around to look like a diamond, making sure the existing fold-line is running horizontally across the paper.

Body

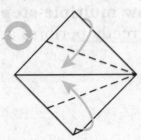 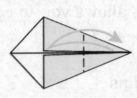 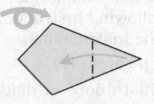

5 From the right-hand corner, valley fold the top and bottom sloping edges over to meet the middle fold-line, thereby making the kite base.

6 Valley fold the right-hand point over to meet the vertical edges. Press it flat and unfold it.

7 Turn the paper over. Valley fold the right-hand point over along the fold-line made in step 6.

8 Valley fold the point over back out toward the right.

 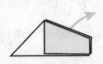 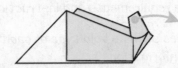

9 Valley fold the paper in half from bottom to top.

10 Reach inside the model and pull out the . . .

11 dinosaur's neck. Press it flat, into the position shown in step 12.

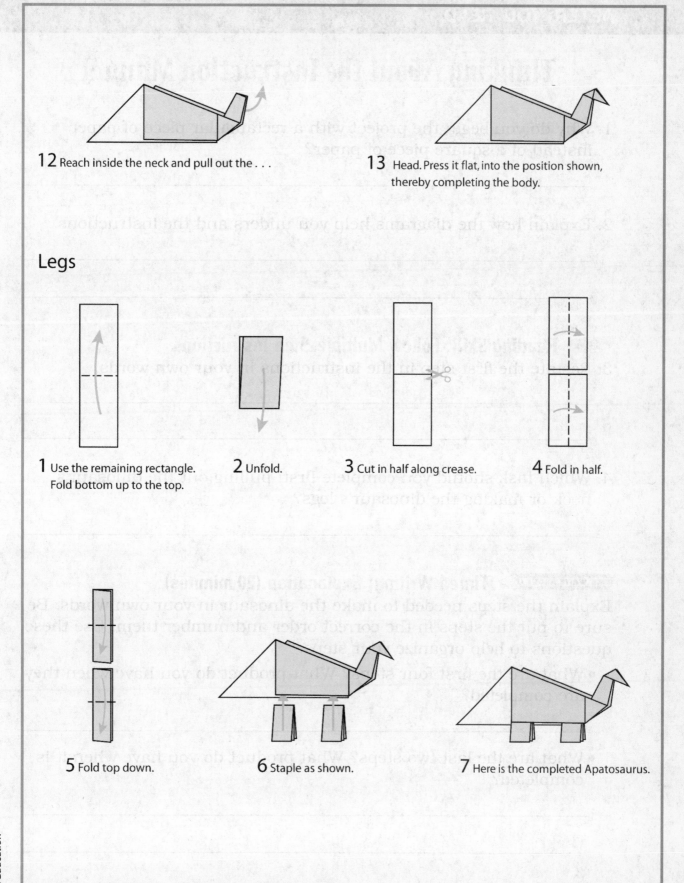

12 Reach inside the neck and pull out the . . .

13 Head. Press it flat, into the position shown, thereby completing the body.

Legs

1 Use the remaining rectangle. Fold bottom up to the top.

2 Unfold.

3 Cut in half along crease.

4 Fold in half.

5 Fold top down.

6 Staple as shown.

7 Here is the completed Apatosaurus.

Thinking About the Instruction Manual

1. Why do you begin the project with a rectangular piece of paper instead of a square piece of paper?

   _____

2. Explain how the diagrams help you understand the instructions.

   _____

   _____

TALK ABOUT IT **Reading Skill: Follow Multiple-Step Instructions**

3. Restate the first step in the instructions in your own words.

   _____

   _____

4. Which task should you complete first: pulling out the dinosaur's neck or making the dinosaur's legs?

   _____

WRITE ABOUT IT **Timed Writing: Explanation (20 minutes)**

Explain the steps needed to make the dinosaur in your own words. Be sure to put the steps in the correct order and number them. Use these questions to help organize your steps.

- What are the first four steps? What product do you have when they are completed?

   _____

- What are the last two steps? What product do you have when it is completed?

   _____

   _____

Poetry Collection 5 • Poetry Collection 6

Reading Skill

Paraphrasing is restating an author's words in your own words. Paraphrasing difficult or confusing passages in a poem helps you clarify the meaning. Use these steps to help you:

- Stop and **reread** any difficult lines or passages.
- Identify unfamiliar words, find their meanings, and replace them with words that mean nearly the same thing.
- Reread to see whether your paraphrase makes sense.

Note the paraphrasing sample in the chart. Use the chart to help you paraphrase difficult lines as you read.

Literary Analysis

Poets use different **forms of poetry** suited to the ideas, images, and feelings they want to express. Here are three poetic forms:

- In a **concrete poem**, words are arranged in a shape that reflects the subject of the poem.
- A **haiku** is a Japanese verse form with three lines. Line 1 has five syllables, line 2 has seven, and line 3 has five.
- A **limerick** is a funny poem of five lines. Lines 1, 2, and 5 rhyme and have three beats, or stressed syllables. Lines 3 and 4 rhyme and have two beats.

Line
Afoot and lighthearted, I take to the open road.

Unfamiliar Word(s)
afoot = on foot lighthearted = happy take to = start out on

Paraphrase
On foot and happy, I start out on the road.

Poetry Collection 5

Summaries Matsuo Bashō's "Haiku" describes a quiet moment in nature. The anonymous limerick plays with words to create a fun scene. "The Sidewalk Racer or On the Skateboard" is shaped like a skateboard. The poem describes the feeling of skateboarding.

Writing About the Big Question

Do we need words to communicate well? A writer's toolbox always contains words, but poets use more than just words to communicate. Poets also use line length, rhyme, and rhythm to convey ideas. Complete this sentence:

The **language** of poetry is unique because _____

_____.

Note-taking Guide
Use this chart to record what each poem is about.

Poem Title	What Poem Is About
Haiku	
Limerick	
The Sidewalk Racer or On the Skateboard	

Haiku
Matsuo Bashō

An old silent pond . . .
A frog jumps into the pond,
splash! Silence again.

Limerick
Anonymous

A flea and a fly in a flue
Were caught, so what could they do?
Said the fly, "Let us flee."
"Let us fly," said the flea.
5 So they flew through a flaw in the flue.

The Sidewalk Racer
or On the Skateboard
Lillian Morrison

Skimming
an asphalt sea
I swerve, I curve, I
sway; I speed to whirring
5 sound an inch above the
ground; I'm the sailor
and the sail, I'm the
driver and the wheel
I'm the one and only
10 single engine
human auto
mobile.

Vocabulary Development

flee (flee) *v.* to run or escape from danger

flaw (flaw) *n.* break; crack

skimming (SKIM ing) *adj.* gliding; moving swiftly and lightly over a surface

Activate Prior Knowledge

Think about something you do often. Describe how you can look at it in a different way.

_____

_____

_____

Literary Analysis

The **haiku form of poetry** has a special number of syllables. Bashō's poem follows the syllable rule. Mark the syllables in each line.

Reading Skill

Paraphrasing is restating an author's words in your own words. How would you paraphrase lines 3–5 of the limerick?

_____

_____

_____

Stop to Reflect

Would it be possible to write a serious limerick? Explain.

_____

_____

Poetry Collection 5

1. **Analyze:** The limerick repeats the sound of the letter blend *fl*. How does this sound contribute to the humor in the poem?

_____

_____

2. **Support:** The speaker in "The Sidewalk Racer" loves skateboarding. Which details in the poem support this?

_____

_____

3. **Reading Skill: Paraphrase** lines 6–12 of "The Sidewalk Racer."

_____

_____

_____

4. **Literary Analysis:** What image or word picture is presented in each line of the **haiku**? Use this web to record your answer.

```
┌──────────────────────────────────────────────┐
│                    Haiku                       │
└──────────────────────────────────────────────┘
        │                │                │
        ▼                ▼                ▼
┌───────────┐    ┌───────────┐    ┌───────────┐
│  Line 1:  │    │  Line 2:  │    │  Line 3:  │
│           │    │           │    │           │
│           │    │           │    │           │
└───────────┘    └───────────┘    └───────────┘
```

Support for Writing: Poem

Write your own **poem**. First, choose a topic for your poem. Then, choose the form that will work best for your topic: haiku, limerick, or concrete poem. Use the chart to help you plan ideas for your poem.

Topic of Poem:	
Form of Poem (haiku, limerick, or concrete poem):	
Style or Pattern of Form:	
Ideas for Word Choices:	

Research and Technology: Presentation of a Poem

Use a computer to design a **presentation of a poem** from this collection.

- Which poem will you design?

  _____

- Choose a font, or letter style, that is easy to read. It should fit with the tone of the poem. Think about the tone of the poem. Is it silly, serious, sad, or happy?

  _____

- Choose some art, or draw your own pictures that fit with the poem. What images will fit with your poem?

  _____

  _____

Use these notes to complete your presentation.

Poetry Collection 6

Summaries Musō Soseki's "Haiku" brings winter to life. The anonymous limerick uses rhyme and words with more than one meaning to describe an accident in a funny way. "Concrete Cat" uses nouns linked to cats. The poet lines up her words to create an image of a cat.

Writing About the Big Question

Do we need words to communicate well? Poets go beyond words to convey their ideas. Haikus use patterns of syllables, limericks use rhythm and rhyme and concrete poems use a visual arrangement of their words. Complete this sentence:

When visual images accompany text, they help convey meaning by

_____.

Note-taking Guide
Use this chart to record what each poem is about.

Poem Title	What Poem Is About
Haiku	
Limerick	
Concrete Cat	

Poetry Collection 6

1. **Infer:** The haiku describes winter winds howling through a forest. Why are there no leaves for the wind to blow in the haiku?

_____

_____

2. **Analyze:** *Spring* and *fall* have double meanings in the limerick. How do both meanings contribute to the humor in the limerick?

_____

_____

_____

3. **Reading Skill:** Review "Concrete Cat." In your own words, **paraphrase** the meaning of the words that form the cat's head.

_____

_____

_____

4. **Literary Analysis:** What image or word picture is presented in each line of the **haiku**? Use this web to record your answer.

```
                        Haiku
        ┌─────────────────┼─────────────────┐
        ▼                 ▼                 ▼
    Line 1:           Line 2:           Line 3:
```

Support for Writing: Poem

Write your own **poem**. First, choose a topic for your poem. Then, choose the form that will work best for your topic: haiku, limerick, or concrete poem. Use the chart to help you plan ideas for your poem.

Topic of Poem:	
Form of Poem (haiku, limerick, or concrete poem):	
Style or Pattern of Form:	
Ideas for Word Choices:	

Research and Technology: Presentation of a Poem

Use the space provided to sketch how you want your poem to look. Consider where you will place images as well as the poem itself.

Poetry Collection 7 • Poetry Collection 8

Reading Skill

Paraphrasing is restating something in your own words. To paraphrase a poem, you must first understand it. Then, use simpler language to restate its meaning. **Reading aloud fluently according to punctuation** will help you group words for meaning.

- Do not automatically stop at the end of each line.
- Use the chart shown here to decide where to pause.

Poetry Reading Guide	
Punctuation	How to Read
no punctuation	Do not pause. Keep reading.
comma (,)	slight pause
colon (:) semicolon (;) dash (—)	longer pause
period (.) question mark (?) exclamation point (!)	longest pause

Literary Analysis

Sound devices are a writer's tools for bringing out the music in words and for expressing feelings. Sound devices commonly used in poetry include the following:

- **Repetition:** the use, more than once, of any element of language—a sound, word, phrase, clause, or sentence—as in *of the people, by the people, and for the people*
- **Alliteration:** the repetition of initial consonant sounds, such as the *b* sound in *big bad wolf*
- **Onomatopoeia:** the use of a word that sounds like what it means, such as *roar* and *buzz*

Poetry Collection 7

Summaries "No Thank You" is a long list of reasons why the speaker does not want a kitten. "Wind and water and stone" describes how these three elements interact with one another. The playful language in "Parade" shows the excitement of a circus parade coming to town.

 **Writing About the Big Question**

Do we need words to communicate well? Poets can make the ordinary— a kitten; a scene in nature; or a parade—seem extraordinary. Complete this sentence:

When a poet writes about ordinary things he or she is **sharing** we

understand _____.

Note-taking Guide

Use this chart to record important images from each poem.

Poem Title	Images
No Thank You	long hair in cornflakes sofas chewed to shreds
Wind and water and stone	
Parade	

Please, see
"No Thank You"
by Shel Silverstein
on page 590 in the
Student Edition.

Activate Prior Knowledge

Think about your favorite song or poem. Why do you like it?

_____

_____

_____

Literary Analysis

Poets use **sound devices** such as **repetition**, **alliteration,** and **onomatopoeia** to bring out the music in the words. What sound device is used in lines 5 and 6?

_____

Reading Skill

Reading aloud fluently according to punctuation can help you find clues to the poem's meaning. What should you do when you come to the ellipsis points (. . .) in the last line?

_____

_____

Reading Check

What is one thing the speaker does not like about cats? Write down a line that tells you.

_____

_____

_____

Wind and water and stone
Octavio Paz

The water hollowed the stone,
the wind <u>dispersed</u> the water,
the stone stopped the wind.
Water and wind and stone.

5　The wind sculpted the stone,
the stone is a cup of water,
the water runs off and is wind.
Stone and wind and water.

The wind sings in its turnings,
10　the water <u>murmurs</u> as it goes,
the motionless stone is quiet.
Wind and water and stone.

One is the other, and is neither:
among their empty names
15　they pass and disappear,
water and stone and wind.

Literary Analysis

Using a word or phrase more than once is called **repetition**. What effect is created by the repetition of words in the fourth line of each stanza?

_____

_____

_____

Reading Skill

Paraphrasing is restating something in your own words. Paraphrase lines 9–11.

_____

_____

Stop to Reflect

The poet compares wind, water, and stone throughout the poem. Underline one of these examples. What is another way that you could compare wind, water, and stone?

_____

_____

_____

Reading Check

What familiar thing is used to describe the stone? Circle the line that tells you.

Vocabulary Development

dispersed (di SPERST) *v.* distributed in many directions
murmurs (MER merz) *v.* makes a soft, continuous sound

Parade
Rachel Field

Background

"Parade" describes an old tradition—the circus parade. Before television and radio, the best way to advertise coming attractions was a march down Main Street featuring clowns, wild animals in cages, and a giant musical instrument called a calliope.

This is the day the circus comes
With blare of brass, with beating drums,
And clashing cymbals, and with roar
Of wild beasts never heard before
5 Within town limits. Spick and span
Will shine each gilded cage and van;
Cockades at every horse's head
Will nod, and riders dressed in red
Or blue trot by. There will be floats
10 In shapes like dragons, thrones and boats,
And clowns on stilts; freaks big and small,
Till <u>leisurely</u> and last of all
Camels and elephants will pass
Beneath our elms, along our grass.

Reader's Response: Did any of these poems end in a way that surprised you? Explain your answer.

_____

_____

_____

_____

Reading Skill

Would you stop or keep reading at the end of line 3? Explain.

_____

_____

_____

Stop to Reflect

The poem describes what you see and hear at the parade. What might you smell and taste at the parade?

_____

_____

_____

Literary Analysis

Circle the words in line 12 of "Parade" that show an example of alliteration.

Vocabulary Development
leisurely (LEE zher lee) *adv.* in an unhurried way

Poetry Collection 7

1. **Speculate:** Why do you think the speaker of "No Thank You" says that he would prefer an ape, lion, pig, or boar to a cat?

_____

_____

2. **Infer:** What do the details about the town in "Parade" suggest about the town?

_____

_____

3. **Reading Skill: Paraphrase** the poem "No Thank You."

_____

_____

4. **Literary Analysis:** Complete this chart by listing examples of **sound devices** in each poem.

	Wind and water and stone	Parade	No Thank You
Repetition			
Alliteration			
Onomatopoeia			

Writing: Prose Description

Write a **prose description** of the scene suggested by one of the poems in this collection. In other words, write a description in your own words, using regular sentences. First, choose the poem you will write about. Then, answer the following questions:

• What details from the poem do you plan to include?

_____

_____

• What details do you plan to leave out? Explain why.

_____

_____

• How would the scene in the poem make you feel if you were there?

_____

Research and Technology: Résumé

Prepare a **résumé** for one of the poets in this collection. Answer the following questions as you look for information about the poet's life:

• Where did the poet grow up? _____

_____

• Did the poet go to college? Where? _____

_____

• What other jobs has the poet had? _____

_____

• What are some of the poet's major accomplishments? _____

_____

Poetry Collection 8

Summaries Fairies warn snakes and other creatures to stay away from the sleeping Queen in "The Fairies' Lullaby." "Saying Yes" is about the speaker's struggle to express herself as a Chinese American. The speaker of "Cynthia in the Snow" enjoys the sight and sound of falling snow.

? Writing About the Big Question

Do we need words to communicate well?

The poems in Poetry Collection 8 all communicate experiences and feelings. Complete this sentence:

Reading about someone else's experiences helps readers feel a **connection**

to _____

_____.

Note-taking Guide

Use the chart to record important details about the three poems.

Who are the fairies protecting in "The Fairies' Lullaby"?	The fairies are protecting the fairy Queen.
What creatures do the fairies warn?	
Where is the speaker of "Saying Yes" from?	
Why does the speaker of "Cynthia in the Snow" like snow?	

Poetry Collection 8

1. **Evaluate:** Do you think that the speaker in "Saying Yes" has a good attitude toward her identity? Why or why not?

_____

_____

_____

2. **Analyze:** In "Cynthia in the Snow," what is the speaker's overall reaction to the snow?

_____

_____

3. **Reading Skill: Paraphrase** the chorus's lines from "The Fairies' Lullaby."

_____

_____

_____

4. **Literary Analysis:** Complete this chart by listing examples of **sound devices** in each poem.

	The Fairies' Lullaby	Cynthia in the Snow	Saying Yes
Repetition			
Alliteration			
Onomatopoeia			

Writing: Prose Description

Write a **prose description** of the scene suggested by one of the poems in this collection. In other words, write a description in your own words, using regular sentences. First, choose the poem you will write about. Then, answer the following questions:

• What details from the poem do you plan to include?

_____

_____

• What details do you plan to leave out? Explain why.

_____

_____

• How would the scene in the poem make you feel if you were there?

_____

_____

Use your notes to write your description.

Research and Technology: Résumé

Complete the following chart as you find information for your poet's **résumé**.

Education:

Work Experience:

Published Works:

Awards:

Features:
- statements regarding policies and required documents
- spaces for providing required information
- a line for the applicant's signature

San Francisco Public Library
LIBRARY CARD APPLICATION

Date: _____

This paragraph gives special instructions for applicants of certain ages.

Photo identification and proof of address are required for all registrations. If you are 12 years of age or under, your parent/guardian must sign the application form.

PLEASE PRINT

Last Name	First Name	Middle

Mailing Address _____ Apt. # _____

City	County	State	ZIP Code

Residence Address *(if different from above)* _____ Apt. # _____

City	County	State	ZIP Code

Telephone 1 _____ Telephone 2 _____

Driver License/ID _____ Student ID _____

Date of Birth _____ / _____ / _____   Age *(circle one)*   0–12 years   13–17   18–64   65 and over
    Month   Day   Year

PIN # ____ ____ ____ ____
    (Choose a 4-digit number)

E-mail _____ @ _____
    (Only include if you wish to receive library notices by e-mail instead of U.S. Mail)

I agree to abide by library rules and to pay for any loss of, or damage to library materials and to pay for overdue fines accumulated on this card. I understand I am responsible for notifying the Library in case of loss or theft of this card. Failure to do so will result in my being held liable for materials on this card and for fines incurred on the card. I also agree to inform the Library of any street address or e-mail changes or change in the status of parent/guardian.

By signing on this line, the applicant agrees to the terms stated in the paragraph above.

Your Signature _____

Signature of Parent/Guardian _____ Print Name _____
(If applicant is 12 years of age or younger)

Do we need words to communicate well?

Why does the library request that the applicant print when communicating his or her information?

Features:

- information regarding what documents or items must be included with the application
- directions about whether the informa-

SARASOTA COUNTY LIBRARY SYSTEM

Library Card Application

Labels and lines are provided for placing all required information.

Please print

Last Name:	First Name:	Middle Name:	Birth Date:

Local Address (number, street, P.O. Box, Apt #)			

City :	State:	ZIP Code:	County (if other than Sarasota)

Telephone Number (with area code) ( )	E-mail Address:

Permanent Address (if different than above):	Telephone Number (with area code) ( )

City:	State:	ZIP Code	

This section is to be completed by a parent or legal guardian if the applicant is under the age of 18.

Please print

Last Name	First Name	Middle Name

Address	Telephone Number: ( )

Please read this before signing!

I verify that the above information is correct. I am aware that by signing this application, I assume responsibility for all use of this card, including internet usage and internet use policies. I agree to pay fines for any items returned overdue and to pay replacement charges for any materials lost, damaged or stolen on this account. I agree to report immediately the loss of this card, otherwise the library will assume its use to be authorized by me. A replacement fee is charged for lost cards.

The Sarasota County Library System has an open access policy. Parents or guardians, not library staff, are responsible for library materials and Internet resources selected and used by children.

By signing the agreement, the applicant agrees to follow the rules of the organization.

_____   _____   _____   _____
Signature of Applicant   Date   Signature of Parent or Guardian   Date
                                                    (If applicant is under 18)

Do we need words to communicate?

(a) Why might the library want the applicant to print when communicating his or her personal information?

Thinking About the Application

1. Paraphrase the responsibilities a library cardholder accepts.

_____

_____

2. Why would a library require a library card upon checkout of library materials?

_____

TALK ABOUT IT **Reading Skill**

3. What information is required in order to complete the library applications?

_____

4. Who must also sign if the applicant is under a certain age?

_____

WRITE ABOUT IT **Timed Writing: Explanation** (15 minutes)

Paraphrase the information on the library card application.
Answer the following questions to help you write your explanation.

• A privilege is a benefit or advantage. What can someone do with a library card?

_____

• Having responsibilities means that you are trustworthy or reliable. Reread the library card application. What are the responsibilities that come with having a library card?

_____

Rewrite your answers in your own words. Then, use your notes to write your explanation.

Gluskabe and Old Man Winter

Drama is different from other types of literature because it is written to be performed. You should imagine that you are seeing and hearing the action as you read a play. Drama and other forms of literature have the following things in common:

- **Characters:** people who take part in the action

- **Conflict:** a problem between two characters or forces

- **Theme:** a message about life

Read this chart to understand the elements of drama.

Elements of Drama	Definition	Example
Acts	units of action in drama	Act 1
Scenes	smaller parts of acts	Act 1, Scene 1
Dialogue	• words that characters say • no quotation marks used • character's name placed in front of character's words	**GLUSKABE:** It is very cold this winter, Grandmother.
Script	printed form of a play, or drama	the physical copy of the play *Gluskabe and Old Man Winter*
Stage directions	• written as information in brackets • describe what stage looks like • describe how characters should act	[Dark room with one lamp glowing; Jeb looks tired.]
Set	arrangement of scenery that shows time and place of action	wigwam in corner with bare trees, snow on the ground
Props	objects on the stage that actors use	book, suitcase, flashlight

There are three types of plays, or drama:

- **Drama** is a word often used to describe a play with a serious subject.

- **Comedy** is a type of drama that has a happy ending. The audience laughs at the characters' dialogue and at the situations in which characters find themselves. Some comedies are written for entertainment. Others are written to address serious issues in a humorous way.

- **Tragedy** is a drama in which events lead to the downfall of the main character. This character is usually a very important person, such as a king.

Drama is often written for stage performance. The dramatic format is also used for scripts written for other types of performances:

- **Screenplays** are scripts for movies. They include camera angles and scene changes that are not usually in a stage play.

- **Teleplays** are screenplays written for television.

- **Radio plays** are scripts written for radio broadcast. They sometimes include sound effects. Radio plays do not include scenery description.

Gluskabe and Old Man Winter

Joseph Bruchac

Summary Old Man Winter stays too long. A human being asks Gluskabe and Grandmother Woodchuck to end winter so his people will live. Gluskabe goes to Old Man Winter after getting advice from Grandmother Woodchuck. Gluskabe has to be clever. He ends winter with the help of Grandmother Woodchuck's advice.

Note-taking Guide

Fill in this chart with details about Gluskabe.

What is Gluskabe's job?	His job is to help the people.
Why does Gluskabe go to Old Man Winter's wigwam?	
Who gives Gluskabe advice?	
How does Gluskabe trick the Summer People?	
Where does Gluskabe take the summerstick?	

Gluskabe and Old Man Winter
Joseph Bruchac

Characters

Speaking Roles	Non-speaking Roles
NARRATOR	SUN
GLUSKABE	FLOWERS
GRANDMOTHER WOODCHUCK	PLANTS
HUMAN BEING	
OLD MAN WINTER	
FOUR OR MORE SUMMER LAND PEOPLE INCLUDING THE LEADER	
FOUR CROWS	

Scene I. Gluskabe and Grandmother Woodchuck's Wigwam

<u>GLUSKABE *and* GRANDMOTHER WOODCHUCK *sit inside with their blankets over their shoulders.*</u>

NARRATOR. Long ago GLUSKABE (gloo-SKAH-bey) lived with his grandmother, Woodchuck, who was old and very wise. Gluskabe's job was to help the people.

GLUSKABE. It is very cold this winter, Grandmother.

GRANDMOTHER WOODCHUCK. *Ni ya yo* (nee yah yo), Grandson. You are right!

GLUSKABE. The snow is very deep, Grandmother.

GRANDMOTHER WOODCHUCK. *Ni ya yo*, Grandson.

GLUSKABE. It has been winter for a very long time, Grandmother.

GRANDMOTHER WOODCHUCK. *Ni ya yo*, Grandson. But look, here comes one of those human beings who are our friends.

HUMAN BEING. *Kwai, kwai, nidobak.* (kwy kwy nee-DOH-bahk). Hello, my friends.

GLUSKABE AND GRANDMOTHER WOODCHUCK. *Kwai, kwai, nidoba* (kwy kwy nee-DOH-bah).

Activate Prior Knowledge

Which season of the year might you want to change? Explain why.

_____

_____

_____

_____

Drama

Stage directions give information about what is on the stage. Stage directions in this play are in italics. Read the underlined stage directions. Which element of drama are the blankets?

_____

_____

_____

Reading Check

What is Gluskabe's job? Circle the text that tells the answer.

Vocabulary Development

wigwam (WIG wahm) *n.* a Native American hut

Drama

Dialogue is what characters say. What important information do you learn from the bracketed dialogue between Grandmother Woodchuck and Gluskabe?

_____

_____

_____

Drama

What do the underlined **stage directions** on this page tell the reader that dialogue cannot?

_____

_____

_____

Drama

Conflict is a problem between characters or between a character and a force. What is the conflict of this play?

_____

_____

Reading Check

What is Old Man Winter's fire made of? Circle the answer.

HUMAN BEING. Gluskabe, I have been sent by the other human beings to ask you for help. This winter has been too long. If it does not end soon, we will all die.

GLUSKABE. I will do what I can. I will go to the wigwam of Old Man Winter. He has stayed here too long. I will ask him to go back to his home in the Winter Land to the north.

GRANDMOTHER WOODCHUCK. Be careful, Gluskabe.

GLUSKABE. Don't worry, Grandmother. Winter cannot beat me.

Scene II. The Wigwam of Old Man Winter
OLD MAN WINTER _sits in his wigwam, "warming" his hands over his fire made of ice. The four balls of summer are on one side of the stage._ GLUSKABE _enters stage carrying his bag and stands to the side of the wigwam door. He taps on the wigwam._

GLUSKABE. Who is there!

GLUSKABE. It is Gluskabe.

OLD MAN WINTER. Ah, come inside and sit by my fire.

GLUSKABE _enters the wigwam._

GLUSKABE. The people are suffering. You must go back to your home in the Winter Land.

OLD MAN WINTER. Oh, I must, eh? But tell me, do you like my fire?

GLUSKABE. I do not like your fire. Your fire is not warm. It is cold.

OLD MAN WINTER. Yes, my fire is made of ice. And so are you!

OLD MAN WINTER _throws his white sheet over_ GLUSKABE. GLUSKABE _falls down._ OLD MAN WINTER _stands up._

OLD MAN WINTER. No one can defeat me!

OLD MAN WINTER _pulls_ GLUSKABE _out of the lodge. Then he goes back inside and closes the door flap. The Sun comes out and shines on_ GLUSKABE. GLUSKABE _sits up and looks at the Sun._

GLUSKABE. Ah, that was a good nap! But I am not going into Old Man Winter's lodge again until I talk with my grandmother.

GLUSKABE *begins walking across the stage toward the four balls.* GRANDMOTHER WOODCHUCK *enters.*

GRANDMOTHER WOODCHUCK. It is still winter, Gluskabe! Did Old Man Winter refuse to speak to you?

GLUSKABE. We spoke, but he did not listen. I will speak to him again; and I will make him listen. But tell me, Grandmother, where does the warm weather come from?

GRANDMOTHER WOODCHUCK. It is kept in the Summer Land.

GLUSKABE. I will go there and bring summer back here.

GRANDMOTHER WOODCHUCK. Grandson, the Summer Land people are strange people. Each of them has one eye. They are also greedy. They do not want to share the warm weather. It will be dangerous.

GLUSKABE. Why will it be dangerous?

GRANDMOTHER WOODCHUCK. The Summer Land people keep the summer in a big pot. They dance around it. Four giant crows guard the pot full of summer. Whenever a stranger tries to steal summer, those crows fly down and pull off his head!

GLUSKABE. Grandmother, I will go to the Summer Land. I will cover up one eye and look like the people there. And I will take these four balls of sinew with me.

GLUSKABE *picks up the four balls, places them in his bag, and puts the bag over his shoulder.*

Scene III. The Summer Land Village
The SUMMER LAND PEOPLE *are dancing around the pot full of summer. They are singing a snake dance song, following their leader, who shakes a rattle in one hand. Four Crows stand guard around the pot as the people dance.*

SUMMER LAND PEOPLE. *Wee gai wah neh*
    (wee guy wah ney),
Wee gai wah neh,

Vocabulary Development
sinew (SIN yoo) *adj.* muscular power, strength; any source of power or strength

---

Drama

Another possible **conflict** exists in this play. Who is the conflict between?

_____

_____

_____

Drama 📖

What does the bracketed **dialogue** tell you about the Summer Land people?

_____

_____

_____

_____

Reading Check

Where is the warm weather kept? Circle the answer in the text.

Stop to Reflect

Why do you think the Summer Land people stop dancing and look at Gluskabe when he speaks to them?

_____

_____

_____

_____

Drama

Stage directions tell the reader information that people in the play do not know. What does the reader know that the Summer Land people do not know?

_____

_____

_____

_____

Drama

Props are objects on the stage that actors use. What props does Gluskabe use to escape from the crows? Circle the answer in the text. How does he use these props to trick the crows?

_____

_____

_____

_____

Wee gai wah neh, wee gai wah neh,
Wee gai wah neh, wee gai wah neh,
Wee gai wah neh.

GLUSKABE *enters, wearing an eye patch and carrying his bag with the balls in it.*

GLUSKABE. *Kwai, kwai, nidobak!* Hello, my friends.

Everyone stops dancing. They gather around GLUSKABE.

LEADER OF THE SUMMER LAND PEOPLE. Who are you?

GLUSKABE. I am not a stranger. I am one of you. See, I have one eye.

SECOND SUMMER LAND PERSON. I do not remember you.

GLUSKABE. I have been gone a long time.

THIRD SUMMER LAND PERSON. He does have only one eye.

FOURTH SUMMER LAND PERSON. Let's welcome him back. Come join in our snake dance.

The singing and dancing begin again: "Wee gai wah neh," etc. GLUSKABE *is at the end of the line as the dancers circle the pot full of summer. When* GLUSKABE *is close enough, he reaches in, grabs one of the summersticks, and breaks away, running back and forth.*

LEADER OF THE SUMMER LAND PERSON. He has taken one of our summersticks!

SECOND SUMMER LAND PERSON. Someone stop him!

THIRD SUMMER LAND PERSON. Crows, catch him!

FOURTH SUMMER LAND PERSON. Pull off his head!

The Crows swoop after GLUSKABE. *He reaches into his pouch and pulls out one of the balls. As each Crow comes up to him, he ducks his head down and holds up the ball. The Crow grabs the ball.* GLUSKABE *keeps running, and pulls out another ball, repeating his actions until each of the Crows has grabbed a ball.*

FIRST CROW. *Gah-gah!* I have his head.

SECOND CROW. *Gah-gah!* No, I have his head!

THIRD CROW. *Gah-gah!* Look, I have his head!

FOURTH CROW. *Gah-gah!* No, look-I have it too!

LEADER OF THE SUMMER LAND PEOPLE. How many heads did that stranger have?

SECOND SUMMER LAND PERSON. He has tricked us. He got away.

Scene IV. The Wigwam of Old Man Winter
GLUSKABE *walks up to Old Man Winter's wigwam. He holds the summerstick in his hand and taps on the door.*

OLD MAN WINTER. Who is there!

GLUSKABE. It is Gluskabe.

OLD MAN WINTER. Ah, come inside and sit by my fire.

GLUSKABE *enters, sits down, and places the summerstick in front of* OLD MAN WINTER.

GLUSKABE. You must go back to your home in the Winter Land.

OLD MAN WINTER. Oh, I must, eh? But tell me, do you like my fire?

GLUSKABE. Your fire is no longer cold. It is getting warmer. Your wigwam is melting away. You are getting weaker.

OLD MAN WINTER. No one can defeat me!

GLUSKABE. Old Man, you are defeated. Warm weather has returned. Go back to your home in the north.

The blanket walls of Old Man Winter's wigwam collapse. OLD MAN WINTER *stands up and walks away as swiftly as he can, crouching down as if getting smaller. People carrying the cutouts of the Sun, Flowers, and Plants come out and surround* GLUSKABE *as he sits there, smiling.*

NARRATOR. So Gluskabe defeated Old Man Winter. Because he brought only one small piece of summer, winter still returns each year. But, thanks to Gluskabe, spring always comes back again.

Reader's Response: How do you feel at the end of winter when the weather gets warmer?

_____

_____

_____

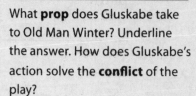

TAKE NOTES

Drama

The **set** is the scenery that shows the time and place of the action. How does the set change at the beginning of Scene IV?

_____

_____

Drama

What **prop** does Gluskabe take to Old Man Winter? Underline the answer. How does Gluskabe's action solve the **conflict** of the play?

_____

_____

_____

_____

_____

Stop to Reflect

What connection can you make between the summerstick that Gluskabe grabs and the four seasons?

_____

_____

_____

_____

Drama

1. **Infer:** Why does Gluskabe need Grandmother Woodchuck's advice before he can defeat Old Man Winter?

   _____

   _____

2. **Analyze:** After Gluskabe receives Grandmother's advice, what is his plan?

   _____

   _____

3. **Drama:** What is the main **conflict** in this **drama**?

   _____

   _____

4. **Drama:** List actions taken by Old Man Winter and the Summer Land people in the second column of this chart. Then, list **dialogue** about Old Man Winter and the Summer Land people in the third column. Examples of each have been given in the chart.

Character	Actions of the Character	Dialogue About the Character
Old Man Winter	warms his hands over fire made of ice	**GRANDMOTHER WOODCHUCK:** "Be careful, Gluskabe."
Summer Land People	dance around the pot full of summer	**GRANDMOTHER WOODCHUCK:** "The Summer Land people are strange people."

Storytelling Program

Plan a **storytelling program** that features traditional tales by Joseph Bruchac. Follow these steps:

• Search the Internet for information about Joseph Bruchac. Look for stories that he has written and performed. Use word searches with "Joseph Bruchac," "Joseph Bruchac stories," and "Joseph Bruchac perform." Bruchac has his own Web site at www.josephbruchac.com. However, it is important to search other sites for additional information about him.

What I learned: _____

_____

_____

_____

• Read as many of Bruchac's Native American stories as you can. Become familiar with his characters and the ways they speak. Read a few of the stories aloud. Listen for the way that the language sounds as you read. Try to pay attention to how you think the story would sound best out loud.

What I learned: _____

_____

_____

_____

• Watch the video interview with Joseph Bruchac. Review your source material. Use this information to answer the following questions.

1. Why does Joseph Bruchac like to tell stories?

_____

_____

2. How does the storyteller turn folk tales into plays?

_____

_____

The Phantom Tollbooth, Act I

Reading Skill

A **summary** of a piece of writing is a short statement that presents the main ideas and most important points. To summarize a drama, first **reread to identify main events**. Include only major events that move the story forward. Then, organize events in the order in which they happen. As you read, use the chart below to record the major events in Act I. Refer to your chart when you write a summary.

Event 1	Event 2	Event 3

Literary Analysis

A **drama** is a story that is written to be performed. Like short stories, dramas have characters, a setting, and a plot. In dramas, however, these elements are developed mainly through **dialogue**, the words spoken by the characters. In the **script**, or written form, of a drama, the characters' names appear before their dialogue. Look at this example:

> **KATRINA.** I can't believe you said that!
> **WALLACE.** I was only kidding.

Paying attention to what the characters say will help you to understand and enjoy the script of a drama.

The Phantom Tollbooth, Act I

Susan Nanus
Based on the book by Norton Juster

Summary A bored young boy named Milo comes home from school. He finds a wrapped gift in his room. Inside the box he finds a tollbooth. Milo sets off on an adventure into a fantasy world. Read Act I, Scene ii on the following pages.

Writing About the Big Question

How do we decide who we are? In *The Phantom Tollbooth Act I*, we meet Milo, a bored and unmotivated boy who receives an unexpected gift that leads him to take an amazing trip and to discover an adventurous side of himself. Complete this sentence:

Experiences such as _____ can help

people discover new aspects of their personalities because _____

_____.

Note-taking Guide

Fill in this chart with some details about the main characters in the story. Briefly describe their behavior in the space provided.

Character	Behavior
Milo	Confused about being in strange places and talking to strange people
Tock	Encourages Milo to keep moving along
Azaz	
Mathemagician	
Spelling Bee	
Humbug	

Activate Prior Knowledge

Describe the setting of a fantasy world you have encountered in a book or a movie.

_____

_____

_____

Literary Analysis 🔍

A **drama** is a story written to be performed. Elements of drama include character, setting, and plot. The **cast** is the list of characters in the drama. What is unusual about the names of the cast in this play?

_____

_____

_____

_____

_____

Reading Check

In what order is the cast listed? Circle the answer in the text.

The Phantom Tollbooth, Act I
Susan Nanus
Based on the book by Norton Juster

Cast (in order of appearance)

THE CLOCK

MILO, A BOY

THE WHETHER MAN

SIX LETHARAGARIANS

TOCK, THE WATCHDOG (SAME AS THE CLOCK)

AZAZ THE UNABRIDGED, KING OF DICTIONOPOLIS

THE MATHEMAGICIAN, KING OF DIGITOPOLIS

PRINCESS SWEET RHYME

PRINCESS PURE REASON

GATEKEEPER OF DICTIONOPOLIS

THREE WORD MERCHANTS

THE LETTERMAN (FOURTH WORD MERCHANT)

SPELLING BEE

THE HUMBUG

THE DUKE OF DEFINITION

THE MINISTER OF MEANING

THE EARL OF ESSENCE

THE COUNT OF CONNOTATION

THE UNDERSECRETARY OF UNDERSTANDING

A PAGE

KAKAFONOUS A. DISCHORD, DOCTOR OF DISSONANCE

THE AWFUL DYNNE

THE DODECAHEDRON

MINERS OF THE NUMBERS MINE

THE EVERPRESENT WORDSNATCHER

THE TERRIBLE TRIVIUM

THE DEMON OF INSINCERITY

SENSES TAKER

The Sets

1. MILO'S BEDROOM—with shelves, pennants, pictures on the wall, as well as suggestions of the characters of the Land of Wisdom.

2. THE ROAD TO THE LAND OF WISDOM—a forest, from which the Whether Man and the Lethargarians emerge.

3. DICTIONOPOLIS—A marketplace full of open air stalls as well as little shops. Letters and signs should abound.[1]

1. **abound** (uh BOWND) v. be plentiful.

4. DIGITOPOLIS—a dark, glittering place without trees or greenery, but full of shining rocks and cliffs, with hundreds of numbers shining everywhere.

5. THE LAND OF IGNORANCE—a gray, gloomy place full of cliffs and caves, with frightening faces. Different levels and heights should be suggested through one or two platforms or risers, with a set of stairs that lead to the castle in the air.

ACT I SCENE ii THE ROAD TO DICTIONOPOLIS.
(ENTER MILO in his car.)

MILO. This is weird! I don't recognize any of this scenery at all. *(A SIGN is held up before MILO, startling him.)* Huh? *(Reads.)* WELCOME TO EXPECTATIONS. INFORMATION, PREDICTIONS AND ADVICE CHEERFULLY OFFERED. PARK HERE AND BLOW HORN. *(MILO blows horn.)*

WHETHER MAN. *(A little man wearing a long coat and carrying an umbrella pops up from behind the sign that he was holding. He speaks very fast and excitedly.)* My, my, my, my, my, welcome, welcome, welcome, welcome to the Land of Expectations, Expectations, Expectations! We don't get many travelers these days; we certainly don't get many travelers. Now what can I do for you? I'm the whether man.

MILO. *(Referring to map.)* Uh . . . is this the right road to Dictionopolis?

WHETHER MAN. Well now, well now, well now, I don't know of any wrong road to Dictionopolis, so if this road goes to Dictionopolis at all, it must be the right road, and if it doesn't, it must be the right road to somewhere else, because there are no wrong roads to anywhere. Do you think it will rain?

MILO. I thought you were the Weather Man.

Vocabulary Development

ignorance (IG nuh ruhns) *n.* lack of knowledge, education, or experience
expectations (ek spek TAY shuhnz) *n.* feelings or beliefs about the way things should be

---

TAKE NOTES

Literary Analysis

Dialogue is the words spoken by characters in a drama. Describe the character of the Whether Man. Underline dialogue that supports your description.

_____

_____

_____

Stop to Reflect

Why would talking to the Whether Man be difficult?

_____

_____

_____

Reading Check

Where does Milo meet the Whether Man? Circle the answer in the text.

TAKE NOTES

Stop to Reflect

Read the underlined sentence. What do you think the Whether Man means by "some people never go beyond Expectations"? Explain why people should or should not try to go beyond expectations.

_____

_____

_____

_____

Reading Skill

A **summary** is a short statement that contains the main ideas and important points of a piece of writing. Summarize what happens on this page.

_____

_____

_____

_____

Reading Check

How does the Whether Man describe the Land of Expectations? Underline the answer.

WHETHER MAN. Oh, no, I'm the Whether Man, not the weather man. _(Pulls out a SIGN or opens a FLAP of his coat, which reads: "WHETHER.")_ After all, it's more important to know whether there will be weather than what the weather will be.

MILO. What kind of place is Expectations?

WHETHER MAN. Good question, good question! Expectations is the place you must always go to before you get to where you are going. Of course, some people never go beyond Expectations, but my job is to hurry them along whether they like it or not. Now what else can I do for you? _(Opens his umbrella.)_

MILO. I think I can find my own way.

WHETHER MAN. Splendid, splendid, splendid! Whether or not you find your own way, you're bound to find some way. If you happen to find my way, please return it. I lost it years ago. I imagine by now it must be quite rusty. You did say it was going to rain, didn't you? _(Escorts MILO to the car under the open umbrella.)_ I'm glad you made your own decision. I do so hate to make up my mind about anything, whether it's good or bad, up or down, rain or shine. Expect everything, I always say, and the unexpected never happens. Goodbye, goodbye, goodbye, good . . .

(A loud CLAP of THUNDER is heard.) Oh dear! _(He looks up at the sky, puts out his hand to feel for rain, and RUNS AWAY. MILO watches puzzledly and drives on.)_

MILO. I'd better get out of Expectations, but fast. Talking to a guy like that all day would get me nowhere for sure. _(He tries to speed up, but finds instead that he is moving slower and slower.)_ Oh, oh, now what? _(He can barely move. Behind MILO, the LETHARGARIANS begin to enter from all parts of the stage. They are dressed to blend in with the scenery and carry small pillows that look like rocks. Whenever they fall asleep, they rest on the pillows.)_ Now I really am getting nowhere. I hope I didn't take a wrong turn. _(The car stops. He tries to start it. It won't move. He gets out and begins to tinker with it.)_ I wonder where I am.

LETHARGARIAN 1. You're . . . in . . . the . . . Dol . . . drums . . . (MILO *looks around.*)

LETHARGARIAN 2. Yes . . . the . . . Dol . . . drums . . . (*A YAWN is heard.*)

MILO. (*Yelling.*) WHAT ARE THE DOLDRUMS?

LETHARGARIAN 3. The Doldrums, my friend, are where nothing ever happens and nothing ever changes. (*Parts of the Scenery stand up or Six People come out of the scenery colored in the same colors of the trees or the road. They move very slowly and as soon as they move, they stop to rest again.*) Allow me to introduce all of us. We are the Lethargarians at your service.

MILO. (*Uncertainly.*) Very pleased to meet you. I think I'm lost. Can you help me?

LETHARGARIAN 4. Don't say think. (*He yawns.*) It's against the law.

LETHARGARIAN 1. No one's allowed to think in the Doldrums. (*He falls asleep.*)

LETHARGARIAN 2. Don't you have a rule book? It's local ordinance 175389-J. (*He falls asleep.*)

MILO. (*Pulls out rule book and reads.*) Ordinance 175389-J: "It shall be unlawful, illegal and unethical to think, think of thinking, surmise, presume, reason, meditate or speculate while in the Doldrums. Anyone breaking this law shall be severely punished." That's a ridiculous law! Everybody thinks.

ALL THE LETHARGARIANS. We don't!

LETHARGARIAN 2. And most of the time, you don't, that's why you're here. You weren't thinking and you weren't paying attention either. People who don't pay attention often get stuck in the Doldrums. Face it, most of the time, you're just like us. (*Falls, snoring, to the ground.* MILO *laughs.*)

LETHARGARIAN 5. Stop that at once. Laughing is against the law. Don't you have a rule book? It's local ordinance 574381-W.

MILO. (OPENS RULE BOOK AND READS.) "In the Doldrums, laughter is frowned upon and smiling is permitted only on alternate Thursdays." Well, if you can't laugh or think, what can you do?

Literary Analysis

Ellipsis points (…) often show a pause or an unfinished thought. Read the bracketed passage. How does this punctuation help you understand the way the **dialogue** should be read?

_____

_____

_____

Reading Skill 📖

Summarize what is not allowed in the Doldrums. Include at least two rules.

1. _____

_____

_____

2. _____

_____

_____

Reading Check

What will happen to anyone caught thinking in the Doldrums? Underline the sentence that tells you.

Reading Skill

Summarize in one sentence what Lethargarians do each day.

_____

_____

_____

_____

_____

Literary Analysis

A **script** is the written form of a **drama**. This script includes descriptions of the characters' actions. How do the Lethargarians' actions support what they say about themselves?

_____

_____

_____

_____

Reading Check

The Lethargarians are not allowed to laugh or think. What can they do instead? Underline the sentence that tells the answer.

LETHARGARIAN 6. Anything as long as it's nothing, and everything as long as it isn't anything. There's lots to do. We have a very busy schedule . . .

LETHARGARIAN 1. At 8:00 we get up and then we spend from 8 to 9 daydreaming.

LETHARGARIAN 2. From 9:00 to 9:30 we take our early mid-morning nap . . .

LETHARGARIAN 3. From 9:30 to 10:30 we dawdle and delay . . .

LETHARGARIAN 4. From 10:30 to 11:30 we take our late early morning nap . . .

LETHARGARIAN 5. From 11:30 to 12:00 we bide our time and then we eat our lunch.

LETHARGARIAN 6. From 1:00 to 2:00 we linger and loiter . . .

LETHARGARIAN 1. From 2:00 to 2:30 we take our early afternoon nap . . .

LETHARGARIAN 2. From 2:30 to 3:30 we put off for tomorrow what we could have done today . . .

LETHARGARIAN 3. From 3:30 to 4:00 we take our early late afternoon nap . . .

LETHARGARIAN 4. From 4:00 to 5:00 we loaf and lounge until dinner . . .

LETHARGARIAN 5. From 6:00 to 7:00 we dilly-dally . . .

LETHARGARIAN 6. From 7:00 to 8:00 we take our early evening nap and then for an hour before we go to bed, we waste time.

LETHARGARIAN 1. *(Yawning.)* You see, it's really quite strenuous doing nothing all day long, and so once a week, we take a holiday and go nowhere.

LETHARGARIAN 5. Which is just where we were going when you came along. Would you care to join us?

MILO. *(Yawning.)* That's where I seem to be going, anyway. *(Stretching.)* Tell me, does everyone here do nothing?

LETHARGARIAN 3. Everyone but the terrible watchdog. He's always sniffing around to see that nobody wastes time. A most unpleasant character.

MILO. The Watchdog?

LETHARGARIAN 6. THE WATCHDOG!

ALL THE LETHARGARIANS. *(Yelling at once.)* RUN! WAKE UP! RUN! HERE HE COMES! THE WATCHDOG! *(They all run off and ENTER a large dog with the head, feet, and tail of a dog, and the body of a clock, having the same face as the character* THE CLOCK.*)*

WATCHDOG. What are you doing here?

MILO. Nothing much. Just killing time. You see . . .

WATCHDOG. KILLING TIME! *(His ALARM RINGS in fury.)* It's bad enough wasting time without killing it. What are you doing in the Doldrums, anyway? Don't you have anywhere to go?

MILO. I think I was on my way to Dictionopolis when I got stuck here. Can you help me?

WATCHDOG. Help you! You've got to help yourself. I suppose you know why you got stuck.

MILO. I guess I just wasn't thinking.

WATCHDOG. Precisely. Now you're on your way.

MILO. I am?

WATCHDOG. Of course. Since you got here by not thinking, it seems reasonable that in order to get out, you must start thinking. Do you mind if I get in? I love automobile rides. *(He gets in. They wait.)* Well?

MILO. All right. I'll try. *(Screws up his face and thinks.)* Are we moving?

WATCHDOG. Not yet. Think harder.

MILO. I'm thinking as hard as I can.

WATCHDOG. Well, think just a little harder than that. Come on, you can do it.

MILO. All right, all right. . . . I'm thinking of all the planets in the solar system, and why water expands when it turns to ice, and all the words that begin with "q," and . . . *(The wheels begin to move.)* We're moving! We're moving!

WATCHDOG. Keep thinking.

MILO. *(Thinking.)* How a steam engine works and how to bake a pie and the difference between Fahrenheit and Centigrade. . .

Reading Skill

Would you include the arrival of the Watchdog in a **summary** of this scene? Why or why not?

_____

_____

_____

_____

Reading Check

How does Milo get out of the Doldrums? Underline the sentence that tells you the answer.

Literary Analysis

Read the **dialogue** between Milo and the Watchdog. How does the Watchdog help Milo?

_____

_____

_____

_____

Reading Skill

Summarize the job of Princesses Rhyme and Reason.

_____

_____

_____

Literary Analysis

Stage directions are in italics—slanted font—in the brackets of the **script**. What do the stage directions in the bracketed text tell you about the lights onstage?

_____

_____

_____

Reading Skill

Summarize the argument between Azaz and the Mathemagician.

_____

_____

_____

Reading Check

What does Azaz look like? Underline the sentence that tells you.

WATCHDOG. Dictionopolis, here we come.

MILO. Hey, Watchdog, are you coming along?

TOCK. You can call me Tock, and keep your eyes on the road.

MILO. What kind of place is Dictionopolis, anyway?

TOCK. It's where all the words in the world come from. It used to be a marvelous place, but ever since Rhyme and Reason left, it hasn't been the same.

MILO. Rhyme and Reason?

TOCK. The two princesses. They used to settle all the arguments between their two brothers who rule over the Land of Wisdom. You see, Azaz is the king of Dictionopolis and the Mathemagician is the king of Digitopolis and they almost never see eye to eye on anything. It was the job of the Princesses Sweet Rhyme and Pure Reason to solve the differences between the two kings, and they always did so well that both sides usually went home feeling very satisfied. But then, one day, the kings had an argument to end all arguments. . . .

(The LIGHTS DIM on TOCK *and* MILO, *and come up on* KING AZAZ *of Dictionopolis on another part of the stage.* AZAZ *has a great stomach, a grey beard reaching to his waist, a small crown and a long robe with the letters of the alphabet written all over it.)*

AZAZ. Of course, I'll abide by the decision of Rhyme and Reason, though I have no doubt as to what it will be. They will choose words, of course. Everyone knows that words are more important than numbers any day of the week.

(The MATHEMAGICIAN *appears opposite* AZAZ. *The* MATHEMAGICIAN *wears a long flowing robe covered entirely with complex mathematical equations, and a tall pointed hat. He carries a long staff with a pencil point at one end and a large rubber eraser at the other.)*

MATHEMAGICIAN. That's what you think, Azaz. People wouldn't even know what day of the week it is without numbers. Haven't you ever looked at a calendar? Face it, Azaz. It's numbers that count.

AZAZ. Don't be ridiculous. *(To audience, as if leading a cheer.)* Let's hear it for WORDS!

MATHEMAGICIAN. *(To audience, in the same manner.)* Cast your vote for NUMBERS!

AZAZ. A, B, C's!

MATHEMAGICIAN. 1, 2, 3's! *(A FANFARE is heard.)*

AZAZ AND MATHEMAGICIAN. *(To each other.)* Quiet! Rhyme and Reason are about to announce their decision.

(RHYME and REASON appear.)

RHYME. Ladies and gentlemen, letters and numerals, fractions and punctuation marks-may we have your attention, please. After careful <u>consideration</u> of the problem set before us by King Azaz of Dictionopolis *(AZAZ bows.)* and the Mathemagician of Digitopolis *(MATHEMAGICIAN raises his hands in a victory salute.)* we have come to the following conclusion:

REASON. Words and numbers are of equal value, for in the cloak of knowledge, one is the warp and the other is the woof.

RHYME. It is no more important to count the sands than it is to name the stars.

RHYME AND REASON. Therefore, let both kingdoms, Dictionopolis and Digitopolis, live in peace.

(The sound of CHEERING is heard.)

AZAZ. Boo! is what I say. Boo and Bah and Hiss!

MATHEMAGICIAN. What good are these girls if they can't even settle an argument in anyone's favor? I think I have come to a decision of my own.

AZAZ. So have I.

AZAZ AND MATHEMAGICIAN. *(To the PRINCESSES.)* You are hereby <u>banished</u> from this land to the Castle-in-the-Air. *(To each other.)* And as for you, KEEP OUT OF MY WAY! *(They stalk off in opposite directions.)*

Vocabulary Development

consideration (kuhn sid er AY shuhn) *n.* painstaking thought or attention
banished (BAN isht) *v.* forced to leave

Literary Analysis

What are two details that you learn about the **dialogue** from the stage directions in the bracketed text? Underline the answers in the text.

Reading Skill

Summarize the decision of Rhyme and Reason in one sentence.

_____

_____

_____

Stop to Reflect

Why do you think Azaz and the Mathemagician disagree with the Princesses' decision?

_____

_____

_____

_____

Reading Skill

Summarize in one sentence Tock's dialogue in the bracketed passage.

_____

_____

Literary Analysis

How does the Gatekeeper's **dialogue** show that the role of his character is to guard the gate?

_____

_____

_____

Reading Check

Why would it be difficult to rescue Rhyme and Reason? Underline the answer.

(During this time, the set has been changed to the Market Square of Dictionopolis. LIGHTS come UP on the deserted square.)

TOCK. And ever since then, there has been neither Rhyme nor Reason in this kingdom. Words are misused and numbers are mismanaged. The argument between the two kings has divided everyone and the real value of both words and numbers has been forgotten. What a waste!

MILO. Why doesn't somebody rescue the Princesses and set everything straight again?

TOCK. That is easier said than done. The Castle-in-the-Air is very far from here, and the one path which leads to it is guarded by <u>ferocious</u> demons. But hold on, here we are. *(A Man appears, carrying a Gate and a small Tollbooth.)*

GATEKEEPER. AHHHHREMMMM! This is Dictionopolis, a happy kingdom, advantageously located in the foothills of Confusion and caressed by gentle breezes from the Sea of Knowledge. Today, by royal <u>proclamation</u>, is Market Day. Have you come to buy or sell?

MILO. I beg your pardon?

GATEKEEPER. Buy or sell, buy or sell. Which is it? You must have come here for a reason.

MILO. Well, I . . .

GATEKEEPER. Come now, if you don't have a reason, you must at least have an explanation or certainly an excuse.

MILO. *(Meekly.)* Uh . . . no.

GATEKEEPER. *(Shaking his head.)* Very serious. You can't get in without a reason. *(Thoughtfully.)* Wait a minute. Maybe I have an old one you can use. *(Pulls out an old suitcase from the tollbooth and rummages through it.)* No . . . no . . . no . . . this won't do . . . hmmm . . .

Vocabulary Development

ferocious (fuh ROH shuhs) *adj.* wild and dangerous

proclamation (prahk luh MAY shuhn) *n.* official public announcement

MILO. *(To TOCK.)* What's he looking for? *(TOCK shrugs.)*

GATEKEEPER. Ah! This is fine. *(Pulls out a Medallion on a chain. Engraved in the Medallion is: "WHY NOT?")* Why not. That's a good reason for almost anything . . . a bit used, perhaps, but still quite serviceable. There you are, sir. Now I can truly say: Welcome to Dictionopolis.

(He opens the Gate and walks off. CITIZENS and MERCHANTS appear on all levels of the stage, and MILO and TOCK find themselves in the middle of a noisy marketplace. As some people buy and sell their wares, others hang a large banner which reads: WELCOME TO THE WORD MARKET.)

MILO. Tock! Look!

MERCHANT 1. Hey-ya, hey-ya, hey-ya, step right up and take your pick. Juicy tempting words for sale. Get your fresh-picked "if's," "and's" and "but's"! Just take a look at these nice ripe "where's" and "when's."

MERCHANT 2. Step right up, step right up, fancy, best-quality words here for sale. Enrich your vocabulary and expand your speech with such elegant items as "quagmire," "flabbergast," or "upholstery."

MERCHANT 3. Words by the bag, buy them over here. Words by the bag for the more talkative customer. A pound of "happy's" at a very reasonable price . . . very useful for "Happy Birthday," "Happy New Year," "happy days," or "happy-go-lucky." Or how about a package of "good's," always handy for "good morning," "good afternoon," "good evening," and "goodbye."

MILO. I can't believe it. Did you ever see so many words?

TOCK. They're fine if you have something to say. *(They come to a Do-It-Yourself Bin.)*

MILO. *(To MERCHANT 4 at the bin.)* Excuse me, but what are these?

MERCHANT 4. These are for people who like to make up their own words. You can pick any assortment you like or buy a special box complete with all the letters and a book of instructions. Here, taste

Literary Analysis

This **script** includes stage directions. List two details that you learn about the setting from the stage directions in the bracketed text.

_____

_____

_____

_____

Reading Skill

Summarize what happens at the World Market. Underline three things that the merchants sell.

_____

_____

_____

_____

Reading Check

Who sells the "if's," "and's," and "but's"? Circle the answer.

© Pearson Education

Choose a letter that has not been mentioned. Describe how you think it would taste.

_____

_____

_____

Literary Analysis

The stage directions suggest that Milo asks the audience for assistance. What might be the purpose of including the audience in the **drama**?

_____

_____

_____

_____

Reading Check ✏

What does the Spelling Bee look like? Circle the answer.

an "A." They're very good. (He pops one into MILO's mouth.)

MILO. (Tastes it hesitantly.) It's sweet! (He eats it.)

MERCHANT 4. I knew you'd like it. "A" is one of our best-sellers. All of them aren't that good, you know. The "Z," for instance—very dry and sawdusty. And the "X"? Tastes like a trunkful of stale air. But most of the others aren't bad at all. Here, try the "I."

MILO. (Tasting.) Cool! It tastes icy.

MERCHANT 4. (To TOCK.) How about the "C" for you? It's as crunchy as a bone. Most people are just too lazy to make their own words, but take it from me, not only is it more fun, but it's also de-lightful, (Holds up a "D.") e-lating, (Holds up an "E.") and extremely useful! (Holds up a "U.")

MILO. But isn't it difficult? I'm not very good at making words.

(The SPELLING BEE, a large colorful bee, comes up from behind.)

SPELLING BEE. Perhaps I can be of some assistance . . . a-s-s-i-s-t-a-n-c-e. (The Three turn around and see him.) Don't be alarmed . . . a-l-a-r-m-e-d. I am the Spelling Bee. I can spell anything. Anything. A-n-y-t-h-i-n-g. Try me. Try me.

MILO. (Backing off, TOCK on his guard.) Can you spell goodbye?

SPELLING BEE. Perhaps you are under the misapprehension . . . m-i-s-a-p-p-r-e-h-e-n-s-i-o-n that I am dangerous. Let me assure you that I am quite peaceful. Now, think of the most difficult word you can, and I'll spell it.

MILO. Uh . . . o.k. (At this point, MILO may turn to the audience and ask them to help him choose a word or he may think of one on his own.) How about . . . "Curiosity"?

SPELLING BEE. (Winking.) Let's see now . . . uh . . . how much time do I have?

Vocabulary Development
misapprehension (mis ap ree HEN shuhn) n. misunderstanding

MILO. Just ten seconds. Count them off, Tock.

SPELLING BEE. *(As* TOCK *counts.)* Oh dear, oh dear. *(Just at the last moment, quickly.)* C-u-r-i-o-s-i-t-y.

MERCHANT 4. Correct! (ALL *Cheer.*)

MILO. Can you spell anything?

SPELLING BEE. *(Proudly.)* Just about. You see, years ago, I was an ordinary bee minding my own business, smelling flowers all day, occasionally picking up part-time work in people's bonnets. Then one day, I realized that I'd never amount to anything without an education, so I decided that . . .

HUMBUG. *(Coming up in a booming voice.)* BALDERDASH! *(He wears a lavish coat, striped pants, checked vest, spats and a derby hat.)* Let me repeat . . . BALDERDASH! *(Swings his cane and clicks his heels in the air.)* Well, well, what have we here? Isn't someone going to introduce me to the little boy?

SPELLING BEE. *(Disdainfully.)* This is the Humbug. You can't trust a word he says.

HUMBUG. NONSENSE! Everyone can trust a Humbug. As I was saying to the king just the other day . . .

SPELLING BEE. You've never met the king. *(To* MILO.*)* Don't believe a thing he tells you.

HUMBUG. Bosh, my boy, pure bosh. The Humbugs are an old and noble family, honorable to the core. Why, we fought in the Crusades with Richard the Lionhearted, crossed the Atlantic with Columbus, blazed trails with the pioneers. History is full of Humbugs.

SPELLING BEE. A very pretty speech . . . s-p-e-e-c-h. Now, why don't you go away? I was just advising the lad of the importance of proper spelling.

HUMBUG. BAH! As soon as you learn to spell one word, they ask you to spell another. You can never catch up, so why bother? *(Puts his arm around* MILO.*)* Take my advice, boy, and forget about it. As my great-great-great-grandfather George Washington Humbug used to say. . .

SPELLING BEE. You, sir, are an impostor i-m-p-o-s-t-o-r who can't even spell his own name!

© Pearson Education

TAKE NOTES

Literary Analysis

This **drama** includes a character named Humbug. The word *humbug* means "nonsense" or "trickery." Why is Humbug a good name for this character?

_____

_____

_____

_____

Reading Skill

Reread to identify main events on this page to help you **summarize**. Then, list in order the two main things that happen on this page.

1. _____

_____

2. _____

_____

Reading Check

Who are the Humbugs? Underline the sentences that tell you the answer.

The Phantom Tollbooth, Act I 279

Stop to Reflect

Describe how the Ministers act.

_____

_____

_____

_____

Reading Skill

Summarize what the Ministers have said to Milo so far.

_____

_____

_____

Reading Check

Who are the Ministers? Underline the answer.

HUMBUG. What? You dare to doubt my word? The word of a Humbug? The word of a Humbug who has direct access to the ear of a King? And the king shall hear of this, I promise you . . .

VOICE 1. Did someone call for the King?

VOICE 2. Did you mention the monarch?

VOICE 3. Speak of the sovereign?

VOICE 4. Entreat the Emperor?

VOICE 5. Hail his highness?

(Five tall, thin gentlemen regally dressed in silks and satins, plumed hats and buckled shoes appear as they speak.)

MILO. Who are they?

SPELLING BEE. The King's advisors. Or in more formal terms, his cabinet.

MINISTER 1. Greetings!

MINISTER 2. Salutations!

MINISTER 3. Welcome!

MINISTER 4. Good Afternoon!

MINISTER 5. Hello!

MILO. Uh . . . Hi.

(All the MINISTERS, from here on called by their numbers, unfold their scrolls and read in order.)

MINISTER 1. By the order of Azaz the Unabridged . . .

MINISTER 2. King of Dictionopolis . . .

MINISTER 3. Monarch of letters . . .

MINISTER 4. Emperor of phrases, sentences, and miscellaneous figures of speech . . .

MINISTER 5. We offer you the hospitality of our kingdom . . .

MINISTER 1. Country

MINISTER 2. Nation

MINISTER 3. State

MINISTER 4. Commonwealth

MINISTER 5. Realm

MINISTER 1. Empire

MINISTER 2. Palatinate

MINISTER 3. Principality.

MILO. Do all those words mean the same thing?

MINISTER 1. Of course.

MINISTER 2. Certainly.

MINISTER 3. Precisely.

MINISTER 4. Exactly.

MINISTER 5. Yes.

MILO. Then why don't you use just one? Wouldn't that make a lot more sense?

MINISTER 1. Nonsense!

MINISTER 2. Ridiculous!

MINISTER 3. Fantastic!

MINISTER 4. Absurd!

MINISTER 5. Bosh!

MINISTER 1. We're not interested in making sense. It's not our job.

MINISTER 2. Besides, one word is as good as another, so why not use them all?

MINISTER 3. Then you don't have to choose which one is right.

MINISTER 4. Besides, if one is right, then ten are ten times as right.

MINISTER 5. Obviously, you don't know who we are.

(Each presents himself and MILO *acknowledges the introduction.)*

MINISTER 1. The Duke of Definition.

MINISTER 2. The Minister of Meaning.

MINISTER 3. The Earl of Essence.

MINISTER 4. The Count of Connotation.

MINISTER 5. The Undersecretary of Understanding.

ALL FIVE. And we have come to invite you to the Royal Banquet.

SPELLING BEE. The banquet! That's quite an honor, my boy. A real h-o-n-o-r.

HUMBUG. DON'T BE RIDICULOUS! Everybody goes to the Royal Banquet these days.

SPELLING BEE. *(To the* HUMBUG.*)* True, everybody does go. But some people are invited and others simply push their way in where they aren't wanted.

HUMBUG. HOW DARE YOU? You buzzing little upstart, I'll show you who's not wanted . . .
(Raises his cane threateningly.)

Reading Check

What do the Ministers invite Milo to come to? Circle the answer in the text.

Reading Skill

Summarize the information in the first bracketed passage.

_____

_____

_____

Literary Analysis

Read the bracketed stage directions. How do the stage directions reinforce Spelling Bee's words?

_____

_____

_____

Reading Skill

Summarize the first bracketed passage.

_____

_____

_____

_____

_____

Reading Check

Where does the banquet take place? Underline the sentence that tells you the answer.

Literary Analysis 🔍

Read the second bracketed passage. What does King Azaz's **dialogue** stress about Dictionopolis?

_____

_____

_____

_____

SPELLING BEE. You just watch it! I'm warning w-a-r-n-i-n-g you! *(At that moment, an ear-shattering blast of TRUMPETS, entirely off-key, is heard, and a PAGE appears.)*

PAGE. King Azaz the Unabridged is about to begin the Royal banquet. All guests who do not appear promptly at the table will automatically lose their place. *(A huge Table is carried out with KING AZAZ sitting in a large chair, carried out at the head of the table.)*

AZAZ. Places. Everyone take your places. *(All the characters, including the HUMBUG and the SPELLING BEE, who forget their quarrel, rush to take their places at the table. MILO and TOCK sit near the king. AZAZ looks at MILO.)* And just who is this?

MILO. Your Highness, my name is Milo and this is Tock. Thank you very much for inviting us to your banquet, and I think your palace is beautiful!

MINISTER 1. Exquisite.

MINISTER 2. Lovely.

MINISTER 3. Handsome.

MINISTER 4. Pretty.

MINISTER 5. Charming.

AZAZ. SILENCE! Now tell me, young man, what can you do to entertain us? Sing songs? Tell stories? Juggle plates? Do tumbling tricks? Which is it?

MILO. I can't do any of those things.

AZAZ. What an ordinary little boy. Can't you do anything at all?

MILO. Well . . . I can count to a thousand.

AZAZ. AARGH, numbers! Never mention numbers here. Only use them when we absolutely have to. Now, why don't we change the subject and have some dinner? Since you are the guest of honor, you may pick the menu.

MILO. Me? Well, uh . . . I'm not very hungry. Can we just have a light snack?

AZAZ. A light snack it shall be!

(AZAZ claps his hands. Waiters rush in with covered trays. When they are uncovered, Shafts of Light pour out. The light may be created through the use of

battery-operated flashlights which are secured in the trays and covered with a false bottom. The Guests help themselves.)

HUMBUG. Not a very substantial meal. Maybe you can suggest something a little more filling.

MILO. Well, in that case, I think we ought to have a square meal . . .

AZAZ. *(Claps his hands.)* A square meal it is! *(Waiters serve trays of Colored Squares of all sizes. People serve themselves.)*

SPELLING BEE. These are awful. *(*HUMBUG *coughs and all the Guests do not care for the food.)*

AZAZ. *(Claps his hands and the trays are removed.)* Time for speeches. *(To* MILO.*)* You first.

MILO. *(Hesitantly.)* Your Majesty, ladies and gentlemen, I would like to take this opportunity to say that . . .

AZAZ. That's quite enough. Mustn't talk all day.

MILO. But I just started to . . .

AZAZ. NEXT!

HUMBUG. *(Quickly.)* Roast turkey, mashed potatoes, vanilla ice cream.

SPELLING BEE. Hamburgers, corn on the cob, chocolate pudding p-u-d-d-i-n-g. *(Each Guest names two dishes and a dessert.)*

AZAZ. *(The last.)* Pâté de foie gras, soupe à l'oignon, salade endives, fromage et fruits et demi-tasse. *(He claps his hands. Waiters serve each Guest his Words.)* Dig in. *(To* MILO.*)* Though I can't say I think much of your choice.

MILO. I didn't know I was going to have to eat my words.

AZAZ. Of course, of course, everybody here does. Your speech should have been in better taste.

MINISTER 1. Here, try some somersault. It improves the flavor.

MINISTER 2. Have a rigamarole.[2] *(Offers breadbasket.)*

MINISTER 3. Or a ragamuffin.

MINISTER 4. Perhaps you'd care for a synonym bun.

---

2. **rigamarole** (RIG uh muh rohl) *n.* silly actions, here playing off the idea of a bread roll.

Reading Skill

Summarize what happens after Milo asks for "a square meal."

_____

_____

_____

_____

Stop to Reflect

The common expression *eat my words* means "admit I was wrong." How is this meaning different from Milo's meaning in the underlined passage?

_____

_____

_____

Literary Analysis

What do you learn about Azaz from his **dialogue**? What kind of person is he?

_____

_____

_____

Reading Check ✏️

How do the guests react to the "square meal"? Underline the words that tell you.

Literary Analysis

Read the **dialogue** in the first bracketed passage. What is a "half-baked" idea, according to the dialogue?

_____

_____

_____

_____

Reading Skill

Read the second bracketed passage. **Summarize** this passage in two sentences.

_____

_____

_____

_____

_____

_____

Reading Check

Underline two examples of a "half-baked idea."

MINISTER **5.** Why not wait for your just desserts?

AZAZ. Ah yes, the dessert. We're having a special treat today . . . freshly made at the half-bakery.

MILO. The half-bakery?

AZAZ. Of course, the half-bakery! Where do you think half-baked ideas come from? Now, please don't interrupt. By royal command, the pastry chefs have . . .

MILO. What's a half-baked idea?

(AZAZ *gives up the idea of speaking as a cart is wheeled in and the Guests help themselves.*)

HUMBUG. They're very tasty, but they don't always agree with you. Here's a good one. (HUMBUG *hands one to* MILO.)

MILO. (*Reads.*) "The earth is flat."

SPELLING BEE. People swallowed that one for years. (*Picks up one and reads.*) "The moon is made of green cheese." Now, there's a half-baked idea.

(*Everyone chooses one and eats. They include: "It Never Rains But Pours," "Night Air Is Bad Air," "Everything Happens for the Best," "Coffee Stunts Your Growth."*)

AZAZ. And now for a few closing words. Attention! Let me have your attention! (*Everyone leaps up and Exits, except for* MILO, TOCK, *and the* HUMBUG.) Loyal subjects and friends, once again on this gala occasion, we have . . .

MILO. Excuse me, but everybody left.

AZAZ. (*Sadly.*) I was hoping no one would notice. It happens every time.

HUMBUG. They're gone to dinner, and as soon as I finish this last bite, I shall join them.

MILO. That's ridiculous. How can they eat dinner right after a banquet?

AZAZ. SCANDALOUS! We'll put a stop to it at once. From now on, by royal command, everyone must eat dinner before the banquet.

MILO. But that's just as bad.

HUMBUG. Or just as good. Things which are equally bad are also equally good. Try to look at the bright side of things.

MILO. I don't know which side of anything to look at. Everything is so confusing, and all your words only make things worse.

AZAZ. How true. There must be something we can do about it.

HUMBUG. Pass a law.

AZAZ. We have almost as many laws as words.

HUMBUG. Offer a reward. *(AZAZ shakes his head and looks madder at each suggestion.)* Send for help? Drive a bargain? Pull the switch? Lower the boom? Toe the line?

(As AZAZ continues to scowl, the HUMBUG loses confidence and finally gives up.)

MILO. Maybe you should let Rhyme and Reason return.

AZAZ. How nice that would be. Even if they were a bother at times, things always went so well when they were here. But I'm afraid it can't be done.

HUMBUG. Certainly not. Can't be done.

MILO. Why not?

HUMBUG. *(Now siding with MILO.)* Why not, indeed?

AZAZ. Much too difficult.

HUMBUG. Of course, much too difficult.

MILO. You could, if you really wanted to.

HUMBUG. By all means, if you really wanted to, you could.

AZAZ. *(To HUMBUG.)* How?

MILO. *(Also to HUMBUG.)* Yeah, how?

HUMBUG. Why . . . uh, it's a simple task for a brave boy with a stout heart, a steadfast dog and a serviceable small automobile.

AZAZ. Go on.

HUMBUG. Well, all that he would have to do is cross the dangerous, unknown countryside between here and Digitopolis, where he would have to persuade the Mathemagician to release the Princesses, which we know to be impossible because the Mathemagician will never agree with Azaz about anything. Once achieving that, it's a simple matter of entering the Mountains of Ignorance from where no one has ever returned

Reading Skill

Summarize what Humbug is doing in the bracketed passage.

_____

_____

_____

Literary Analysis

Read the **dialogue** on this page. What problem must be solved in this **drama**? Underline the words that tell you the answer.

_____

_____

_____

Stop to Reflect

How would you feel about rescuing Rhyme and Reason? Would you be frightened if you were Milo?

_____

_____

_____

Reading Skill

Summarize the difficulties that must be overcome to rescue the princesses.

_____

_____

_____

_____

_____

_____

Literary Analysis

Read the bracketed **dialogue**. How does Azaz feel about the power of words?

_____

_____

_____

Reading Check ✎

What gift does King Azaz give Milo for protection on his journey? Circle the answer.

alive, an effortless climb up a two thousand foot stairway without railings in a high wind at night to the Castle-in-the-Air. After a pleasant chat with the Princesses, all that remains is a leisurely ride back through those chaotic crags where the frightening fiends have sworn to tear any intruder from limb to limb and devour him down to his belt buckle. And finally after doing all that, a triumphal parade! If, of course, there is anything left to parade . . . followed by hot chocolate and cookies for everyone.

AZAZ. I never realized it would be so simple.

MILO. It sounds dangerous to me.

TOCK. And just who is supposed to make that journey?

AZAZ. A very good question. But there is one far more serious problem.

MILO. What's that?

AZAZ. I'm afraid I can't tell you that until you return.

MILO. But wait a minute, I didn't . . .

AZAZ. Dictionopolis will always be grateful to you, my boy, and your dog. (AZAZ *pats* TOCK *and* MILO.)

TOCK. Now, just one moment, sire . . .

AZAZ. You will face many dangers on your journey, but fear not, for I can give you something for your protection. (AZAZ *gives* MILO *a box.*) In this box are the letters of the alphabet. With them you can form all the words you will ever need to help you overcome the obstacles that may stand in your path. All you must do is use them well and in the right places.

MILO. (*Miserably.*) Thanks a lot.

AZAZ. You will need a guide, of course, and since he knows the obstacles so well, the Humbug has cheerfully volunteered to accompany you.

HUMBUG. Now, see here . . . !

AZAZ. You will find him dependable, brave, resourceful and loyal.

HUMBUG. (*Flattered.*) Oh, your Majesty.

MILO. I'm sure he'll be a great help. (*They approach the car.*)

TOCK. I hope so. It looks like we're going to need it.

(The lights darken and the KING *fades from view.)*

AZAZ. Good luck! Drive carefully! *(The three get into the car and begin to move. Suddenly a thunderously loud NOISE is heard. They slow down the car.)*

MILO. What was that?

TOCK. It came from up ahead.

HUMBUG. It's something terrible, I just know it. Oh, no. Something dreadful is going to happen to us. I can feel it in my bones. *(The NOISE is repeated. They all look at each other fearfully as the lights fade.)*

> Reader's Response: Which character in this drama would you most like to be? Explain you choice.
>
> _____
>
> _____
>
> _____

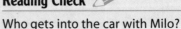

TAKE NOTES

Literary Analysis

What in the **script** tells the audience that danger may lie ahead?

_____

_____

_____

_____

Reading Check

Who gets into the car with Milo? Circle the answer in the text.

The Phantom Tollbooth, Act I

1. **Identify Cause and Effect:** What effect does the absence of Rhyme and Reason have on Dictionopolis?

   _____

   _____

2. **Predict:** In Act II, Milo will start his journey. What do you think his journey will be like? Give three details from Act I to support your answer.

   _____

   _____

   _____

3. **Reading Skill:** What events would you include in a **summary** of Act I?

   _____

   _____

4. **Literary Analysis:** Fill in this chart to explain how the **dialogue** shows something about a character's personality, the setting, and an action. An example has been provided.

Dialogue	What It Suggests
MILO: Will, it doesn't matter anyway. Dictionopolis. That's a weird name. I might as well go there.	**Character:** Milo is bored. He does not care about anything.
GATEKEEPER: This is Dictionopolis, a happy kingdom, advantageously located in the foothills of confusion and caressed by gentle breezes from the Sea of Knowledge.	**Setting:**
WATCHDOG: Do you mind if I get in? I love automobile rides.	**Action:**

Writing: Summary

Write a **summary** of Act I. A summary includes the most important events. Answer the following questions to help you write your summary.

- Why is Dictionopolis such an unusual place?

_____

_____

_____

- Which details make the story interesting?

_____

_____

_____

- Which information from the stage directions should you include in your summary?

_____

_____

_____

Listening and Speaking: Speech

Use the following lines to write ideas for your **speech.** Make sure that you include key events and ideas that Milo would mention.

- Milo's experiences: _____

_____

_____

_____

_____

Write your speech on another sheet of paper. Then, practice reading it several times. Use gestures and changes in tone to reinforce the meaning of your words.

The Phantom Tollbooth, Act II

Reading Skill

When you **compare** two things, you tell how they are alike. When you **contrast** two things, you tell how they are different. As you read drama, **picture the action** to compare and contrast characters, situations, and events. To picture the action, pay attention to the dialogue and the descriptions of how characters speak and act.

Literary Analysis

Stage directions are the words in a drama that the characters do not say. They tell performers how to move and speak, and they help readers picture the action, sounds, and scenery. Stage directions are usually printed in italics and set between brackets, as in this example.

CARLOS. *(To* ISABEL.*)* Remember, don't make a sound! *(He tiptoes offstage.)*

As you read, use this chart to record stage directions that help you picture the action and understand what the characters are thinking and feeling.

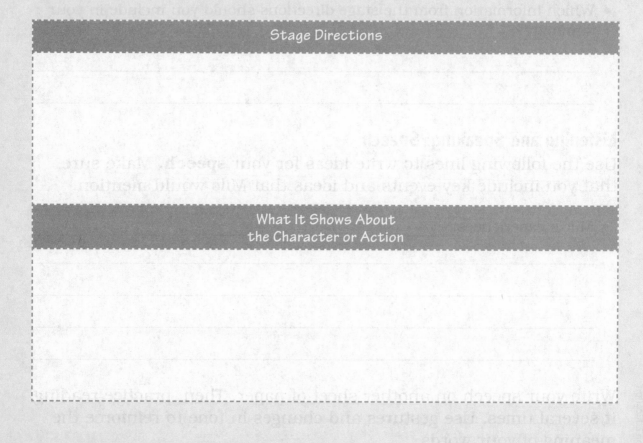

Stage Directions

What It Shows About the Character or Action

The Phantom Tollbooth, Act II

Susan Nanus
Based on the book by Norton Juster

Summary Milo, Tock, and Humbug arrive in Digitopolis in Scene i. They ask the Doctor of Dissonance, the Dodecahedron, and the Mathemagician which road to take to find the princesses. They arrive in the Land of Ignorance to rescue the Princesses. After they succeed, Milo learns an important lesson.

 Writing About the Big Question

How do we decide who we are? In Act II, Milo comes back from his adventure to find that he is not the same boy he used to be. Complete this sentence:

New experiences can give us a new **perspective** on _____

because _____.

Note-taking Guide

Milo, Tock, and Humbug meet many challenges in the Land of Ignorance. Fill in this chart with information about the challenges that the three face.

Character	Challenges to Milo, Tock, and Humbug
Senses Taker	
Demon of Insincerity	
Terrible Trivium	

The Phantom Tollbooth, Act II

Scene ii The Land of Ignorance

Describe a challenge you faced that has made you stronger.

_____

_____

_____

Literary Analysis

Stage directions help readers picture the action, sounds, and scenery. These words are usually printed in italics between brackets. What effect does the stage direction *LIGHTS UP* have on the action?

_____

_____

Reading Skill

Picture the action to help you remember details and events. What single event or detail do you remember best from Act I, Scene ii?

_____

_____

Reading Check

What does Reason say to Rhyme about Milo, Tock, and Humbug's chances of success? Circle the answer.

LIGHTS UP on RHYME *and* REASON, *in their castle, looking out two windows.*

RHYME. *I'm worried sick, I must confess*
I wonder if they'll have success
All the others tried in vain,
And were never seen or heard again.

REASON. Now, Rhyme, there's no need to be so <u>pessimistic</u>. Milo, Tock, and Humbug have just as much chance of succeeding as they do of failing.

RHYME. *But the demons are so deadly smart*
They'll stuff your brain and fill your heart
With <u>petty</u> thoughts and selfish dreams
And trap you with their nasty schemes.

REASON. Now, Rhyme, be reasonable, won't you? And calm down, you always talk in couplets[1] when you get nervous. Milo has learned a lot from his journey. I think he's a match for the demons and that he might soon be knocking at our door. Now come on, cheer up, won't you?

RHYME. I'll try.

(LIGHTS FADE on the PRINCESSES *and COME UP on the little Car, traveling slowly.)*

MILO. So this is the Land of Ignorance. It's so dark. I can hardly see a thing. Maybe we should wait until morning.

VOICE. They'll be <u>mourning</u> for you soon enough.
(They look up and see a large, soiled, ugly bird

Vocabulary Development

pessimistic (pes uh MIS tik) *adj.* always thinking that something bad will happen

petty (PET ee) *adj.* not important

mourning (MAWRN ing) *v.* feeling very sad because someone has died and showing the sadness through actions and words

1. **couplets** (KUP lits) *n.* two lines of poetry in a row that often rhyme.

with a dangerous beak and a <u>malicious</u> expression.)

MILO. I don't think you understand. We're looking for a place to spend the night.

BIRD. *(Shrieking.)* It's not yours to spend!

MILO. That doesn't make any sense, you see . . .

BIRD. Dollars or cents, it's still not yours to spend.

MILO. But I don't mean . . .

BIRD. Of course you're mean. Anybody who'd spend a night that doesn't belong to him is very mean.

TOCK. Must you interrupt like that?

BIRD. Naturally, it's my job. I take the words right out of your mouth. Haven't we met before? I'm the Everpresent Wordsnatcher.

MILO. Are you a demon?

BIRD. I'm afraid not. I've tried, but the best I can manage to be is a nuisance. *(<u>Suddenly gets nervous as he looks beyond the three.</u>)* And I don't have time to waste with you. *(Starts to leave.)*

TOCK. What is it? What's the matter?

MILO. Hey, don't leave. I wanted to ask you some questions. . . . Wait!

BIRD. Weight? Twenty-seven pounds. Bye-bye. *(Disappears.)*

MILO. Well, he was no help.

MAN. Perhaps I can be of some assistance to you? *(There appears a beautifully dressed man, very polished and clean.)* Hello, little boy. *(Shakes* MILO's *hand.)* And how's the faithful dog? *(Pats* TOCK.*)* And who is this handsome creature? *(Tips his hat to* HUMBUG.*)*

HUMBUG. *(To others.)* What a pleasant surprise to meet someone so nice in a place like this.

MAN. But before I help you out, I wonder if first you could spare me a little of your time, and help me with a few small jobs?

HUMBUG. Why, certainly.

Vocabulary Development
malicious (muh LISH uhs) *adj.* having or showing evil intentions

---

Reading Skill

When you **compare** two things, you tell how they are alike. When you **contrast** two things, you tell how they are different. Compare and contrast the two ways that the word *spend* is used in the first bracketed passage.

_____

_____

_____

Literary Analysis 🔍

What does the underlined **stage direction** tell you about upcoming action in the play?

_____

_____

_____

Reading Skill

Read the second bracketed passage. **Contrast** the effects of Man and Bird on Milo, Tock, and Humbug.

_____

_____

_____

_____

_____

Literary Analysis

How do the **stage directions** in the bracketed passage move the action along?

_____

_____

_____

_____

Stop to Reflect

Why do you think Milo, Tock, and Humbug take on Man's tasks?

_____

_____

_____

_____

Reading Check

What does Man want Milo to do? Underline the answer in the text.

TOCK. Gladly.

MILO. Sure, we'd be happy to.

MAN. Splendid, for there are just three tasks. First, I would like to move this pile of sand from here to there. *(Indicates through pantomime a large pile of sand.)* But I'm afraid that all I have is this tiny tweezers. *(Hands it to* MILO, *who begins moving the sand one grain at a time.)* Second, I would like to empty this well and fill that other, but I have no bucket, so you'll have to use this eyedropper. *(Hands it to* TOCK, *who begins to work.)* And finally, I must have a hole in this cliff, and here is a needle to dig it. *(*HUMBUG *eagerly begins. The man leans against a tree and stares vacantly off into space. The LIGHTS indicate the passage of time.)*

MILO. You know something? I've been working steadily for a long time, now, and I don't feel the least bit tired or hungry. I could go right on the same way forever.

MAN. Maybe you will. *(He yawns.)*

MILO. *(Whispers to* TOCK.*)* Well, I wish I knew how long it was going to take.

TOCK. Why don't you use your magic staff and find out?

MILO. *(Takes out pencil and calculates. To* MAN.*)* Pardon me, sir, but it's going to take 837 years to finish these jobs.

MAN. Is that so? What a shame. Well then you'd better get on with them.

MILO. But . . . it hardly seems worthwhile.

MAN. WORTHWHILE! Of course they're not worthwhile. I wouldn't ask you to do anything that was worthwhile.

TOCK. Then why bother?

MAN. Because, my friends, what could be more important than doing unimportant things? If you stop to do enough of them, you'll never get where you are going. *(Laughs villainously.)*

MILO. *(Gasps.)* Oh, no, you must be . . .

MAN. Quite correct! I am the Terrible Trivium, demon of petty tasks and worthless jobs, ogre of wasted effort and monster of habit. *(They start to back away from him.)* Don't try to leave, there's so much to do, and you still have 837 years to go on the first job.

MILO. But why do unimportant things?

MAN. Think of all the trouble it saves. If you spend all your time doing only the easy and useless jobs, you'll never have time to worry about the important ones which are so difficult. *(Walks toward them whispering.)* Now do come and stay with me. We'll have such fun together. There are things to fill and things to empty, things to take away and things to bring back, things to pick up and things to put down . . . *(They are transfixed by his soothing voice. He is about to embrace them when a* VOICE *screams.)*

VOICE. Run! Run! *(They all wake up and run with the Trivium behind. As the voice continues to call out directions, they follow until they lose the Trivium.)* RUN! RUN! This way! This way! Over here! Over here! Up here! Down there! Quick, hurry up!

TOCK. *(Panting.)* I think we lost him.

VOICE. Keep going straight! Keep going straight! Now step up! Now step up!

MILO. Look out! *(They all fall into a Trap.)* But he said "up!"

VOICE. Well, I hope you didn't expect to get anywhere by listening to me.

HUMBUG. We're in a deep pit! We'll never get out of here.

VOICE. That is quite an accurate evaluation of the situation.

MILO. *(Shouting angrily.)* Then why did you help us at all?

VOICE. Oh, I'd do as much for anybody. Bad advice is my specialty. *(A Little Furry Creature appears.)* I'm the demon of Insincerity. I don't mean what I say; I don't mean what I do; and I don't mean what I am.

Reading Skill

Compare the Terrible Trivium to the Lethargarians, who appear in Act I. How are they the same?

_____

_____

_____

_____

Literary Analysis

What do the underlined **stage directions** tell you about how Milo, Tock, and Humbug feel about the Terrible Trivium?

_____

_____

_____

Stop to Reflect

Would you have listened to the Voice if you were Milo? Why or why not?

_____

_____

_____

_____

Reading Check

Where are Milo, Humbug, and Tock stuck? Circle the answer.

Vocabulary Development
transfixed (trans FIKST) *adj.* not able to move

© Pearson Education

Stop to Reflect

Why do you think Milo is beginning to realize the dangers in the Land of Ignorance?

_____

_____

_____

_____

_____

Reading Skill

Compare and contrast the ways in which Milo and Humbug react to the Demon of Insincerity.

_____

_____

_____

_____

_____

Reading Check

How do Milo, Humbug, and Tock get out? Underline the answer.

MILO. Then why don't you go away and leave us alone!

INSINCERITY. *(VOICE)* Now, there's no need to get angry. You're a very clever boy and I have complete confidence in you. You can certainly climb out of that pit . . . come on, try. . .

MILO. I'm not listening to one word you say! You're just telling me what you think I'd like to hear, and not what is important.

INSINCERITY. Well, if that's the way you feel about it . . .

MILO. That's the way I feel about it. We will manage by ourselves without any unnecessary advice from you.

INSINCERITY. *(Stamping his foot.)* Well, all right for you! Most people listen to what I say, but if that's the way you feel, then I'll just go home. *(Exits in a huff.[2])*

HUMBUG. *(Who has been quivering with fright.)* And don't you ever come back! Well, I guess we showed him, didn't we?

MILO. You know something? This place is a lot more dangerous than I ever imagined.

TOCK. *(Who's been surveying the situation.)* I think I figured a way to get out. Here, hop on my back. *(MILO does so.)* Now, you, Humbug, on top of Milo. *(He does so.)* Now hook your umbrella onto that tree and hold on. *(They climb over* HUMBUG, *then pull him up.)*

HUMBUG. *(As they climb.)* Watch it! Watch it, now. Ow, be careful of my back! My back! Easy, easy . . . oh, this is so difficult. Aren't you finished yet?

TOCK. *(As he pulls up* HUMBUG.*)* There. Now, I'll lead for a while. Follow me, and we'll stay out of trouble. *(They walk and climb higher and higher.)*

HUMBUG. Can't we slow down a little?

TOCK. Something tells me we better reach the Castle-in-the-Air as soon as possible, and not stop to rest for a single moment. *(They speed up.)*

MILO. What is it, Tock? Did you see something?

---

2. **in a huff** (huf) feeling angry.

TOCK. Just keep walking and don't look back.

MILO. You did see something!

HUMBUG. What is it? Another demon?

TOCK. Not just one, I'm afraid. If you want to see what I'm talking about, then turn around. *(They turn around. The stage darkens and hundreds of Yellow Gleaming Eyes can be seen.)*

HUMBUG. Good grief! Do you see how many there are? Hundreds! The Overbearing Know-it-all, the Gross Exaggeration, the Horrible Hopping Hindsight, . . . and look over there! The Triple Demons of Compromise! Let's get out of here! *(Starts to scurry.)* Hurry up, you two! Must you be so slow about everything?

MILO. Look! There it is, up ahead! The Castle-in-the-Air! *(They all run.)*

HUMBUG. They're gaining!

MILO. But there it is!

HUMBUG. I see it! I see it!

(They reach the first step and are stopped by a little man in a frock coat, sleeping on a worn ledger. He has a long quill pen and a bottle of ink at his side. He is covered with ink stains over his clothes and wears spectacles.)

TOCK. Shh! Be very careful. *(They try to step over him, but he wakes up.)*

SENSES TAKER. *(From sleeping position.)* Names? *(He sits up.)*

HUMBUG. Well, I . . .

SENSES TAKER. NAMES? *(He opens book and begins to write, splattering himself with ink.)*

HUMBUG. Uh . . . Humbug, Tock and this is Milo.

SENSES TAKER. Splendid, splendid. I haven't had an "M" in ages.

MILO. What do you want our names for? We're sort of in a hurry.

SENSES TAKER. Oh, this won't take long. I'm the official Senses Taker and I must have some information before I can take your sense. Now if

Literary Analysis

List two details that you learn about the setting from the **stage directions** in the first bracketed passage.

1. _____

_____

2. _____

_____

Reading Check

What demons does Humbug see? Circle the answers in the text.

Reading Skill

The Senses Taker shows excitement in the underlined text. How does he **compare** with characters in Dictionopolis?

_____

_____

_____

Reading Skill

Compare what the Senses Taker says in the bracketed passage to what Insincerity says.

_____

_____

_____

Stop to Reflect

Is the information the Senses Taker requests useful or useless? Explain.

_____

_____

_____

_____

Reading Check

What is Milo nervous about as the Senses Taker starts asking questions? Underline the answer.

---

you'll just tell me: *(Handing them a form to fill. Speaking slowly and <u>deliberately</u>.)* When you were born, where you were born, why you were born, how old you are now, how old you were then, how old you'll be in a little while . . .

MILO. I wish he'd hurry up. At this rate, the demons will be here before we know it!

SENSES TAKER. . . . Your mother's name, your father's name, where you live, how long you've lived there, the schools you've attended, the schools you haven't attended . . .

HUMBUG. I'm getting writer's cramp.

TOCK. I smell something very evil and it's getting stronger every second. *(To SENSES TAKER.)* May we go now?

SENSES TAKER. Just as soon as you tell me your height, your weight, the number of books you've read this year . . .

MILO. We have to go!

SENSES TAKER. All right, all right, I'll give you the short form. *(Pulls out a small piece of paper.)* Destination?

MILO. But we have to . . .

SENSES TAKER. *DESTINATION?*

MILO, TOCK AND HUMBUG. The Castle-in-the-Air! *(They throw down their papers and run past him up the first few stairs.)*

SENSES TAKER. Stop! I'm sure you'd rather see what I have to show you. *(Snaps his fingers; they freeze.)* A circus of your very own. *(CIRCUS MUSIC is heard. MILO seems to go into a trance.)* And wouldn't you enjoy this most wonderful smell? *(TOCK sniffs and goes into a trance.)* And here's something I know you'll enjoy hearing . . . *(To HUMBUG. The sound of CHEERS and APPLAUSE for HUMBUG is heard, and he goes into a trance.)* There we are. And now, I'll just sit back and let the demons catch up with you.

Vocabulary Development

deliberately (di LIB er it lee) *adv.* carefully

(MILO *accidentally drops his package of gifts. The Package of Laughter from* DR. DISCHORD *opens and the Sounds of Laughter are heard. After a moment,* MILO, TOCK *and* HUMBUG *join in laughing and the spells are broken.)*

MILO. There was no circus.

TOCK. There were no smells.

HUMBUG. The applause is gone.

SENSES TAKER. I warned you I was the Senses Taker. I'll steal your sense of Purpose, your sense of Duty, destroy your sense of Proportion—and but for one thing, you'd be helpless yet.

MILO. What's that?

SENSES TAKER. As long as you have the sound of laughter, I cannot take your sense of Humor. Agh! That horrible sense of humor.

HUMBUG. HERE THEY COME! LET'S GET OUT OF HERE!

(The demons appear in nasty slithering hordes, running through the audience and up onto the stage, trying to attack TOCK, MILO *and* HUMBUG. *The three heroes run past the* SENSES TAKER *up the stairs toward the Castle-in-the-Air with the demons snarling behind them.)*

MILO. Don't look back! Just keep going! *(They reach the castle. The two princesses appear in the windows.)*

PRINCESSES. Hurry! Hurry! We've been expecting you.

MILO. You must be the Princesses. We've come to rescue you.

HUMBUG. And the demons are close behind!

TOCK. We should leave right away.

PRINCESSES. We're ready anytime you are.

MILO. Good, now if you'll just come out. But wait a minute—there's no door! How can we rescue you from the Castle-in-the-Air if there's no way to get in or out?

HUMBUG. Hurry, Milo! They're gaining on us.

REASON. Take your time, Milo, and think about it.

MILO. Ummm, all right . . . just give me a second or two. *(He thinks hard.)*

Literary Analysis 🔍

Read the first bracketed passage. Would you be able to **picture the action** without the **stage directions?** Explain.

_____

_____

_____

_____

Stop to Reflect 📖

What effect might the demons' actions in the second bracketed passage have on the audience?

_____

_____

_____

Reading Skill 📖

What advice does Reason give Milo in the third bracketed passage?

_____

_____

_____

How does Reason's advice help you **picture the action**?

_____

_____

_____

© Pearson Education

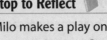

Stop to Reflect

Milo makes a play on words. The expression "time flies" is used to mean "time goes by quickly." What meaning does Milo use here?

_____

_____

_____

_____

Literary Analysis

Read the **stage directions** in the bracketed passage to **picture the action**. Describe the action in your own words.

_____

_____

_____

_____

_____

_____

_____

Reading Check

Who arrives to battle the demons? Circle the answer in the text.

HUMBUG. I think I feel sick.

MILO. I've got it! Where's that package of presents? *(Opens the package of letters.)* Ah, here it is. *(Takes out the letters and sticks them on the door, spelling:)* E-N-T-R-A-N-C-E. Entrance. Now, let's see. *(Rummages through and spells in smaller letters:)* P-u-s-h. Push. *(He pushes and a door opens. The* PRINCESSES *come out of the castle. Slowly, the demons ascend the stairway.)*

HUMBUG. Oh, it's too late. They're coming up and there's no other way down!

MILO. Unless . . . *(Looks at* TOCK.*)* Well . . . Time flies, doesn't it?

TOCK. Quite often. Hold on, everyone, and I'll take you down.

HUMBUG. Can you carry us all?

TOCK. We'll soon find out. Ready or not, here we go! *(His alarm begins to ring. They jump off the platform and disappear. The demons, howling with rage, reach the top and find no one there. They see the* PRINCESSES *and the heroes running across the stage and bound down the stairs after them and into the audience. There is a mad chase scene until they reach the stage again.)*

HUMBUG. I'm exhausted! I can't run another step.

MILO. We can't stop now . . .

TOCK. Milo! Look out there! *(The armies of* AZAZ *and* MATHEMAGICIAN *appear at the back of the theater, with the Kings at their heads.)*

AZAZ. *(As they march toward the stage.)* Don't worry, Milo, we'll take over now.

MATHEMAGICIAN. Those demons may not know it, but their days are numbered!

SPELLING BEE. Charge! C-H-A-R-G-E! Charge! *(They rush at the demons and battle until the demons run off howling. Everyone cheers. The* FIVE MINISTERS OF AZAZ *appear and shake* MILO's *hand.)*

MINISTER 1. Well done.

MINISTER 2. Fine job.

MINISTER 3. Good work!

MINISTER 4. Congratulations!

MINISTER 5. CHEERS! *(Everyone cheers again. A fanfare interrupts. A* PAGE *steps forward and reads from a large scroll:)*

PAGE. Henceforth, and forthwith,
Let it be known by one and all,
That Rhyme and Reason
Reign once more in Wisdom.

(The PRINCESSES *bow gratefully and kiss their brothers, the Kings.)*

And furthermore,
The boy named Milo,
The dog known as Tock,
And the insect hereinafter referred to as
the Humbug
Are hereby declared to be Heroes of the Realm.

(All bow and salute the heroes.)

MILO. But we never could have done it without a lot of help.

REASON. That may be true, but you had the courage to try, and what you can do is often a matter of what you will do.

AZAZ. That's why there was one very important thing about your quest we couldn't discuss until you returned.

MILO. I remember. What was it?

AZAZ. Very simple. It was impossible!

MATHEMAGICIAN. Completely impossible!

HUMBUG. Do you mean . . . ? *(Feeling faint.)* Oh . . . I think I need to sit down.

AZAZ. Yes, indeed, but if we'd told you then, you might not have gone.

MATHEMAGICIAN. And, as you discovered, many things are possible just as long as you don't know they're impossible.

MILO. I think I understand.

RHYME. I'm afraid it's time to go now.

REASON. And you must say goodbye.

MILO. To everyone? *(Looks around at the crowd. To* TOCK *and* HUMBUG.*)* Can't you two come with me?

HUMBUG. I'm afraid not, old man. I'd like to, but I've

TAKE NOTES

Reading Check

Contrast the views that Milo and Reason have of Milo's bravery.

_____

_____

_____

_____

_____

Stop to Reflect

Read the bracketed passage. What is the lesson that Milo learns?

_____

_____

_____

_____

Reading Check

What statement could Mathemagician not discuss with Milo until after the mission? Circle the answer.

© Pearson Education

Stop to Reflect

Read the bracketed passage. Do you agree more with Reason's or Rhyme's advice? Explain.

_____

_____

_____

_____

_____

Reading Skill

Contrast Azaz's and Mathemagician's behavior now with their behavior at the beginning of the play.

_____

_____

_____

_____

Reading Check

Does Milo understand what Rhyme tells him? Underline the answer.

arranged for a lecture tour which will keep me occupied for years.

TOCK. And they do need a watchdog here.

MILO. Well, O.K., then. *(MILO hugs the HUMBUG.)*

HUMBUG. *(Sadly.)* Oh, bah.

MILO. *(He hugs TOCK, and then faces everyone.)* Well, goodbye. We all spent so much time together, I know I'm going to miss you. *(To the PRINCESSES.)* I guess we would have reached you a lot sooner if I hadn't made so many mistakes.

REASON. You must never feel badly about making mistakes, Milo, as long as you take the trouble to learn from them. Very often you learn more by being wrong for the right reasons than you do by being right for the wrong ones.

MILO. But there's so much to learn.

RHYME. That's true, but it's not just learning that's important. It's learning what to do with what you learn and learning why you learn things that matters.

MILO. I think I know what you mean, Princess. At least, I hope I do. *(The car is rolled forward and MILO climbs in.)* Goodbye! Goodbye! I'll be back someday! I will! Anyway, I'll try. *(As MILO drives the set of the Land of Ignorance begins to move offstage.)*

AZAZ. Goodbye! Always remember. Words! Words! Words!

MATHEMAGICIAN. And numbers!

AZAZ. Now, don't tell me you think numbers are as important as words?

MATHEMAGICIAN. Is that so? Why I'll have you know . . . *(The set disappears, and MILO's Room is seen onstage.)*

MILO. *(As he drives on.)* Oh, oh, I hope they don't start all over again. Because I don't think I'll have much time in the near future to help them out. *(The sound of loud ticking is heard. MILO finds himself in his room. He gets out of the car and looks around.)*

THE CLOCK. Did someone mention time?

MILO. Boy, I must have been gone for an awful long time. I wonder what time it is. *(Looks at clock.)* Five o'clock. I wonder what day it is. *(Looks at calendar.)* It's still today! I've only been gone for an hour! *(He continues to look at his calendar, and then begins to look at his books and toys and maps and chemistry set with great interest.)*

CLOCK. An hour. Sixty minutes. How long it really lasts depends on what you do with it for some people, an hour seems to last forever. For others, just a moment, and so full of things to do.

MILO. *(Looks at clock.)* Six o'clock already?

CLOCK. In an instant. In a <u>trice</u>. Before you have time to blink. *(The stage goes black in less than no time at all.)*

Reader's Response: Which character in this drama would you most like to meet? Explain why.

_____

_____

_____

_____

Vocabulary Development

trice (trys) *n.* a very short time; a moment

Literary Analysis

On the basis of the stage directions in the bracketed passage, how do you think Milo now feels about time?

_____

_____

_____

_____

Stop to Reflect 📖

Milo has left the Land of Ignorance and all of its characters. What happens in Milo's room that tells you that a bit of the fantasy world is still with him?

_____

_____

_____

Reading Check ✏️

How long has Milo been gone? Circle the answer in the text.

The Phantom Tollbooth, Act II

1. **Deduce:** What will be the result if Milo, Tock, and Humbug follow the Terrible Trivium's directions?

_____

_____

_____

2. **Draw Conclusions:** What does Milo learn about humor from his encounter with the Senses Taker?

_____

_____

_____

3. **Reading Skill:** Fill in this Venn diagram with details from Act II, Scene ii to **compare** and **contrast** the Senses Taker and the Terrible Trivium.

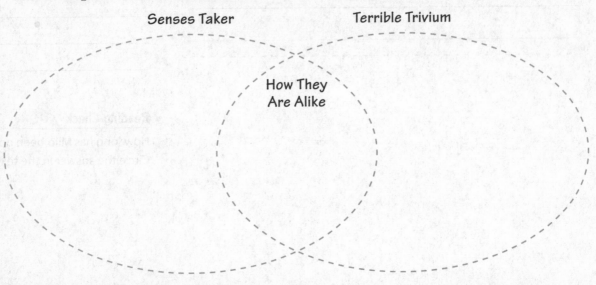

Senses Taker   Terrible Trivium

How They
Are Alike

4. **Literary Analysis:** Describe one place in the play where **stage directions** are necessary for understanding the events.

_____

_____

_____

Writing: Review

Write a **review** of *The Phantom Tollbooth*. Answer the following questions to help you present your opinions in your review.

- Which characters are the most exciting? Why?

_____

_____

_____

- Do any characters become more interesting as you think about them? If so, which characters?

_____

_____

_____

- Which events are the funniest? The most confusing?

_____

_____

_____

Research and Technology: Multimedia Report

Use the following chart to gather information for your **multimedia presentation**.

What is infinity?	
What is the largest number?	
What is the smallest number?	
Three main ideas you learned from your research.	1. 2. 3.

Online Articles

About Online Articles

An **online article** is an article that appears on a Web site. It may cover a variety of topics. Some online articles cover current events. Others may discuss historical, scientific, or technical topics. Online articles may contain features such as graphics, links, or sound to provide additional information.

Different organizations publish online articles. Some organizations are more reliable than others. Reliable organizations usually include:

- educational institutions
- government agencies
- newspapers and magazines

Reading Skill

Not all online articles contain correct information. To decide if an online article has correct information, **evaluate the evidence** for the author's conclusions. Reliable evidence includes facts, examples, quotations, and expert opinions. A fact is a statement that can be proved. An expert opinion is a statement by someone with extensive knowledge about a topic. Opinions that are not supported by facts may not be correct. To learn more about how to evaluate evidence, study the graphic organizer below.

Checklist for Evaluating Evidence

❑ Does the author provide concrete evidence, such as facts, statistics, and expert opinions?

❑ Does the author identify the sources of his or her evidence?

❑ Can the author's evidence be verified?

❑ Does the author's evidence logically support his or her conclusions?

Features:
- informative title
- brief opener that states the main idea
- facts, statistics, and direct quotations that support main idea
- specialized and technical language
- text written for a general audience

NASA Finally Goes Metric

by *SPACE* Staff

When NASA returns astronauts to the moon, the mission will be measured in kilometers, not miles.

The agency has decided to use metric units for all operations on the lunar surface, according to a statement released today.

These brief opening paragraphs give the main idea.

The change will standardize parts and tools. It means Russian wrenches could be used to fix an air leak in a U.S.-built habitat. It will also make communications easier, such as when determining how far to send a rover for a science project.

NASA has ostensibly used the metric system since about 1990, the statement said, but English units are still employed on some missions, and a few projects use both. NASA uses both English and metric aboard the International Space Station.

The dual strategy led to the loss of the Mars Climate Orbiter robotic probe in 1999; a contractor provided thruster firing data in English units while NASA was calculating in metric.

The decision comes after a series of meetings between NASA and 13 other space agencies around the world, where metric measurements rule.

These paragraphs give information on the history behind the NASA decision.

"When we made the announcement at the meeting, the reps for the other space agencies all gave a little cheer," said Jeff Volosin, strategy development lead for NASA's Exploration Systems Mission Directorate. "I think NASA has been seen as maybe a bit stubborn by other space agencies in the past, so this was important as a gesture of our willingness to be cooperative when it comes to the Moon."

Informally, the space agencies have also discussed using Internet protocols for lunar communications, the statement said.

"That way, if some smaller space agency or some private company wants to get involved in something we're doing on the Moon, they can say, 'Hey, we already know how to do internet communications,'" Volosin said. "It lowers the barrier to entry."

THE BIG ?

How do we decide who we are?
(a) Did NASA decide to be an independent or a cooperative space agency? Explain. **(b)** How did a catastrophe help them to make that decision?

Thinking About the Online Article

1. What organization published this article?

_____

2. What is NASA's purpose in using only metric units?

_____

TALK ABOUT IT **Reading Skill**

3. What kinds of evidence does the author use in this article?

_____

_____

4. What facts support the opinion that *NASA has been seen as maybe a bit stubborn?*

_____

_____

WRITE ABOUT IT **Timed Writing: Summary (20 minutes)**

Explain the process you used to evaluate the evidence in this online article.

• Reread the article. List some pieces of evidence that support the information and the author's conclusions.

_____

_____

• How did you decide whether the evidence was based on fact or opinion?

_____

_____

Black Cowboy, Wild Horses

People told stories long before there were books to read. People who tell stories aloud follow what is called the **oral tradition**. Most folk tales, fables, myths, legends, folk songs, and fairy tales come from the oral tradition. Look for these characteristics in stories from the oral tradition:

- A **universal theme** is a message about life that most people understand.

- **Fantasy** is a type of imaginative writing. Fantasy contains elements that are not found in real life.

- **Personification** is a special type of language. Writers use personification to give human characteristics, such as speech, to nonhuman subjects, such as animals.

- **Irony** is a surprising event that is the opposite of what you expect. Unexpected endings are called **ironic** endings.

- **Hyperbole** is an exaggeration. Hyperbole in folk literature is usually meant to be funny.

- **Dialect** is the form of language spoken by people of a certain region. Storytellers use dialect to make **characters** seem real.

- **Local customs** are the traditions of a group of people. Details of local customs help build the time and place, or **setting**, of a story's action.

This chart describes the different types of stories found in the oral tradition.

Type of Oral Tradition	Definition	Example
Folk Tales	• entertaining stories that tell about shared ideas of a culture • often have heroes, adventure, magic, or romance • Details change over time. • were later written down	*The Ant and the Dove*
Fables	• brief stories or poems • teach a lesson or moral • usually have animal characters	*The Lion and the Bulls*
Myths	• fictional tales about gods and heroes or natural events • A collection of myths is a culture's **mythology**.	*Arachne*
Legends	• a culture's familier and traditional stories • often based on fact • change to include more fictional details over time • may become subject of an **allusion**, a reference to a well-known person, place, event, or literary work .	*The Legend of Sleepy Hollow*

Black Cowboy, Wild Horses
Julius Lester

Summary Bob Lemmons is a cowboy who tracks a herd of wild horses. He rides his black stallion, Warrior, who knows how to blend in among wild horses. Bob and Warrior fight the wild herd's leader for control of the herd. They lead the herd on an exciting run.

Note-taking Guide

Fill in the cause-and-effect chart to show how Bob and Warrior take over the herd.

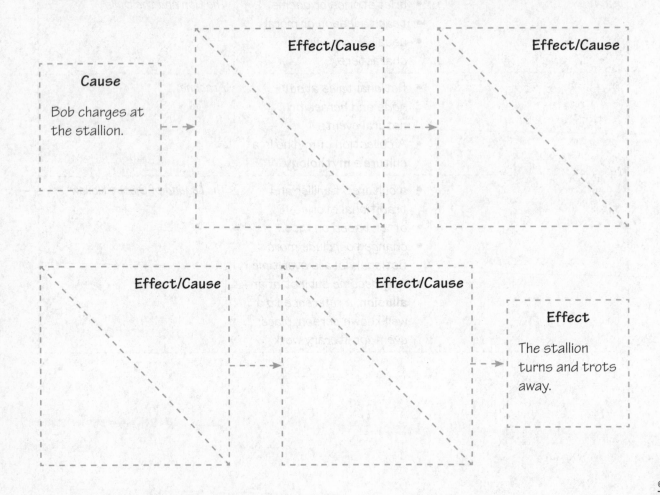

Cause

Bob charges at the stallion.

Effect/Cause

Effect/Cause

Effect/Cause

Effect/Cause

Effect

The stallion turns and trots away.

Black Cowboy, Wild Horses
Julius Lester

FIRST LIGHT. Bob Lemmons rode his horse slowly up the rise. When he reached the top, he stopped at the edge of the bluff. He looked down at the corral where the other cowboys were beginning the morning chores, then turned away and stared at the land stretching as wide as love in every direction. The sky was curved as if it were a lap on which the earth lay napping like a curled cat. High above, a hawk was suspended on cold threads of unseen winds. Far, far away, at what looked to be the edge of the world, land and sky kissed.

He guided Warrior, his black stallion, slowly down the bluff. When they reached the bottom, the horse reared, eager to run across the vastness of the plains until he reached forever. Bob smiled and patted him gently on the neck. "Easy. Easy," he whispered. "We'll have time for that. But not yet."

He let the horse trot for a while, then slowed him and began peering intently at the ground as if looking for the answer to a question he scarcely understood.

It was late afternoon when he saw them—the hoof-prints of mustangs, the wild horses that lived on the plains. He stopped, dismounted, and walked around carefully until he had seen all the prints. Then he got down on his hands and knees to examine them more closely.

Some people learned from books. Bob had been a slave and never learned to read words. But he could look at the ground and read what animals had walked on it, their size and weight, when they had passed by, and where they were going. No one he knew could bring in mustangs by themselves, but Bob could make horses think he was one of them—because he was.

He stood, reached into his saddlebag, took out an apple, and gave it to Warrior, who chewed with noisy enthusiasm. It was a herd of eight mares, a colt, and a stallion. They had passed there two days ago. He would see them soon. But he needed to smell of sun, moon, stars, and wind before the mustangs would accept him.

Activate Prior Knowledge

This story is about a cowboy and horses. Briefly describe a story you know about cowboys or horses.

_____

_____

_____

_____

Oral Traditions

Personification is a type of figurative language in which a nonhuman subject is given human characteristics. Read the first bracketed paragraph. Underline the part that shows personification.

Oral Traditions

Hyperbole is an exaggeration. Read the second bracketed paragraph. What information is exaggerated in this paragraph?

_____

_____

_____

Reading Check

What is Warrior eager to do? Underline the answer in the text.

Oral Traditions

The author uses many examples of **personification** in his descriptions on this page. Circle three examples of personification.

Oral Traditions

Setting is the time and place in a story. What is the setting in this story?

_____

_____

_____

_____

Stop to Reflect

Why do you think Bob sleeps in the saddle?

_____

_____

_____

_____

Reading Check

Why does Bob decide not to make a fire? Circle the answer.

The sun went down and the chilly night air came quickly. Bob took the saddle, saddlebag, and blanket off Warrior. He was cold, but could not make a fire. The mustangs would smell the smoke in his clothes from miles away. He draped a thick blanket around himself, then took the cotton sack of dried fruit, beef jerky, and nuts from his saddlebag and ate. When he was done, he lay his head on his saddle and was quickly asleep. Warrior grazed in the tall, sweet grasses.

As soon as the sun's round shoulders came over the horizon, Bob awoke. He ate, filled his canteen, and saddling Warrior, rode away. All day he followed the tracks without hurrying.

Near dusk, clouds appeared, piled atop each other like mountains made of fear. Lightning flickered from within them like candle flames shivering in a breeze. Bob heard the faint but distinct rumbling of thunder. Suddenly lightning vaulted from cloud to cloud across the curved heavens.

Warrior reared, his front hooves pawing as if trying to knock the white streaks of fire from the night sky. Bob raced Warrior to a nearby ravine as the sky exploded sheets of light. And there, in the distance, beneath the ghostly light, Bob saw the herd of mustangs. As if sensing their presence, Warrior rose into the air once again, this time not challenging the heavens but almost in greeting. Bob thought he saw the mustang stallion rise in response as the earth shuddered from the sound of thunder.

Then the rain came as hard and stinging as remorse. Quickly Bob put on his poncho, and turning Warrior away from the wind and the rain, waited. The storm would pass soon. Or it wouldn't. There was nothing to do but wait.

Finally the rain slowed and then stopped. The clouds thinned, and there, high in the sky, the moon appeared as white as grief. Bob slept in the saddle while Warrior grazed on the wet grasses.

Vocabulary Development

ravine (ruh VEEN) _n._ a long, deep hollow in Earth's surface
remorse (rih MAWRS) _n._ a deep sense of guilt felt over a wrong one has done
canteen (kan TEEN) _n._ small container used to hold water

The sun rose into a clear sky and Bob was awake immediately. The storm would have washed away the tracks, but they had been going toward the big river. He would go there and wait.

By mid-afternoon he could see the ribbon of river shining in the distance. He stopped, needing only to be close enough to see the horses when they came to drink. Toward evening he saw a trail of rolling, dusty clouds.

In front was the mustang herd. As it reached the water, the stallion slowed and stopped. He looked around, his head raised, nostrils flared, smelling the air. He turned in Bob's direction and sniffed the air again.

Bob tensed. Had he come too close too soon? If the stallion smelled anything new, he and the herd would be gone and Bob would never find them again. The stallion seemed to be looking directly at him. Bob was too far away to be seen, but he did not even blink his eyes, afraid the stallion would hear the sound. Finally the stallion began drinking and the other horses followed. Bob let his breath out slowly. He had been accepted.

The next morning he crossed the river and picked up the herd's trail. He moved Warrior slowly, without sound, without dust. Soon he saw them grazing. He stopped. The horses did not notice him. After a while he moved forward, slowly, quietly. The stallion raised his head. Bob stopped.

When the stallion went back to grazing, Bob moved forward again. All day Bob watched the herd, moving only when it moved but always coming closer. The mustangs sensed his presence. They thought he was a horse.

So did he.

The following morning Bob and Warrior walked into the herd. The stallion eyed them for a moment. Then, as if to test this newcomer, he led the herd off in a gallop. Bob lay flat across Warrior's back and moved with the herd. If anyone had been watching, they would not have noticed a man among the horses.

When the herd set out early the next day, it was moving slowly. If the horses had been going faster, it would not have happened.

TAKE NOTES

Stop to Reflect

What causes the "rolling, dusty clouds" that Bob sees in the distance?

_____

_____

_____

Oral Traditions

Folk tales often feature heroes, adventure, magic, or romance. Which two characteristics appear in the story?

_____

_____

Briefly describe each characteristic.

_____

_____

_____

_____

_____

Reading Check

Why does Bob think he has come too close to the herd of wild horses? Underline the answer in the text.

Oral Traditions

Folk tales are entertaining stories that tell about shared ideas of a culture. What cultural value is described in the bracketed paragraph?

_____

_____

_____

_____

Oral Traditions

A **universal theme** includes a message about life that most people understand. A conflict between people or animals is a common theme in literature. Three separate conflicts occur in the text on this page. Write who is involved in each conflict.

_____

_____

_____

Reading Check ✏️

Why does Bob try to take over the herd when he does? Circle the answer in the text.

The colt fell to the ground as if she had stepped into a hole and broken her leg. Bob and the horses heard the chilling sound of the rattles. Rattlesnakes didn't always give a warning before they struck. Sometimes, when someone or something came too close, they bit with the fury of fear.

The horses whinnied and pranced nervously, smelling the snake and death among them. Bob saw the rattler, as beautiful as a necklace, sliding silently through the tall grasses. He made no move to kill it. Everything in nature had the right to protect itself, especially when it was afraid.

The stallion galloped to the colt. He pushed at her. The colt struggled to get up, but fell to her side, shivering and kicking feebly with her thin legs. Quickly she was dead.

Already vultures circled high in the sky. The mustangs milled aimlessly. The colt's mother whinnied, refusing to leave the side of her colt. The stallion wanted to move the herd from there, and pushed the mare with his head. She refused to budge, and he nipped her on the rump. She skittered away. Before she could return to the colt, the stallion bit her again, this time harder. She ran toward the herd. He bit her a third time, and the herd was off. As they galloped away, Bob looked back. The vultures were descending from the sky as gracefully as dusk.

It was time to take over the herd. The stallion would not have the heart to fight fiercely so soon after the death of the colt. Bob galloped Warrior to the front and wheeled around, forcing the stallion to stop quickly. The herd, confused, slowed and stopped also.

Bob raised Warrior to stand high on his back legs, fetlocks pawing and kicking the air. The stallion's eyes widened. He snorted and pawed the ground, surprised and uncertain. Bob charged at the stallion.

Both horses rose on hind legs, teeth bared as they kicked at each other. When they came down, Bob charged Warrior at the stallion again, pushing him backward. Bob rushed yet again.

The stallion neighed loudly, and nipped Warrior on the neck. Warrior snorted angrily, reared, and kicked out with his forelegs, striking the stallion on the nose. Still maintaining his balance, Warrior struck again and again. The mustang stallion cried out in pain. Warrior pushed hard against the stallion. The stallion lost his footing and fell to the earth. Warrior rose, neighing triumphantly, his front legs pawing as if seeking for the rungs on which he could climb a ladder into the sky.

The mustang scrambled to his feet, beaten. He snorted weakly. When Warrior made as if to attack again, the stallion turned, whinnied weakly, and trotted away.

Bob was now the herd's leader, but would they follow him? He rode slowly at first, then faster and faster. The mustangs followed as if being led on ropes.

Throughout that day and the next he rode with the horses. For Bob there was only the bulging of the horses' dark eyes, the quivering of their flesh, the rippling of muscles and bending of bones in their bodies. He was now sky and plains and grass and river and horse.

When his food was almost gone, Bob led the horses on one last ride, a dark surge of flesh flashing across the plains like black lightning. Toward evening he led the herd up the steep hillside, onto the bluff, and down the slope toward the big corral. The cowboys heard him coming and opened the corral gate. Bob led the herd, but at the last moment he swerved Warrior aside, and the mustangs flowed into the fenced enclosure. The cowboys leaped and shouted as they quickly closed the gate.

Bob rode away from them and back up to the bluff. He stopped and stared out onto the plains. Warrior reared and whinnied loudly.

"I know," Bob whispered. "I know. Maybe someday."

Maybe someday they would ride with the mustangs, ride to that forever place where land and sky kissed, and then ride on. Maybe someday.

Reader's Response: How would you feel if you rode for days with a herd of wild mustangs?

_____

_____

_____

Oral Traditions

It seems that the *opposite* of **personification** happens in the bracketed passage. Bob takes on certain traits of the horse. What are these traits?

_____

_____

_____

_____

Stop to Reflect

Bob and Warrior want to ride free with the mustangs. What do Bob and Warrior find attractive about a mustang's life?

_____

_____

_____

_____

Oral Traditions

This **folk tale** uses vivid images to tell an entertaining story. The author describes Warrior as "neighing triumphantly." What image does the author use to show Warrior's feeling of triumph? Underline the answer in the text.

Folk Literature

1. **Infer:** What danger does Bob face in approaching the mustangs too soon?

_____

_____

2. **Compare:** Why does it seem that Warrior's goals or dreams are the same as Bob's?

_____

_____

3. **Oral Tradition:** List qualities about cowboy Bob that make him seem real. List qualities that exaggerate his abilities and make him a **legend**. Complete this diagram.

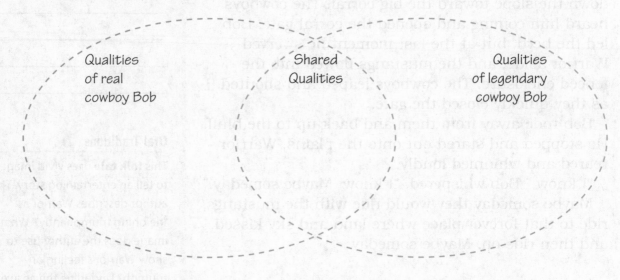

Qualities of real cowboy Bob

Shared Qualities

Qualities of legendary cowboy Bob

4. **Oral Tradition:** What is the **universal theme** in this **folk tale**?

_____

_____

Reading

Follow these steps to gather information for a **reading** of passages from some of Julius Lester's books.

- Search the Internet to find background information about Julius Lester and his books. Begin by finding Lester's home page. Type the following in your browser's address box: http://members.authorsguild.net/ juliuslester/. Press the enter key. Click on the "My Books" link to see a list of Lester's books and a brief description of each book. Also, select a search engine for further research. Type "*Julius Lester*" AND *books* or "*Julius Lester*" AND "*folk tales*" in the search box. Choose reliable sites when the results come up. These include sites about the author and the sources used to make the site. Write the titles of books that interest you and a description of each book.

Book: _____

_____

Book: _____

_____

Book: _____

_____

- Go to the library. Find a computer and the online catalogue. Select an author search. Type *Lester, Julius* in the search box. Press the enter key. A list of Lester's books will come up. Write the titles of the books you want and the information that will help you find each book. Then find the books on the shelf.

- Read as many of Lester's stories as interest you. Look for interesting **dialect**. Dialect is the language spoken in a particular region. Choose one of Lester's books to read. Then read the entire book.

- Select some passages that interest you. Practice reading the passages aloud.

- Watch the video interview with Julius Lester. Then review your source material. Use this information to help prepare for your reading.

The Tiger Who Would Be King • The Ant and the Dove • The Lion and the Bulls • A Crippled Boy

Reading Skill

A **cause** is an event, an action, or a feeling that produces a result. The result is called an **effect**. Sometimes an effect is the result of a number of causes. To help you identify the relationship between an event and its causes, **reread** important passages in the work, looking for connections. Use this chart to record the events and actions that produce an effect.

Cause	Cause	Cause

Effect

Literary Analysis

Fables and folk tales are part of the oral tradition of passing songs, stories, and poems from generation to generation by word of mouth.

- **Fables** are brief stories that teach a lesson or contain a moral. They often feature animal characters.

- **Folk tales** feature heroes, adventure, magic, and romance. These stories often entertain while teaching a lesson.

Some fables and folk tales have **ironic**, or surprising, endings because they do not turn out as you expect.

The Tiger Who Would Be King • The Ant and the Dove

Summary "The Tiger Who Would Be King" tells the story of a fight among the animals to show that sometimes no one wins. "The Ant and the Dove" shows that a good deed can be repaid at an unexpected time.

 ## Writing About the Big Question

How much do our communities shape us? These tales use animal characters to teach lessons about people struggling against each other and about people working together. Complete this sentence:

When members of a **community** cooperate and **support** one another, they

can _____.

Note-taking Guide

Use this chart to list the actions taken by the characters in "The Tiger Who Would Be King" and "The Ant and the Dove". Then, list why each character takes the actions.

Character	Action taken	Motivation, or why the action is taken
Tiger	Fights the lion	Wants to be king of the beasts
Lion		
Dove		
Ant		

The Tiger Who Would Be King
James Thurber

Activate Prior Knowledge

Describe a time when you wanted something so badly that you thought you would do anything to get it.

_____

_____

_____

Reading Skill

A **cause** is an event, an action, or a feeling that produces a result. The result is called an **effect**. What causes Leo to defend his crown?

_____

_____

Literary Analysis

A **fable** uses animals to tell a story that teaches a lesson or a moral. What conflict or problem does this fable address?

_____

_____

Reading Check

Why do the animals of the jungle begin to fight? Underline the text that tells you.

One morning the tiger woke up in the jungle and told his mate that he was king of beasts.

"Leo, the lion, is king of beasts," she said.

"We need a change," said the tiger. "The creatures are crying for a change."

The tigress listened but she could hear no crying, except that of her cubs.

"I'll be king of beasts by the time the moon rises," said the tiger. "It will be a yellow moon with black stripes, in my honor."

"Oh, sure," said the tigress as she went to look after her young, one of whom, a male, very like his father, had got an imaginary thorn in his paw.

The tiger <u>prowled</u> through the jungle till he came to the lion's den. "Come out," he roared, "and greet the king of beasts! The king is dead, long live the king!"

Inside the den, the lioness woke her mate. "The king is here to see you," she said.

"What king?" he inquired, sleepily.

"The king of beasts," she said.

"I am the king of beasts," roared Leo, and he charged out of the den to defend his crown against the pretender.

It was a terrible fight, and it lasted until the setting of the sun. All the animals of the jungle joined in, some taking the side of the tiger and others the side of the lion. Every creature from the aardvark to the zebra took part in the struggle to overthrow the lion or to <u>repulse</u> the tiger, and some did not know which they were fighting for, and some fought for both, and some fought whoever was nearest, and some fought for the sake of fighting.

"What are we fighting for?" someone asked the aardvark.

"The old order," said the aardvark.

"What are we dying for?" someone asked the zebra.

Vocabulary Development

prowled (prowld) *v.* moved around quietly and secretly

repulse (ri PULS) *v.* drive back; repel an attack

"The new order," said the zebra.

When the moon rose, fevered and gibbous,[1] it shone upon a jungle in which nothing stirred except a macaw[2] and a cockatoo,[3] screaming in horror. All the beasts were dead except the tiger, and his days were numbered and his time was ticking away. He was monarch of all he surveyed, but it didn't seem to mean anything.

MORAL: You can't very well be king of beasts if there aren't any.

The Ant and the Dove
Russian Folk Tale
Leo Tolstoy

A thirsty ant went to the stream to drink. Suddenly it got caught in a whirlpool and was almost carried away.

At that moment a dove was passing by with a twig in its beak. The dove dropped the twig for the tiny insect to grab hold of. So it was that the ant was saved.

A few days later a hunter was about to catch the dove in his net. When the ant saw what was happening, it walked right up to the man and bit him on the foot. <u>Startled</u>, the man dropped the net. And the dove, thinking that you never can tell how or when a kindness may be repaid, flew away.

Vocabulary Development
startled (STAHRT uhld) *adj.* surprised

1. **gibbous** (GIB uhs) *adj.* more than half but less than completely illuminated.
2. **macaw** (muh KAW) *n.* bright-colored, harsh-voiced parrot of Central or South America.
3. **cockatoo** (kahk uh TOO) *n.* crested parrot with white plumage tinged with yellow or pink.

© Pearson Education

Stop to Reflect

What lesson can readers learn from "The Tiger Who Would Be King"?

_____

_____

_____

Literary Analysis

A **folk tale** often has heroes, adventure, magic, and romance to tell a story that teaches a lesson. Who is the hero of "The Ant and the Dove"?

_____

_____

Reading Skill

What is the **effect** of the dove's action in "The Ant and the Dove"?

_____

_____

Reading Check

How did the ant save the dove? Underline the text that tells you.

The Tiger Who Would Be King • The Ant and the Dove

1. **Apply:** Some animals in "The Tiger Who Would Be King" fight without thinking about the outcome of their actions. What human qualities does Thurber show in these animals?

   _____

   _____

2. **Infer:** The dove in "The Ant and the Dove" drops a twig for the ant. How does this action save the ant?

   _____

3. **Reading Skill:** Identify several **causes** of the fight in the jungle in "The Tiger Who Would Be King."

   _____

   _____

4. **Literary Analysis:** Use this chart to identify the elements of **fables** and **folk tales** in the two stories.

Title	Characters	Moral or Lesson

Writing: Fable

Write a **fable** that teaches the same lesson as either "The Tiger Who Would Be King" or "The Ant and the Dove." Answer the following questions to help you write your fable.

- What is the lesson that you want your readers to learn?

  _____

- Who are the characters in your fable?

  _____

- How do the characters get in trouble?

  _____

  _____

- How do the characters learn a lesson?

  _____

  _____

Listening and Speaking: Oral Report

Prepare an **oral report** on the life of either James Thurber or Leo Tolstoy. Complete the following chart to prepare your oral report.

Author:		
Childhood Events	Life as a Writer	Photos or images
Other pieces to read by this auther:		

The Lion and the Bulls • A Crippled Boy

Summary A lion spreads rumors to break apart a group of bulls in "The Lion and the Bulls." "A Crippled Boy" shows a lonely, disabled boy with a great skill. His skill earns him a place at the king's palace.

Writing About the Big Question

How much do our communities shape us? In both of these tales, characters look for ways to achieve a goal. Complete this sentence:

If a person achieves success by taking advantage of others in his or her

group, the result can be _____.

Note-taking Guide

Use this chart to record details from "The Lion and the Bulls" and "A Crippled Boy."

Character	What problem does he face?	How does he solve his problem?
Lions		
Theo		

The Lion and the Bulls • A Crippled Boy

1. **Infer:** What human qualities does Aesop give the animals in "The Lion and the Bulls"?

_____

_____

2. **Analyze:** Name two ways in which Theo in "A Crippled Boy" benefits from developing his talent.

_____

_____

3. **Reading Skill:** What is the **effect** of the bulls' moving away from one another in "The Lion and the Bulls"?

_____

_____

4. **Literary Analysis:** Use this chart to identify the elements of **fable** and **folk tale** in the two stories.

Title	Characters	Moral or Lesson

Writing: Fable

Write a **fable** that teaches the same lesson as either "The Lion and the Bulls" or "A Crippled Boy." Answer the following questions to help you write your fable.

- What is the lesson that you want your readers to learn?

  _____

- Who are the characters in your fable?

  _____

- How do the characters get in trouble?

  _____

  _____

- How do the characters learn a lesson?

  _____

  _____

Listening and Speaking: Oral Report

Use the following activity to record information for your **report** about one of the authors.

- Give some information about the author.

  _____

  _____

- Why did this person become a writer?

  _____

  _____

- What will you read and why?

  _____

  _____

Prologue from The Whale Rider • Arachne

Reading Skill

A **cause** is an event, an action, or a feeling that makes something happen. An **effect** is what happens. Sometimes an **effect** can become the cause of another event. For example, seeing a person lift a heavy object can cause you to offer help. Your help can then cause that person to feel good.

As you read, look for clue words such as *because*, *so*, and *as a result* to signal a cause-and-effect relationship. **Ask questions** such as "What happened?" and "Why did this happen?" to help you follow the cause-and-effect relationships.

Literary Analysis

Myths are fictional tales that describe the actions of gods or heroes. Every culture has its own myths. A myth can do one or more of the following:

- tell how the universe or culture began
- explain something in nature, such as thunder
- teach a lesson
- express a value, such as courage

As you read, use this chart to analyze the characteristics of myths.

Characters	Explanation

Myth

Value	Lesson

Arachne
Olivia E. Coolidge

Summary This myth describes how spiders came to be. In this tale, a young girl named Arachne weaves a beautiful cloth. She brags because she is proud of her cloth. Her bragging makes the goddess Athene angry. Athene punishes Arachne for her pride.

❓ Writing About the Big Question

How much do our communities shape us?
Like many myths, "Arachne" teaches an important lesson. Complete this sentence:

Stories that are passed down from **generation** to generation often teach

lessons about such **values** as _____

_____.

Note-taking Guide
Use this chart to record details about Arachne and Athene from the myth.

	Arachne	Athene
Who she is	Young Greek woman	Greek goddess of wisdom, skills, and warfare
What she looks like		
How she acts		

Arachne
Olivia E. Coolidge

Arachne was a maiden who became famous throughout Greece, though she was neither wellborn nor beautiful and came from no great city. She lived in an <u>obscure</u> little village, and her father was a humble dyer of wool. In this he was very skillful, producing many varied shades, while above all he was famous for the clear, bright scarlet which is made from shellfish, and which was the most glorious of all the colors used in ancient Greece. Even more skillful than her father was Arachne. It was her task to spin the fleecy wool into a fine, soft thread and to weave it into cloth on the high, standing loom within the cottage. Arachne was small and pale from much working. Her eyes were light and her hair was a dusty brown, yet she was quick and graceful, and her fingers, roughened as they were, went so fast that it was hard to follow their flickering movements. So soft and even was her thread, so fine her cloth, so gorgeous her embroidery, that soon her products were known all over Greece. No one had ever seen the like of them before.

At last Arachne's fame became so great that people used to come from far and wide to watch her working. Even the graceful nymphs[1] would steal in from stream or forest and peep shyly through the dark doorway, watching in wonder the white arms of Arachne as she stood at the loom and threw the shuttle from hand to hand between the hanging threads, or drew out the long wool, fine as a hair, from the distaff[2] as she sat spinning. "Surely Athene[3] herself must have taught her," people would murmur to one another. "Who else could know the secret of such marvelous skill?"

Vocabulary Development

obscure (uhb SKYOOR) *adj.* not well-known

1. **nymphs** (nimfz) *n.* minor nature goddesses, represented as beautiful maidens living in rivers, trees, and mountains.
2. **distaff** (DIS taf) *n.* stick on which flax or wool is wound for spinning.
3. **Athene** (uh THEE nuh) *n.* Greek goddess of wisdom, skills, and warfare.

Activate Prior Knowledge

Think about a time when someone you knew was bragging. How did this person's bragging make other people feel?

_____

_____

Reading Skill

A **cause** is an event, an action, or a feeling that makes something happen. An **effect** is what happens. What causes Arachne's work to be known all over Greece?

_____

_____

Literary Analysis

Myths are fictional tales that describe the actions of gods or heroes. Read the bracketed paragraph. Underline a reference that tells you that this story is a myth.

Reading Check

What was Arachne's father famous for? Underline the text that tells you.

Literary Analysis

Myths often teach about values. What value gets Arachne into trouble?

_____

_____

How did the Greeks probably feel about this value?

_____

_____

_____

Stop to Reflect

Why is Arachne upset when people say that Athene must have taught her to spin?

_____

_____

Reading Skill

Why does the old woman speak to Arachne? What **effect** do her words have on Arachne?

_____

_____

_____

Reading Check

What does the text say that Arachne lived for? Underline the sentence that tells you.

Arachne was used to being wondered at, and she was immensely proud of the skill that had brought so many to look on her. Praise was all she lived for, and it displeased her greatly that people should think anyone, even a goddess, could teach her anything. Therefore when she heard them murmur, she would stop her work and turn round indignantly to say, "With my own ten fingers I gained this skill, and by hard practice from early morning till night. I never had time to stand looking as you people do while another maiden worked. Nor if I had, would I give Athene credit because the girl was more skillful than I. As for Athene's weaving, how could there be finer cloth or more beautiful embroidery than mine? If Athene herself were to come down and compete with me, she could do no better than I."

One day when Arachne turned round with such words, an old woman answered her, a gray old woman, bent and very poor, who stood leaning on a staff and peering at Arachne amid the crowd of onlookers. "Reckless girl," she said, "how dare you claim to be equal to the immortal gods themselves? I am an old woman and have seen much. Take my advice and ask pardon of Athene for your words. Rest content with your fame of being the best spinner and weaver that <u>mortal</u> eyes have ever beheld."

"Stupid old woman," said Arachne indignantly, "who gave you a right to speak in this way to me? It is easy to see that you were never good for anything in your day, or you would not come here in poverty and rags to gaze at my skill. If Athene resents my words, let her answer them herself. I have challenged her to a contest, but she, of course, will not come. It is easy for the gods to avoid matching their skill with that of men."

At these words the old woman threw down her staff and stood erect. The wondering onlookers saw her grow tall and fair and stand clad in long robes of dazzling white. They were terribly afraid as they realized that they stood in the presence of Athene. Arachne herself flushed red for a moment, for she had

Vocabulary Development
mortal (MAWR tuhl) *n.* referring to humans, who must eventually die

never really believed that the goddess would hear her. Before the group that was gathered there she would not give in; so pressing her pale lips together in obstinacy and pride, she led the goddess to one of the great looms and set herself before the other. Without a word both began to thread the long woolen strands that hang from the rollers, and between which the shuttle[4] moves back and forth. Many skeins lay heaped beside them to use, bleached white, and gold, and scarlet, and other shades, varied as the rainbow. Arachne had never thought of giving credit for her success to her father's skill in dyeing, though in actual truth the colors were as remarkable as the cloth itself.

Soon there was no sound in the room but the breathing of the onlookers, the whirring of the shuttles, and the creaking of the wooden frames as each pressed the thread up into place or tightened the pegs by which the whole was held straight. The excited crowd in the doorway began to see that the skill of both in truth was very nearly equal, but that, however the cloth might turn out, the goddess was the quicker of the two. A pattern of many pictures was growing on her loom. There was a border of twined branches of the olive, Athene's favorite tree, while in the middle, figures began to appear. As they looked at the glowing colors, the spectators realized that Athene was weaving into her pattern a last warning to Arachne. The central figure was the goddess herself competing with Poseidon[5] for possession of the city of Athens; but in the four corners were mortals who had tried to strive with gods and pictures of the awful fate that had overtaken them. The goddess ended a little before Arachne and stood back from her marvelous work to see what the maiden was doing.

Never before had Arachne been matched against anyone whose skill was equal, or even nearly equal

Vocabulary Development

obstinacy (AHB stuh nuh see) *n.* stubbornness

4. **shuttle** (SHUT uhl) *n.* instrument used in weaving to carry thread back and forth.

5. **Poseidon** (poh SY duhn) *n.* Greek god of the seas and of horses.

Reading Skill

Why does Athene sit down at the loom to weave? What do you think the **effect** of this will be?

Literary Analysis

Myths can describe the actions of gods. What do you think it says about the Greek gods that Athene appears when Arachne is speaking badly about her?

_____

_____

Stop to Reflect

What do you think is the importance of Athene's pattern?

_____

_____

_____

Reading Check

What does Arachne realize about the colors her father creates as she sits down at the loom to weave? Underline the sentence that tells you.

Reading Skill

What **effect** does Arachne's design have on Athene? Underline the text that tells you what happens when Athene realizes what Arachne's design is.

Stop to Reflect

In ancient times, what lessons might this myth have taught readers?

_____

_____

Reading Check ✎

According to this myth, where do spiders come from? Underline the sentence that tells you.

to her own. As she stole glances from time to time at Athene and saw the goddess working swiftly, calmly, and always a little faster than herself, she became angry instead of frightened, and an evil thought came into her head. Thus as Athene stepped back a pace to watch Arachne finishing her work, she saw that the maiden had taken for her design a pattern of scenes which showed evil or unworthy actions of the gods, how they had deceived fair maidens, resorted to trickery, and appeared on earth from time to time in the form of poor and humble people. When the goddess saw this insult glowing in bright colors on Arachne's loom, she did not wait while the cloth was judged, but stepped forward, her gray eyes blazing with anger, and tore Arachne's work across. Then she struck Arachne across the face. Arachne stood there a moment, struggling with anger, fear, and pride. "I will not live under this insult," she cried, and seizing a rope from the wall, she made a noose and would have hanged herself.

The goddess touched the rope and touched the maiden. "Live on, wicked girl," she said. "Live on and spin, both you and your descendants. When men look at you they may remember that it is not wise to strive with Athene." At that the body of Arachne shriveled up, and her legs grew tiny, spindly, and distorted. There before the eyes of the spectators hung a little dusty brown spider on a slender thread.

All spiders descend from Arachne, and as the Greeks watched them spinning their thread wonderfully fine, they remembered the contest with Athene and thought that it was not right for even the best of men to claim equality with the gods.

Reader's Response: If you were Arachne, would you have challenged the goddess Athene? Explain.

_____

_____

_____

Arachne

1. **Analyze:** Arachne refuses to accept the advice of the old woman. What character traits does Arachne reveal through this behavior?

_____

_____

2. **Infer:** What is Athene's original intention toward Arachne?

_____

_____

3. **Reading Skill:** Complete the chart to show **causes** and **effects** in "Arachne."

Causes	Effects
Arachne challenges Athene.	
	Arachne's design shows unworthy actions performed by the gods.
Athene touches the rope and touches Arachne.	

4. **Literary Analysis:** What beliefs and values are taught in this **myth**?

_____

_____

Writing: Essay

Write a brief **essay** about the differences between learning lessons from stories and learning lessons from experience. Answer the following questions to help you organize your essay. Use these notes to help you complete the essay.

- What lessons from your experiences will you write about?

  _____

- How will you introduce these lessons in your essay?

  _____

- How will you compare these lessons with lessons learned from stories?

  _____

- Which do you believe is better: learning a lesson from a story or learning a lesson from experience? Explain your answer.

  _____

  _____

Research and Technology: Annotated Bibliography

Use the following chart to gather information for the annotated bibliography.

Book or Other Source	Description

Prologue from The Whale Rider
Witi Ihimaera

Summary This myth explains the beginnings of the Maori people of New Zealand. It tells of a man who rides a whale through the ocean and onto land. It also explores the wonders of the land and the ocean.

 Writing About the Big Question

How much do our communities shape us? Legends and myths, which are passed down through generations. They reveal the beliefs and ideas that are important to cultural communities. Complete this sentence:

Ancient legends about a culture's **values** can **influence** modern people to

_____

because _____.

Note-taking Guide:
Use this chart to record details about the selection.

What do both the land and sea feel?	Where do the fairy people go?	When is the first sighting made?	How does the flying fish know that the time has come?	Who comes to the land on the whale?
Both land and sea feel a great emptiness and yearning.				

Prologue from The Whale Rider

1. **Analyze:** What effect is created by giving human feelings to nonhuman subjects, such as the land and sea?

_____

_____

2. **Infer:** Why are the land and sea excited about the arrival of the Ancients?

_____

_____

3. **Reading Skill:** Complete the chart to show **causes** and **effects** in _The Whale Rider_ prologue.

Causes	Effects
The land and sea feel a great emptiness.	
	Flying fish leap to look beyond the horizon.
The whale rider says a prayer over the last spear.	

4. **Literary Analysis:** What values are taught in this **myth**?

_____

_____

Writing: Essay

Write a short **essay**. Compare your experience of waiting for something exciting to happen with the sense of anticipation and joy expressed in the selection. Answer the following questions to help you organize your comparison. Use these notes to help you complete the essay.

- What experience will you write about?

  _____

- How will you introduce this experience in your essay?

  _____

- How will you compare your feelings with the feelings expressed in *The Whale Rider* prologue?

  _____

- Compare the lesson you learned from your experience with what is learned in *The Whale Rider* prologue. How will you relate the two in your essay?

  _____

Research and Technology: Annotated Bibliography

Use the following chart to gather information for the annotated bibliography.

Book or Other Source	Description

Press Releases

About Press Releases

A **press release** is a document written by a company. It gives information to news organizations. A press release is also called a news release. It might tell about:

- an upcoming event
- the winners of awards
- a change in leadership at a company

The purpose of a press release is to persuade news organizations to report on an event. Sometimes a newspaper will use a press release to create a short news article.

Reading Skill

An outline is a list of main ideas and important details. When you **create an outline,** it can help you remember the information you read.

Follow these steps to create an outline:

1. Find the main ideas in the text.
2. List subtopics for each main idea.
3. List important details that support the subtopics.

Use the graphic organizer below to help you take notes as you read.

I. First Main Idea
A. First subtopic
1. supporting detail
2. supporting detail
B. Second subtopic
1. supporting detail
2. supporting detail

News Release

Satellites and Sea Lions
Working Together to Improve Ocean Models

Features:
- informational reading
- current or breaking news
- text written for a general or a specific audience

News Release
Updated 2/27/07

The best oceanographers in the world never studied at a university. Yet they know how to navigate expertly along oceanic fronts, the invisible boundaries between waters of different temperatures and densities. These ocean experts can find rich fishing in places and at depths that others would assume are barren. They regularly visit the most interesting and dynamic parts of the sea.

Sea lions, seals, sharks, tuna, and other top ocean predators share some of their experiences with human researchers, thanks to electronic tags. Besides tracking the animals, these sensors also collect oceanographic data, such as temperature and salinity. Scientists are beginning to incorporate this rich store of information into ocean models providing new insights into the inner workings of the ocean and the lives of its creatures.

Note the details about the scientists' goals.

"Our goal is to produce a three-dimensional model of the ocean," says JPL oceanographer Dr. Yi Chao. Chao uses data from satellites, ships, buoys and floats to map the currents, heat content and different water densities beneath the ocean surface. When Chao heard Dr. Dan Costa, a professor of marine biology at the University of California, Santa Cruz, present some of his animal tagging data at a scientific meeting a few years ago, he saw an opportunity to improve his ocean models. Costa recognized a chance to get a clearer picture of the place where his research subjects live. [. . .]

The research collaboration now includes Dr. Barbara Block, a professor of marine sciences at Stanford University, Palo Alto, Calif., and the scientists have added tagging data collected from tuna and sharks to their studies. Together with a group called TOPP, for Tagging of Pacific Pelagics, they are now working to expand the use of environmental and biological data collected by ocean inhabitants.

"We are at the forefront of knowing how animals use the ocean," says Costa. "But we want to understand the environment better. We still see the ocean primarily as deep or shallow or

data sets have small errors, others much larger errors. Figuring out how to put these in our system is a challenge," he says. "But five years from now, we should be able to see the ocean the way a turtle sees it."

"As we are getting more data from the sea and improving our computer models," says Chao, "we should be able to make routine ocean forecasts, similar to what meteorologists have been doing in the past few decades. People who open the newspaper or turn on the TV in the morning will see the updated ocean forecast and make appropriate decisions as they plan their activities on the sea."

near-shore or offshore. But just as there are different habitats on land, the ocean has fine-scale features that are very important to animals," he explains. "We want to be able to look at the ocean and say the equivalent of "this is a grassland" or "this is a forest.""

In late January, Costa and his research group headed up the California coast to begin tagging elephant seals and collecting tags that were deployed last spring. The work is strictly regulated to ensure that the animals are protected from harm, and it requires a permit from the National Marine Fisheries Service. [. . .]

"Marine scientists have been tracking marine animals for years," says Chao. "It's an interesting challenge, though, to use the data. There are all sorts— from tuna, sharks, seals—you name it. Some of these

What is most important about using marine animals as ocean sensors is that the work benefits the animals, Costa explains. "Collaborations between biologists like Barbara Block and me and physical oceanographers like Yi are critical for understanding why the animals go where they go," he says, "as we need to know and understand the ocean physics and its relationship to climate processes. Further, the ability to understand how climate change is affecting the world oceans is not only of benefit to humans, but is vital for trying figure out what is going to happen to habitat of marine animals."

> This paragraph lists details about the research's benefit to animals.

THE BIG ? **How much do our communities shape us?**

(a) According to the news release, what community is conducting the research? **(b)** Why might this community want people to know about their work? Explain.

Red Cross Helps Florida Residents Recover From Tornadoes

by Arindam Mukherjee
Staff Writer, American Red Cross

Residents are beginning to clean up and recover possessions from homes damaged by a series of tornadoes that ripped through four Florida counties on Christmas day.

More than 200 mobile homes in and around DeLand as well as dozens of single-family homes, at least three apartment buildings and a local university and flight school in the area were damaged when four tornadoes blew through Columbia, Pasco, Lake and Volusia counties in Florida on Monday, Dec. 25, 2006. According to the National Weather Service, winds topped 120 mph—strong enough to flip over teaching planes at the flight school in Daytona Beach.

The Red Cross Response

Florida's Coast to Coast chapter of the American Red Cross responded immediately, setting up emergency shelters for those driven from their homes by the tornadoes.

"Our immediate need was to provide shelter and feeding to the people," said the chapter's Director of Public Affairs Pam Hamlin. "We helped open two shelters, one in Daytona Beach and the other in DeLand, Volusia Co., and are feeding people at the affected sites."

Dianna Van Horn, who is a Public Affairs Manager with the American Red Cross currently helping support Florida's Coast to Coast chapter in this response, indicated that the first day that the centers were open, Thursday, was slow. She expects the volume to pick up as word spreads.

Red Cross feeding operations also continue in impacted areas with the chapter delivering meals in Daytona and DeLand, where the bulk of damage occurred, via Red Cross emergency response vehicles. Also, the Red Cross has begun conducting damage assessments that will help in determining what types of assistance residents may need in order to beginning getting their lives back to normal.

Making a Difference

Van Horn expressed pride at seeing the Red Cross volunteers making a difference in the lives of residents in these Florida communities.

"It's interesting to me that we're preparing to end one year and begin another doing what we do best—responding to people in crisis after a disaster," said Van Horn. "Our own volunteers willingly stop their lives—putting everything on hold—to help those who have been forced to restart their lives in the coming year as a result of these tornadoes."

In times of disaster, the Red Cross provides emergency shelter, food, water and can help those affected obtain replacement medications as well as clothing, cleaning supplies and other essentials such as hygiene products, linens and blankets. As important as helping the body is, looking after the emotional and mental well-being of disas-

ter survivors is another priority for the Red Cross. Over the years, the Red Cross has learned that toys such as stuffed animals can bring tremendous comfort to those enduring a disaster. It is one more small way to help get them on the road to recovery.

Staying Safe in the Aftermath

As it becomes safe and accessible, more residents will return to their homes and communities to assess damage, clean up or recover belongings. The Red Cross urges caution and offers the following tips to help residents stay in the aftermath of the tornadoes:

- Listen to local and emergency officials—Continue to use a portable radio or television to monitor local news for updates, and follow instructions from emergency officials.

- Put on protective clothing—Put on long pants, a long-sleeved shirt, sturdy shoes and work gloves to protect yourself from broken items and debris.

- Inspect your home—Inspect your home for damage and get everyone out if it is unsafe.

- Watch for hazards in your neighborhood—Look out for fallen electrical wires, broken gas lines and flash flooding—foliage collecting in sewers this time of year can compound drainage problems. Report downed lines immediately so that utilities can be turned off at the source. Avoid hazardous debris such as broken glass or spilled chemicals and do not go into damaged buildings.

A comprehensive list of tips and additional information about staying safe after a tornado are available online in the "Disaster Services" section of the Red Cross Web site under the heading "After a Disaster."

Weather tragedies such as this are a stark reminder that disaster can strike anywhere and at any time, often without any warning. Preparing ahead of time by getting or assembling an emergency supplies kit, making a plan and being informed about what types of disasters can affect your home and community, can be empowering and make you better able to react when the unexpected occurs.

Thinking About the Press Releases

1. Describe how scientists learn about the experiences of sea lions.

_____

_____

2. List ways to stay safe after tornadoes.

_____

_____

TALK ABOUT IT **Reading Skill**

3. Does the detail *Scientists have added tagging data to their studies* support the idea that "scientists learn much about the ocean from the animals that live there"? Explain.

_____

_____

_____

4. Does the detail *More than 200 mobile homes around DeLand were damaged by tornados* support the idea that "the Red Cross helps Florida resident recover from tornadoes"? Explain.

_____

_____

WRITE ABOUT IT **Timed Writing: Explanation (20 minutes)**

Create an outline of one of the press releases. Then, write a brief summary of the release. Answer the following questions:

• What is the main idea of the press release?

_____

_____

• What are two details that support the main idea?

_____

_____

He Lion, Bruh Bear, and Bruh Rabbit •
Why the Tortoise's Shell Is Not Smooth

Reading Skill

Your **purpose** for reading is the reason you read a text. Sometimes you choose a text based on a purpose you already have. Other times you set a purpose based on the kind of text you are about to read. **Setting a purpose** helps you focus your reading. You might set a purpose to learn about a subject, to gain understanding, to take an action, or simply to read for enjoyment.

Preview the text before you begin to read. Look at the title, the pictures, and the beginnings of paragraphs to get an idea about the focus of the work. This will help you set a purpose or decide whether the text will fit a purpose you already have. Use this chart to record details as you preview the text.

Text Details	What the Details Suggest About the Text
Title	
Pictures	
Beginnings of paragraphs	

Literary Analysis

Personification is the representation of an animal or an object as if it had a human personality, intelligence, or emotions. In folk literature, personification is often used to give human qualities to animal characters. Through the actions of these animal characters, human qualities, behavior, and problems can be illustrated in a humorous way.

Why the Tortoise's Shell Is Not Smooth
Chinua Achebe

Summary All of the birds are invited to a feast in the sky. The hungry, clever tortoise wants to go along. He gets the birds to give him feathers so that he can fly. Tortoise figures out a way to eat the best food before the birds can get to it. The angry birds take back their feathers. Tortoise must figure out how to land softly.

 Writing About the Big Question

How much do our communities shape us? In "Why the Tortoise's Shell is not Smooth," Tortoise tricks the birds and leaves them hungry while he feasts. Complete this sentence:

When an individual takes advantage of the members of his community,

the group may respond by _____

_____.

Note-taking Guide

Fill in this chart with the events that lead to Tortoise's broken shell.

First	Second	Third	Fourth	Last
The birds are invited to a feast in the sky.				Tortoise breaks his shell when he falls to Earth.

Activate Prior Knowledge

Stories grow and change as they are told over and over again. List ways that you have added to a story when you retold it.

_____

_____

_____

Reading Skill

Your **purpose** for reading is the reason that you read a text. What purpose for reading does the story's title present?

_____

_____

Literary Analysis 🔍

The representation of an animal or an object as if it has a human personality, intelligence, or emotions is called **personification**. Circle examples of personification in the bracketed paragraph. What does this personification show about Tortoise?

_____

_____

_____

_____

Why the Tortoise's Shell Is Not Smooth
Chinua Achebe

Low voices, broken now and again by singing, reached Okonkwo (oh KOHN kwoh) from his wives' huts as each woman and her children told folk stories. Ekwefi (e KWE fey) and her daughter, Ezinma (e ZYN mah), sat on a mat on the floor. It was Ekwefi's turn to tell a story.

"Once upon a time," she began, "all the birds were invited to a feast in the sky. They were very happy and began to prepare themselves for the great day. They painted their bodies with red cam wood[1] and drew beautiful patterns on them with dye.

"Tortoise saw all these preparations and soon discovered what it all meant. Nothing that happened in the world of the animals ever escaped his notice; he was full of cunning. As soon as he heard of the great feast in the sky his throat began to itch at the very thought. There was a <u>famine</u> in those days and Tortoise had not eaten a good meal for two moons. His body rattled like a piece of dry stick in his empty shell. So he began to plan how he would go to the sky."

"But he had no wings," said Ezinma.

"Be patient," replied her mother. "That is the story. Tortoise had no wings, but he went to the birds and asked to be allowed to go with them.

"'We know you too well,' said the birds when they had heard him. 'You are full of cunning and you are ungrateful. If we allow you to come with us you will soon begin your mischief.'

"'You do not know me,' said Tortoise. 'I am a changed man. I have learned that a man who makes trouble for others is also making it for himself.'

"Tortoise had a sweet tongue, and within a short time all the birds agreed that he was a changed man,

Vocabulary Development
famine (fam in) _n._ shortage of food

1. **red cam** (kam) **wood** hard West African wood that makes red dye.

and they each gave him a feather, with which he made two wings.

"At last the great day came and Tortoise was the first to arrive at the meeting place. When all the birds had gathered together, they set off in a body. Tortoise was very happy as he flew among the birds, and he was soon chosen as the man to speak for the party because he was a great <u>orator</u>.

"'There is one important thing which we must not forget,' he said as they flew on their way. 'When people are invited to a great feast like this, they take new names for the occasion. Our hosts in the sky will expect us to honor this age-old custom.'

"None of the birds had heard of this custom but they knew that Tortoise, in spite of his failings in other directions, was a widely traveled man who knew the customs of different peoples. And so they each took a new name. When they had all taken, Tortoise also took one. He was to be called All of you.

"At last the party arrived in the sky and their hosts were very happy to see them. Tortoise stood up in his many-colored plumage and thanked them for their invitation. His speech was so <u>eloquent</u> that all the birds were glad they had brought him, and nodded their heads in approval of all he said. Their hosts took him as the king of the birds, especially as he looked somewhat different from the others.

"After kola nuts had been presented and eaten, the people of the sky set before their guests the most delectable dishes Tortoise had ever seen or dreamed of. The soup was brought out hot from the fire and in the very pot in which it had been cooked. It was full of meat and fish. Tortoise began to sniff aloud. There was pounded yam and also yam pottage[2] cooked with palm oil and fresh fish. There were also pots of palm wine. When everything had been set before the

Vocabulary Development

orator (AWR uht uhr) *n.* person who can speak well in public

eloquent (EL uh kwuhnt) *adj.* persuasive and expressive

2. **yam** (yam) **pottage** (PAHT ij) *n.* thick stew made of sweet potatoes.

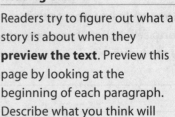

Reading Skill

Readers try to figure out what a story is about when they **preview the text**. Preview this page by looking at the beginning of each paragraph. Describe what you think will happen in this part of the story.

_____

_____

_____

_____

_____

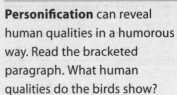

Literary Analysis

Personification can reveal human qualities in a humorous way. Read the bracketed paragraph. What human qualities do the birds show?

_____

_____

_____

Reading Check

Why is Tortoise chosen to speak for the group? Circle the text that tells you.

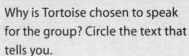

Why the Tortoise's Shell Is Not Smooth **349**

Stop to Reflect

How would you react to the Tortoise's actions if you were one of the birds?

_____

_____

_____

_____

Reading Skill

Read the underlined sentences. What is your **purpose** for continuing to read the story?

_____

_____

_____

_____

Literary Analysis

Personification includes giving human actions and behaviors to animal characters. Circle the text that shows Parrot's cleverness.

guests, one of the people of the sky came forward and tasted a little from each pot. He then invited the birds to eat. But Tortoise jumped to his feet and asked: 'For whom have you prepared this feast?'

"'For all of you,' replied the man.

"Tortoise turned to the birds and said: 'You remember that my name is All of you. The custom here is to serve the spokesman first and the others later. They will serve you when I have eaten.'

"He began to eat and the birds grumbled angrily. The people of the sky thought it must be their custom to leave all the food for their king. And so Tortoise ate the best part of the food and then drank two pots of palm wine, so that he was full of food and drink and his body grew fat enough to fill out his shell.

"The birds gathered round to eat what was left and to peck at the bones he had thrown all about the floor. Some of them were too angry to eat. They chose to fly home on an empty stomach. But before they left, each took back the feather he had lent to Tortoise. And there he stood in his hard shell full of food and wine but without any wings to fly home. He asked the birds to take a message for his wife, but they all refused. In the end Parrot, who had felt more angry than the others, suddenly changed his mind and agreed to take the message.

"'Tell my wife,' said Tortoise, 'to bring out all the soft things in my house and cover the compound[3] with them so that I can jump down from the sky without very great danger.'

"Parrot promised to deliver the message, and then flew away. But when he reached Tortoise's house he told his wife to bring out all the hard things in the house. And so she brought out her husband's hoes, machetes, spears, guns, and even his cannon. Tortoise looked down from the sky and saw his wife bringing things out, but it was too far to see what they were. When all seemed ready he let himself go. He fell and fell and fell until he began to fear that he would never stop falling. And then like the sound of his cannon he crashed on the compound."

"Did he die?" asked Ezinma.

---

3. **compound** (KAHM pownd) *n.* grounds surrounded by buildings.

"No," replied Ekwefi. "His shell broke into pieces. But there was a great medicine man in the neighborhood. Tortoise's wife sent for him and he gathered all the bits of shell and stuck them together. That is why Tortoise's shell is not smooth."

Reader's Response: Do you think the tortoise got what he deserved? Explain your answer.

_____

_____

_____

_____

Reading Skill

Recall the **purpose** you set at the beginning of the story. Restate your purpose here. Did you achieve your purpose while reading? Explain.

_____

_____

_____

_____

_____

Reading Check

Does the Tortoise die? Underline the text that tells you.

Why the Tortoise's Shell Is Not Smooth

1. **Analyze:** Why do the birds decide to help Tortoise go to the feast?

   _____

   _____

2. **Interpret:** Explain how Tortoise's new name allows him to eat before the birds eat.

   _____

   _____

3. **Reading Skill:** Your **purpose** for reading this folk tale may have been to be entertained. How might your purpose be different if you were reading a nonfiction article about tortoises?

   _____

   _____

4. **Literary Analysis:** Complete this chart to analyze the **personification** of one of the animal characters. First, list the ways in which the character behaves like an animal. Then, list the ways in which the character behaves like a human.

Character's Name: Tortoise	
Animal Qualities:	Human Qualities:

Writing: Invitation

Write an **invitation** to the birds' feast in the sky. Use the following questions to help you include details in your invitation.

- What is unusual about the feast?

  _____

- How should guests dress for the feast?

  _____

- What is the reason for such a feast?

  _____

Listening and Speaking: Dramatic Reading

Prepare for the dramatic reading by deciding who will read each part. Make sure that each group member has a copy of the text for the reading. Then, each group member can mark his or her lines on the copy.

- Ekwefi the storyteller (reads the parts that are not dialogue):

  _____

- The Birds: _____

- Tortoise: _____

Answer the following questions about the part that you will read.

- What are my most important lines? _____

- How should I say them? _____

- Which words should I stress for effect? _____

He Lion, Bruh Bear, and Bruh Rabbit
Virginia Hamilton

Summary He Lion scares the animals when he roars. Bruh Bear and Bruh Rabbit try to get he Lion to calm down. They tell him that Man is the king of the forest. He Lion does not believe them. They take him to see Man. Man does something that makes he Lion be quiet.

 Writing About the Big Question

How much do our communities shape us? In "He Lion, Bruh Bear and Bruh Rabbit," all of the animals get together to try to solve a problem. They decide to consult with the wisest members of their community. Complete this sentence:

It makes sense to **involve** a wise member of the **community** in a

problem when _____

_____ .

Note-taking Guide
Fill in this chart to describe each character in the story.

Character	He Lion	Bruh Bear	Bruh Rabbit	Man
Details about the character	He Lion roars loudly and scares the small animals. He thinks that he is king of the forest.			

He Lion, Bruh Bear, and Bruh Rabbit

1. **Infer:** What do Bruh Bear and Bruh Rabbit think of he Lion?

_____

_____

2. **Draw Conclusions:** Based on he Lion's behavior, what lesson does this story appear to teach?

_____

_____

3. **Reading Skill:** What was your **purpose** for reading this folk tale?

_____

_____

4. **Literary Analysis:** Use the chart below to analyze the **personification** of one of the animal characters. First, list the ways in which the character behaves like an animal. Then, list the ways in which the character behaves like a human.

Character's Name: he Lion	
Animal Qualities:	Human Qualities:

Writing: Invitation

Write an **invitation** to the animals' "sit-down talk" at the beginning of the story. Answer the following questions to help you include details in your invitation.

- List a reason for holding the meeting that all of the animals will understand.

  _____

  _____

- Everyone at the meeting should have a chance to speak about his or her concerns. How would you organize the talk so that this can happen?

  _____

  _____

Listening and Speaking: Dramatic Reading

Present a **dramatic reading** of the scene in which he Lion, Bruh Bear, and Bruh Rabbit search for Man. Fill in the spaces in the chart with information about how each character will speak.

he Lion	Bruh Bear	Bruh Rabbit
Tone of voice	Tone of voice	Tone of voice
Speed of speech	Speed of speech	Speed of speech
Level of loudness	Level of loudness	Level of loudness
Words to stress	Words to stress	Words to stress

The Stone • The Three Wishes

Reading Skill

Setting a purpose for reading gives you a focus as you read. One general purpose you may set for all your reading is to **make connections**. Specifically, you can **make connections** between literature and your own experience by identifying the following:

- universal themes about big ideas such as friendship or courage
- details that give you glimpses into cultures other than your own
- ways the ideas in the text apply to your life

Literary Analysis

The theme of a literary work is its central idea or message about life and human nature. A **universal theme** is a message about life that is expressed regularly in many cultures and time periods. Examples of universal themes include the importance of courage, the power of love, and the danger of greed.

Look for a universal theme in a literary work by focusing on the story's main character, conflicts the character faces, changes he or she undergoes, and the effects of these changes. As you read, use this chart to help you determine the universal theme.

Character	
How character changes	
Meaning of change	
Universal theme	

The Three Wishes
Ricardo E. Alegría

Summary A woodsman and his wife live together in the forest. They are poor but happy. One day a stranger gives the wife three wishes. The wishes cause problems for the couple. The woodsman and his wife discover that happiness comes from love and not from riches.

 ## Writing About the Big Question

How much do our communities shape us? This folk tale has a very common theme—a couple is granted three wishes and find that they do not know how to use them well. Complete this sentence:

In many **cultures** stories in which someone is granted three wishes are

passed down through **generations** because these tales teach _____

_____.

Note-taking Guide

Use this chart to record what happens when the characters use each wish.

Wish	Result
The wife accidentally wishes that her husband were with her.	The husband appears in the house.

The Three Wishes
Ricardo E. Alegría

Many years ago, there lived a woodsman and his wife. They were very poor but very happy in their little house in the forest. Poor as they were, they were always ready to share what little they had with anyone who came to their door. They loved each other very much and were quite content with their life together. Each evening, before eating, they gave thanks to God for their happiness.

One day, while the husband was working far off in the woods, an old man came to the little house and said that he had lost his way in the forest and had eaten nothing for many days. The woodsman's wife had little to eat herself, but, as was her custom, she gave a large portion of it to the old man. After he had eaten everything she gave him, he told the woman that he had been sent to test her and that, as a reward for the kindness she and her husband showed to all who came to their house, they would be granted a special grace. This pleased the woman, and she asked what the special grace was.

The old man answered, "Beginning immediately, any three wishes you or your husband may wish will come true."

When she heard these words, the woman was overjoyed and exclaimed, "Oh, if my husband were only here to hear what you say!"

The last word had scarcely left her lips when the woodsman appeared in the little house with the ax still in his hands. The first wish had come true.

The woodsman couldn't understand it at all. How did it happen that he, who had been cutting wood in the forest, found himself here in his house? His wife explained it all as she <u>embraced</u> him. The woodsman just stood there, thinking over what his wife had said. He looked at the old man who stood quietly, too, saying nothing.

Vocabulary Development

embraced (im BRAYSD) *v.* clasped in the arms, usually as an expression of affection

Activate Prior Knowledge

Think about another story in which a strange visitor gives wishes to the characters in the story. Name or describe the story.

_____

_____

_____

Reading Skill

Making connections between a story and your life can help you focus as you read. Which details in the story relate to your life?

_____

_____

_____

Reading Check

What do the woodsman and his wife do before eating each night? Underline the answer in the text.

Reading Skill

One way that an author can **set a purpose** is to show a **connection** to a **universal theme**. Read the bracketed paragraph. What theme is the author trying to connect with? Circle the details that support this theme.

_____

_____

_____

Stop to Reflect

Do you think the woodsman and his wife make a good third wish? Explain.

_____

_____

_____

_____

_____

Reading Check

What does the couple want for their last wish? Underline the answer in the text.

_____

_____

_____

Suddenly he realized that his wife, without stopping to think, had used one of the three wishes, and he became very annoyed when he remembered all of the useful things she might have asked for with the first wish. For the first time, he became angry with his wife. The desire for riches had turned his head, and he scolded his wife, shouting at her, among other things, "It doesn't seem possible that you could be so stupid! You've wasted one of our wishes, and now we have only two left! May you grow ears of a donkey!"

He had no sooner said the words than his wife's ears began to grow, and they continued to grow until they changed into the pointed, furry ears of a donkey.

When the woman put her hand up and felt them, she knew what had happened and began to cry. Her husband was very ashamed and sorry, indeed, for what he had done in his temper, and he went to his wife to comfort her.

The old man, who had stood by silently, now came to them and said, "Until now, you have known happiness together and have never quarreled with each other. Nevertheless, the mere knowledge that you could have riches and power has changed you both. Remember, you have only one wish left. What do you want? Riches? Beautiful clothes? Servants? Power?"

The woodsman tightened his arm about his wife, looked at the old man, and said, "We want only the happiness and joy we knew before my wife grew donkey's ears."

No sooner had he said these words than the donkey ears disappeared. The woodsman and his wife fell upon their knees to ask forgiveness for having acted, if only for a moment, out of covetousness[1] and greed. Then they gave thanks for all their happiness.

Vocabulary Development
greed (greed) *n.* a selfish desire for more than one's share of something

1. **covetousness** (KUV uht uhs nuhs) *n.* envy; wanting what another person has.

The old man left, but before going, he told them that they had undergone this test in order to learn that there can be happiness in poverty just as there can be unhappiness in riches. As a reward for their <u>repentance</u>, the old man said that he would bestow upon them the greatest happiness a married couple could know. Months later, a son was born to them. The family lived happily all the rest of their lives.

Reader's Response: Suppose you were given three wishes. How would you avoid the problems of the woodsman and his wife?

_____

_____

_____

_____

 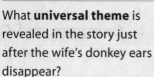
Literary Analysis

What **universal theme** is revealed in the story just after the wife's donkey ears disappear?

_____

_____

_____

Reading Check

What does the couple receive at the end of the story? Circle the sentence that tells you the answer.

Vocabulary Development

repentance (ri PEN tuhns) *n.* feeling of sorrow for wrongdoing

© Pearson Education

The Three Wishes

1. **Compare and Contrast:** How does the behavior of the couple change after they are given the opportunity to make wishes?

_____

_____

_____

2. **Interpret:** How does the saying "Be careful what you wish for" apply to the couple?

_____

_____

3. **Reading Skill:** Use this chart to note how details in the folk tale helped you achieve the **purpose** of making connections.

Universal Theme	Cultural Details	Connections to Life

4. **Literary Analysis:** What **universal theme**, or message about life, does the author suggest in the first paragraph of the story?

_____

_____

_____

Writing: Plot Proposal

Write a **plot proposal**, or plan of story events, that illustrates the universal theme from "The Three Wishes." First, write a sentence that describes the story's theme.

_____

_____

Then, invent a new plot that contains the same theme. Use this chart to organize your notes for your proposal.

	What happens?	How does what happens relate to the story's theme?
Beginning of plot		
Middle of plot		
End of plot		

Listening and Speaking: Oral Response

Present an **oral response** to the theme of "The Three Wishes." First, write a sentence that describes the story's theme.

_____

_____

Then, use this chart to help you organize your response.

	Description	How does the example relate to the story's theme?	Does the example show that you agree or disagree with the story's theme?
Example from another story			
Example from your own life			

The Stone
Lloyd Alexander

Summary Maibon is worried about getting old. He helps a dwarf in exchange for a wish. Maibon asks for a stone that will stop him from growing old. The dwarf tries to warn Maibon about such a stone. Things turn out differently than Maibon expects.

Writing About the Big Question

How much do our communities shape us? In the story, Maibon's wish has a negative effect on his family and his farm. Complete this sentence:

One person's actions can affect others in his **family** and **community**

because _____

_____.

Note-taking Guide

Events cause results in stories. Events from "The Stone" are listed in the left column of the chart. Record details about the results of these events.

Event	Result
Maibon helps the dwarf.	The dwarf rewards him with a wish.
The dwarf gives Maibon a stone that will stop him from growing old.	
Maibon gets rid of the stone.	

The Stone

1. **Infer:** Why does Maibon choose the stone over all of the other gifts?

   _____

   _____

   _____

2. **Analyze:** What new belief does Maibon have that finally allows him to rid himself of the stone?

   _____

   _____

   _____

3. **Reading Skill:** Use this chart to note how details in the story helped you achieve the **purpose** of making connections.

Universal Theme	Cultural Details	Connections to Life

4. **Literary Analysis:** What **universal theme** is revealed in the story, just after Doli explains to Maibon why the stone will not go away?

   _____

   _____

   _____

Writing: Plot Proposal

Write a **plot proposal**, or plan of story events, that illustrates a universal theme from "The Stone." First, write a sentence that describes the story's theme.

_____

_____

Then, invent a new plot that contains the same theme. Use this chart to organize your notes for your proposal.

	What Happens?	How does what happens relate to the story's theme?
Beginning of plot		
Middle of plot		
End of plot		

Research And Technology: Report

Complete the following chart by listing the different areas of Puerto Rico and then describing what each area is like. Use this information in your **report**.

Areas of the Island	Description

Instructions on Using a Map

About Instructions on Using a Map

A **map** is a drawing of an area or country. It may show physical features, such as rivers, or political features, such as cities. Maps usually have the following information:

- a compass rose showing which direction is north
- a scale showing the relationship between the size of the drawing and the actual size of the place
- a key, or legend, shows the various symbols the mapmaker used and what they represent

By understanding this information, you can use a map effectively.

Reading Skill

Instructions explain how to perform a task. In order to perform that task correctly, **connect and clarify the main ideas** in the instructions. A main idea is the most important idea in a text. It is supported by details. To find a main idea, identify all the details. Then summarize them to see what idea they support. Study the graphic organizer below to learn more about main ideas.

Questions to Ask When Using a Map	
Where am I right now?	You must first find your current or starting location.
Where is my destination?	Once you find the second point on the map, you can figure out how to get to where you want to go.
How far do I have to go?	Many maps contain scales and will tell you that an inch on the map is equal to some actual distance.
What is the best route?	The best route is often the most direct one, but study the map to make sure. For example, if the most direct route has you walking through a field with tall grass, you should consider another route.

Britannica Student Encyclopedia

How to Read a Road Map

The main idea of the encyclopedia entry is presented here.

A globe is a small, round model of our round Earth, but maps of all or parts of the Earth are flat. Therefore only a globe can show distances, directions, and shapes as they really are. For most purposes, however, maps are more useful than globes. They can be larger and show more detail. They can be printed in books, such as in this encyclopedia. They can also be carried about easily, folded or rolled.

There are many kinds of maps and each kind tells a different story. For finding directions there are sea charts and aeronautical charts, railroad maps, road maps, and contour maps. Most common of all are the road maps used by automobile drivers.

When you unfold a road map, hold it so that you can read the words on it. North most likely will be at the top of the sheet, but you should check by looking for a direction arrow or a compass rose. If there is none, you can assume that north is at the top of the map.

If north is at the top, the right-hand edge is east, the left-hand edge is west, and south is at the bottom. When you spread a map on a table, turn it so that the map north is toward the north. Then the directions east and west on

your map will be east and west on the Earth. If you hang the map on a wall, try to hang it so that east is to the east as you face the map.

The mapmaker, like the architect, draws to scale. If he decides to make one inch (2.5 centimeters) represent 20 miles (32 kilometers), this must be true on every part of the map. If one inch represents 20 miles, one can easily figure the distance from point to point "as the crow flies." Since roads do not always follow a straight route, one must total the mileage shown on the map along the highways to calculate actual driving distance.

Many state road maps have separate maps of important cities. These maps are very small compared to the state map; but because they are drawn to a much larger scale, they can show streets, parks, and main buildings. The larger the scale, the more details a mapmaker can show.

The information given here can be clarified by looking at a map of a city like the one shown on the next page.

Thinking About Instructions on Using a Map

1. What are some different types of maps?

_____

2. How does scale affect the amount of details on a map?

_____

TALK ABOUT IT **Reading Skill**

3. What is the main idea of the third and fourth paragraphs?

_____

_____

4. How do the main ideas of the first two paragraphs connect?

_____

_____

WRITE ABOUT IT **Timed Writing: Explanation (20 minutes)**

In your own words, explain how to use a map. Answer these questions
to help organize your ideas:

• What do the first two paragraphs tell about maps?

_____

_____

• What do the middle two paragraphs tell about maps?

_____

_____

• What do the last two paragraphs tell about maps?

_____

_____

Word Families

Words that have the same root make up a **word family**. Many English word families are built around Greek roots. Often these roots keep the same spelling in all the words of the word family.

What Can you Learn From Ancient Greek? The words in this list are all part of very common word families built on Greek roots. The Greek root *tele* means "far," *auto* means "self," and *cyc* means "wheel" or "ring." The spelling of these forms does not change from word to word. If you keep this in mind, you will spell the list words and other words in the same word families correctly.

Practice Read the following paragraph. Circle any word that is misspelled. Then, write the misspelled word correctly on the blank.

> Word List
>
> telephone
> television
> telescope
> telecast
> automobile
> automatic
> autograph
> bycycle
> cyclone
> recycle

We entered a contest on televishion. Two weeks. later, we got a telefone call. "You have won a bycycle!" the caller said. "Or you may choose a telascope instead." "I would rather have an autamobile," I said.

_____

_____

_____

_____

The exercises and tools presented here are designed to help you increase your vocabulary. Review the instruction and complete the exercises to build your vocabulary knowledge. Throughout the year, you can apply these skills and strategies to improve your reading, writing, speaking, and listening vocabulary.

The following list contains common word roots with meanings and examples. On the blank lines, write other words you know that have the same roots. Write the meanings of the new words.

Root	Meaning	Example and Meaning	Your Words	Meanings
-brev-	brief; short	*brevity:* the quality of lasting for a short time		
-cede-	go	*recede:* move or go away or move or go back		
-dict-	say or tell	*predict:* tell what might happen next		
-fac-	make	*factory:* place where things are made		
-fer-	bring; carry	*reference:* something you say or write that mentions another person or thing, something that brings or carries more information		
-ject-	throw	*eject:* push or throw out with force		
-manu-	hand	*manual:* operated or done by hand		

Root	Meaning	Example and Meaning	Your Words	Meanings
-phon-	hearing; sound	*telephone:* a device that brings sound over long distances		
-port-	carry	*support:* carry or hold something up		
-scrib-	write	*scribble:* write something quickly in a messy way		
-sequ-	follow	*consequence:* effect that follows a cause		
-similis-	same	*similar:* alike in some way		
-spec-	look; see	*inspect:* look carefully at something		
-sum-	take; use	*assumption:* something that you think is true or take as true		
-tele-	far; distant	*telescope:* instrument that makes distant objects look larger		
-vali-	strong; worth	*valid:* true, based on strong reasons or facts		
-ver-	truth	*verify:* make sure something is true		

© Pearson Education

The following list contains common prefixes with meanings and examples. On the blank lines, write other words you know that begin with the same prefixes. Write the meanings of the new words.

Prefix	Meaning	Example and Meaning	Your Words	Meanings
anti-	against	*antisocial*: not liking to meet and talk to people; against friendliness		
aud-	hearing; sound	*auditorium*: a room for hearing concerts or speeches		
con-	with; together	*concur*: agree with		
de-	down; from	*decrease*: become less		
dis-	not	*disorganized*: not organized		
in-	without; not	*incapable*: not able		
inter-	between	*intermission*: short period of time between the parts of a play or concert		
ir-	without; not	*irregular*: not regular		

Prefix	Meaning	Example and Meaning	Your Words	Meanings
mis-	wrong; bad	*misspell*: spell wrong; spell incorrectly		
multi-	many	*multicolored*: having many colors		
non-	without; not	*nonfat*: without fat		
ob-	against	*obstacle*: something that works against another, something that makes it difficult for you to succeed		
post-	after	*post-test*: a test given after instruction		
pre-	before	*preview*: look before		
re-	again	*remake*: make again		
sub-	below, under	*submarine*: a ship that moves under the ocean		
super-	above; over	*superior*: better than another		
un-/an-/a-	not	*unbelievable*: not believable		

The following list contains common suffixes with meanings and examples. On the blank lines, write other words you know that have the same suffixes. Write the meanings of the new words.

Suffix	Meaning	Example and Meaning	Your Words	Meanings
-able/-ible	able to be	*movable*: able to be moved		
-al	relating to	*financial*: relating to money		
-ance/-ence	act of; state of; quality of	*assistance*: act of giving help		
-ate	make	*motivate*: make someone feel eager to do something		
-en	make	*weaken*: make something less strong		
-er/-or	one who	*actor*: person who acts		
-ful	filled with	*joyful*: filled with happiness		
-hood	state or quality of	*manhood*: the state of being an adult male		

Suffix	Meaning	Example and Meaning	Your Words	Meanings
-ic	like; pertaining to	*heroic*: like a hero; brave		
-ish	resembling	*foolish*: not sensible		
-ist	one who	*violinist*: person who plays the violin		
-ize/-yze	make	*publicize*: make public; tell people about		
-less	without	*powerless*: without power		
-ly	in a way	*quickly*: done in a short amount of time		
-ment	act or quality of	*excitement*: feeling of being excited		
-ness	state or quality of	*kindness*: friendly and caring behavior		
-ous	having; full of	*famous*: having fame; known and recognized by many people		
-sion/-tion	act or process of	*persuasion*: act of convincing someone		

Use a **dictionary** to find the correct spelling, the meaning, the pronunciation, and the part of speech of a word. The dictionary will show you how the plural is formed if it is irregular. You can also find the word's history, or *etymology*, in a dictionary. Etymology explains how words change, how they are borrowed from other languages, and how new words are invented, or "coined."

Here is a sample entry from a dictionary. Notice what it tells about the word. Then, follow the instructions.

lemon (lem´ ən) **n.** [ME *lymon* < MFr *limon* < Ar *laimūn* < Pers *līmūn*] **1** a small, egg-shaped, edible citrus fruit with a yellow rind and a juicy, sour pulp, rich in ascorbic acid **2** the small, spiny, semitropical evergreen citrus tree (*Citrus limon*) bearing this fruit **3** pale yellow **4** [slang] something, esp. a manufactured article, that is defective or imperfect

1. Circle the *n.* in the dictionary entry. It stands for *noun.* Write what these other parts of speech abbreviations mean: *v.* _____, *adv.* _____, *adj.* _____, *prep.* _____.

2. Underline the origins of the word *lemon.* ME stands for Middle English, Ar stands for Arabic, and Pers. stands for Persian. What do you think MFr stands for? _____

3. Put a box around the pronunciation.

4. How many noun definitions does the entry have? _____

5. Which definition is slang? _____

6. Which definition of *lemon* is used in the following sentence? _____

   The car that my dad bought turned out to be a lemon.

Activity: Use a dictionary to learn about the origins of these words.

Activity: Use a dictionary to learn about the origins of these words.

1. literature _____ / _____ / _____
    pronunciation   main part of speech   original language(s)

_____ / _____
        1st meaning   other meanings

_____

_____

_____

2. language _____ / _____ / _____
    pronunciation   main part of speech   original language(s)

_____ / _____
        1st meaning   other meanings

_____

_____

_____

Activity: Look up each of the following words in a dictionary. Then, write a definition of the word and a sentence using the word.

moment _____

_____

popular _____

_____

remedy _____

_____

blur _____

_____

lazy _____

_____

Use these word study cards to break big words into their parts. Write the word at the top of the card. Then, divide the word into its prefix, root, and suffix. Note that not all words have prefixes and suffixes. List the meaning of each part of the word. Next, find three words with the same root and write them on the card. Finally, write the word's part of speech and its definition. Use a dictionary to help you. One example has been done for you.

Word:		invisible	
Prefix		**Root**	**Suffix**
in: not		**vis:** see	**ible**-able to be

Root-related Words
1. vision
2. revise
3. visibility

Definition: invisible *adj.* not able to be seen

Word:			
Prefix		**Root**	**Suffix**

Root-related Words
1.
2.
3.

Definition:

Word:

Prefix	Root	Suffix

Root-related Words
1.
2.
3.

Definition:

Word:

Prefix	Root	Suffix

Root-related Words
1.
2.
3.

Definition:

Word:

Prefix	Root	Suffix

Root-related Words
1.
2.
3.

Definition:

claim (KLAYM) *v.* state as a fact

distinguish (dis TING gwish) *v.* tell the difference

fact (FAKT) *n.* a statement that can be proved

opinion (uh PIN yuhn) *n.* a statement that expresses a person's judgment or belief

predict (pree DIKT) *v.* make a logical assumption about what will happen next

prior (PRY uhr) *adj.* coming before in time; earlier

prove (PROOV) *v.* show evidence

revise (ri VYZ) *v.* think about something again in order to make improvements

support (suh POHRT) *v.* uphold; offer proof

verify (VER uh fy) *v.* prove to be true

A. Completion Complete each sentence that has been started for you. Your sentence completion should be logical and illustrate the meaning of the vocabulary word in italics.

1. You should do your homework *prior* to _____

_____

2. You put *facts* into a report in order to _____

_____

3. He was the first to *claim* _____

4. I tried to *distinguish* between _____

_____

5. In my *opinion*, it is better to be _____

_____

6. By experimenting, the scientist was able to *prove* _____

_____

7. I can *predict* what will happen tomorrow by _____

_____

8. The journalist was able to *support* his story with _____

_____

9. Two good reasons to *revise* an essay before turning it in are _____

_____

10. I was able to *verify* that the story was true by _____

_____

B. Use each academic vocabulary word in an original sentence that illustrates its meaning.

claim/true _____

_____

distinguish/between _____

_____

fact/research _____

_____

opinion/conversation _____

_____

predict/outcome _____

_____

prior/rehearsal _____

_____

prove/theory _____

_____

revise/speech _____

_____

support/examples _____

_____

verify/information _____

_____

apparently (uh PER uhnt lee) *adv.* appearing to be

conclude (kuhn KLOOD) *v.* form an opinion or make judgment, based on evidence presented

detail (di TAYL) *n.* a piece of information

examine (eg ZAM uhn) *v.* look at carefully

identifiable (y DEN tuh FY uh buhl) *adj.* recognizable; able to be identified

infer (in FER) *v.* assume something based on facts

possible (PAHS uh buhl) *adj.* able to be done

refer (ri FER) *v.* look back

speculate (SPEK yuh layt) *v.* make a prediction

support (suh POHRT) *v.* provide evidence for

support (suh POHRT) *n.* evidence or reasons for

A. True/False For each of the following, mark T or F to indicate whether the italicized vocabulary word has been used correctly in the sentence. If you have marked F, correct the sentence by using the word properly.

1. _____ *Refer* to a cookbook for the latest entertainment news.

2. _____ It is important to *support* your opinion with facts.

3. _____ The *details* in the story act as clues for the reader.

4. _____ *Apparently*, the author wanted to surprise the reader.

5. _____ Based on the evidence, Molly was able to *conclude* that her friend was not guilty.

6. _____ If something is *possible*, it cannot be done.

7. _____ Lies are good *support* for an argument.

8. _____ Please, *speculate* the dishes after you are through eating.

9. _____ A doctor will *examine* you to find out if you are sick.

10. _____ Use the left blinker to *infer* that you are going to turn left.

11. _____ There are *identifiable* characters in the story.

B. Use each word pair in a sentence that shows the meaning of the academic vocabulary word.

apparently/surprise _____

_____

conclude/essay _____

_____

detail/story _____

_____

examine/painting _____

_____

identifiable/trees _____

_____

infer/information _____

_____

possible/study _____

_____

refer/instructions _____

_____

speculate/future _____

_____

support (verb)/theory _____

_____

support (noun)/example _____

_____

achievement (uh CHEEV muhnt) *n.* result of achieving or accomplishing

determine (dee TER muhn) *v.* decide or figure out

direction (duh REK shuhn) *n.* act of directing or supervising

essential (uh SEN shuhl) *adj.* basic; necessary

identify (y DEN tuh fy) *v.* recognize or point out

influence (IN floo uhns) *n.* power to affect others

intent (in TENT) *n.* purpose, objective, or aim

key (KEE) *adj.* important

strategy (STRAT uh jee) *n.* a plan for a specific outcome

significant (sig NIF uh kuhnt) *adj.* important

A. Code Name Use the code to figure out each vocabulary word. Each letter is represented by a number or symbol. This exercise will help you learn how to spell and recognize the vocabulary words.

%	5	•	*	2	#	!	7	^	&	9	¶	£	$	3	¥	+	=	?	÷	4	¢	6	§	«	ç
a	b	c	d	e	f	g	h	i	j	k	l	m	n	o	p	q	r	s	t	u	v	w	x	y	z

1. ^ $ ÷ 2 $ ÷ _____

2. 9 2 « _____

3. * 2 ÷ 2 = £ ^ $ 2 _____

4. ? ÷ = % ÷ 2 ! « _____

5. % • 7 ^ 2 ¢ 2 £ 2 $ ÷ _____

6. ^ $ # ¶ 4 2 $ • 2 _____

7. 2 ? ? 2 $ ÷ ^ % ¶ _____

8. ? ^ ! $ ^ # ^ • % $ ÷ _____

9. * ^ = 2 • ÷ ^ 3 $ _____

10. ^ * 2 $ ÷ ^ # « _____

B. Completion Complete each sentence that has been started for you. Your sentence should make sense and illustrate the meaning of the vocabulary word in italics.

1. My greatest *achievement* is _____.

2. Read the recipe to *determine* _____

   _____.

3. For *direction* in writing, I ask _____.

4. Water is *essential* for _____.

5. To *identify* the part of speech of a word, you must _____

   _____.

6. I have *influence* over _____.

7. My *intent* in going to school is _____

   _____.

8. One *key* ingredient in the casserole is _____.

9. A good *strategy* for staying healthy is _____

   _____.

10. The most *significant* event of the day _____

    _____.

C. Write new words that you come across in your reading. Define each word.

_____

_____

_____

_____

context (KAHN tekst) *n.* situation in which a word is used

convey (kuhn VAY) *v.* communicate; carry from place to place

define (dee FYN) *v.* state the meaning

explain (eks PLAYN) *v.* make clear or understandable

paraphrase (PAR uh frayz) *v.* restate in your own words

passage (PAS ij) *n.* a body of text

preview (PREE vyoo) *v.* view, or look at, beforehand

represent (rep ri ZENT) *v.* stand for

restate (ree STAYT) *v.* say something again

A. Unscramble each vocabulary word and write it on the line to the right. This exercise will help you learn how to spell and recognize the vocabulary words.

1. **w e e r p i v** _____

2. **t o c x n e t** _____

3. **c y o v e n** _____

4. **r a s h a p e r p a** _____

5. **s p a g a s e** _____

6. **e d e n i f** _____

7. **s e r e a t t** _____

8. **p a x e l n i** _____

9. **s e r e n p e r t** _____

B. True/False For each of the following, mark T or F to indicate whether the italicized vocabulary word has been used correctly in the sentence. If you have marked F, correct the sentence by changing the words that make the sentence wrong.

1. _____ You can figure out how to spell a word by looking at its *context*.

2. _____ If you speak clearly, you will be able to *convey* your ideas better.

3. _____ If you want to *define* a new word, use an almanac.

4. _____ Joe will *explain* the situation clearly, so that Martha will be able to understand.

5. _____ If you *paraphrase* what an author has written, you copy it word for word.

6. _____ A *passage* in a book is generally much longer than a chapter.

7. _____ It is a good idea for the parents to *preview* a movie before letting young children see it.

8. _____ In that story, the clock *represents* time.

9. _____ To *restate* in your own words means the same thing as to paraphrase.

C. Write new words that you come across in your reading. Define each word.

_____

_____

_____

brief (BREEF) *adj.* short

characteristic (KAR uhk tuhr IS tik) *n.* quality or feature

compare (kuhm PAYR) *v.* show how things are alike

contrast (kuhn TRAST) *v.* show how things are different

describe (di SKRYB) *v.* tell or write about

element (EL uh muhnt) *n.* part of the whole

recall (ri KAWL) *v.* remember

review (ri VYOO) *v.* look at again

summary (SUM uh ree) *n.* the main ideas in brief form

unique (YOO neek) *adj.* one of a kind

A. True/False For each of the following, mark T or F to indicate whether the italicized vocabulary word has been used correctly in the sentence. If you have marked F, correct the sentence by changing the words that make the sentence wrong.

1. _____ Paul wrote a *summary* of the book before he began the first chapter.

2. _____ All of the uniforms were blue, striped, and *unique*.

3. _____ Julia *described* her summer vacation in vivid detail.

4. _____ The *brief* speech lasted more than fours hours, leaving the audience tired.

5. _____ One *characteristic* of my best friend is her sense of humor.

6. _____ Jacob was planning to *review* his essay before he began writing it.

7. _____ Neill showed how both objects were alike by *contrasting* their similar traits.

8. _____ The keypad is another *element* of a cellular phone.

9. _____ After studying hard, Rose was able to *recall* all the dates on her history exam.

10. _____ When you *compare* two houses, you should discuss how they are alike.

B. Completion Complete each sentence that has been started for you. Your sentence completion should be logical and illustrate the meaning of the vocabulary word in italics.

1. The bicycle he rode was considered *unique* because _____

_____.

2. We *compared* the movie to the book to see if _____

_____.

3. We couldn't wait to see the movie after Ralph *described* _____

_____.

4. After Julia *summarized* the story, I _____

_____.

5. There is a great *contrast* between _____

_____.

6. An important *characteristic* of a rain storm is _____

_____.

7. The special effects were a key *element* of _____

_____.

8. Rose made an effort to keep her speech *brief* because _____

_____.

9. One thing that can help you *recall* important information is _____

_____.

10. It is important to *review* your homework in order to _____

_____.

adapt (uh DAPT) *v.* adjust

cause (KAWZ) *n.* the reason something happens

effect (e FEKT) *n.* the consequence of

enable (en AY buhl) *v.* allow; assist

establish (uh STAB lish) *v.* set up; cause to be

focus (FOH kuhs) *adj.* direct one's thoughts or efforts

purpose (PER puhs) *n.* intent; plan

reason (REE zuhn) *v.* why something happens

relationship (ri LAY shuhn ship) *n.* the connection between two things

result (ri ZULT) *n.* the consequence of

A. Code Name Use the code to figure out each vocabulary word. Each letter is represented by a number or symbol. This exercise will help you learn how to spell and recognize the vocabulary words.

%	5	•	*	2	#	!	7	^	&	9	¶	£	$	3	¥	+	=	?	÷	4	¢	6	§	«	ç
a	b	c	d	e	f	g	h	i	j	k	l	m	n	o	p	q	r	s	t	u	v	w	x	y	z

1. # 3 • 4 ? _____

2. 2 ? ÷ % 5 ¶ ^ ? 7 _____

3. ¥ 4 = ¥ 3 ? 2 _____

4. = 2 ¶ % ÷ ^ 3 $? 7 ^ ¥ _____

5. • % 4 ? 2 _____

6. % * % ¥ ÷ _____

7. 2 $ % 5 ¶ 2 _____

8. = 2 % ? 3 $ _____

9. 2 # # 2 • ÷ _____

10. = 2 ? 4 ¶ ÷ _____

B. True/False For each of the following, mark T or F to indicate whether the italicized vocabulary word has been used correctly in the sentence. If you have marked F, correct the sentence by using the word properly.

1. _____ An emergency shelter was *established* before the hurricane.

2. _____ If you *adapt* your behavior, you do not change it at all.

3. _____ The *cause* of the flood was the dam bursting.

4. _____ The principal and teachers have a good *relationship*.

5. _____ I was not prepared as a *result* of studying.

6. _____ I was very distracted by the TV and able to *focus* on my homework.

7. _____ The *effect* of passing a test is studying very hard.

8. _____ The school rules *enabled* us to stay off the grass while playing ball.

9. _____ Ryan had a good *reason* for wanting to delay baseball practice.

10. _____ A common *purpose* for reading a textbook is to be entertained.

C. Write new words that you come across in your reading. Define each word.

_____

_____

_____

_____

_____

_____

_____

_____

Use this page to write down academic words you come across in other subjects, such as social studies or science. When you are reading your textbooks, you may find words that you need to learn. Following the example, write down the word, the part of speech, and an explanation of the word. You may want to write an example sentence to help you remember the word.

dissolve *verb* to make something solid become part of a liquid by putting it in a liquid and mixing it

The sugar *dissolved* in the hot tea.

_____

_____

_____

_____

_____

_____

_____

_____

_____

_____

_____

_____

_____

_____

_____

_____

_____

_____

Use these flash cards to study words you want to remember. The words on this page come from Unit 1. Cut along the dotted lines on pages V25 through V32 to create your own flash cards or use index cards. Write the word on the front of the card. On the back, write the word's part of speech and definition. Then, write a sentence that shows the meaning of the word.

grief	reflection	abruptly
prelude	evident	winced
timidly	grudgingly	ignore

noun
deep sadness

When her husband died, her grief was obvious.

noun
an image of one's self, as seen in a mirror

I saw a reflection of my face in the windowpane.

adverb
suddenly, without warning

The bus stopped so abruptly, I fell off my seat.

noun
introduction to a main event

We sang the school song as a prelude to the big game.

adjective
easy to see; very clear

Her happiness was evident in her cheery smile.

verb
drew back slightly, as if in pain; cringed

The boy winced as the nurse gave him a shot.

adverb
in a way that shows fear or shyness

Frightened, Rosa timidly asked a question.

adverb
in an unwilling or resentful way

Max grudgingly admitted his mistake.

verb
pay no attention to

Anna tried to ignore the car alarm.

Use these flash cards to study words you want to remember. Cut along the dotted lines on pages V25 through V32 to create your own flash cards or use index cards. Write the word on the front of the card. On the back, write the word's part of speech and definition. Then, write a sentence that shows the meaning of the word.

Use a fold-a-list to study the definitions of words. The words on this page come from Unit 1. Write the definition for each word on the lines. Fold the paper along the dotted line to check your definition. Create your own fold-a-lists on pages V31 and V32.

sympathy _____

_____

compulsion _____

_____

intently _____

_____

awed _____

_____

mode _____

_____

frenzied _____

_____

inhabited _____

_____

seized _____

_____

suspended _____

_____

revelation _____

_____

Fold In ↓

Write the word that matches the definition on each line.
Fold the paper along the dotted line to check your work.

shared feeling   _____

driving force   _____

purposefully; earnestly   _____

filled with feelings
of fear and wonder   _____

way of doing something   _____

acting in a wild,
uncontrolled way   _____

lived in; occupied   _____

grabbed; taken hold of   _____

stopped for a time   _____

sudden rush
of understanding   _____

Fold In ←

Write the words you want to study on this side of the page. Write the definitions on the back. Then, test yourself. Fold the paper along the dotted line to check your definition.

Word: _____

_____

Word: _____

_____

Word: _____

_____

Word: _____

_____

Word: _____

_____

Word: _____

_____

Word: _____

_____

Word: _____

_____

Word: _____

_____

Word: _____

_____

Fold In ←

Write the word that matches the definition on each line.
Fold the paper along the dotted line to check your work.

Definition: _____

Definition: _____

Definition: _____

Definition: _____

Definition: _____

Definition: _____

Definition: _____

Definition: _____

Definition: _____

Definition: _____

Fold In ←

The list on these pages presents words that cause problems for many people. Some of these words are spelled according to set rules, but others follow no specific rules. As you review this list, check to see how many of the words give you trouble in your own writing. Then, add your own commonly misspelled words on the lines that follow.

abbreviate	auxiliary	census	deficient
absence	awkward	certain	definitely
absolutely	bandage	changeable	delinquent
abundance	banquet	characteristic	dependent
accelerate	bargain	chauffeur	descendant
accidentally	barrel	chief	description
accumulate	battery	clothes	desert
accurate	beautiful	coincidence	desirable
ache	beggar	colonel	dessert
achievement	beginning	column	deteriorate
acquaintance	behavior	commercial	dining
adequate	believe	commission	disappointed
admittance	benefit	commitment	disastrous
advertisement	bicycle	committee	discipline
aerial	biscuit	competitor	dissatisfied
affect	bookkeeper	concede	distinguish
aggravate	bought	condemn	effect
aggressive	boulevard	congratulate	eighth
agreeable	brief	connoisseur	eligible
aisle	brilliant	conscience	embarrass
all right	bruise	conscientious	enthusiastic
allowance	bulletin	conscious	entrepreneur
aluminum	buoyant	contemporary	envelope
amateur	bureau	continuous	environment
analysis	bury	controversy	equipped
analyze	buses	convenience	equivalent
ancient	business	coolly	especially
anecdote	cafeteria	cooperate	exaggerate
anniversary	calendar	cordially	exceed
anonymous	campaign	correspondence	excellent
answer	canceled	counterfeit	exercise
anticipate	candidate	courageous	exhibition
anxiety	capacity	courteous	existence
apologize	capital	courtesy	experience
appall	capitol	criticism	explanation
appearance	captain	criticize	extension
appreciate	career	curiosity	extraordinary
appropriate	carriage	curious	familiar
architecture	cashier	cylinder	fascinating
argument	catastrophe	deceive	February
associate	category	decision	fiery
athletic	ceiling	deductible	financial
attendance	cemetery	defendant	fluorescent

foreign	minuscule	proceed	_____
fourth	miscellaneous	prominent	
fragile	mischievous	pronunciation	_____
gauge	misspell	psychology	
generally	mortgage	publicly	_____
genius	naturally	pursue	
genuine	necessary	questionnaire	_____
government	neighbor	realize	
grammar	neutral	really	_____
grievance	nickel	recede	
guarantee	niece	receipt	_____
guard	ninety	receive	
guidance	noticeable	recognize	_____
handkerchief	nuisance	recommend	
harass	obstacle	reference	_____
height	occasion	referred	
humorous	occasionally	rehearse	_____
hygiene	occur	relevant	
ignorant	occurred	reminiscence	_____
immediately	occurrence	renowned	
immigrant	omitted	repetition	_____
independence	opinion	restaurant	
independent	opportunity	rhythm	_____
indispensable	optimistic	ridiculous	
individual	outrageous	sandwich	_____
inflammable	pamphlet	satellite	
intelligence	parallel	schedule	_____
interfere	paralyze	scissors	
irrelevant	parentheses	secretary	_____
irritable	particularly	siege	
jewelry	patience	solely	_____
judgment	permanent	sponsor	
knowledge	permissible	subtle	_____
lawyer	perseverance	subtlety	
legible	persistent	superintendent	_____
legislature	personally	supersede	
leisure	perspiration	surveillance	_____
liable	persuade	susceptible	
library	phenomenal	tariff	_____
license	phenomenon	temperamental	
lieutenant	physician	theater	_____
lightning	pleasant	threshold	
likable	pneumonia	truly	_____
liquefy	possess	unmanageable	
literature	possession	unwieldy	_____
loneliness	possibility	usage	
magnificent	prairie	usually	_____
maintenance	precede	valuable	
marriage	preferable	various	_____
mathematics	prejudice	vegetable	
maximum	preparation	voluntary	_____
meanness	previous	weight	
mediocre	primitive	weird	_____
mileage	privilege	whale	
millionaire	probably	wield	_____
minimum	procedure	yield	

When you are reading, you will find many unfamiliar words. Here are some tools that you can use to help you read unfamiliar words.

Phonics

Phonics is the science or study of sound. When you learn to read, you learn to associate certain sounds with certain letters or letter combinations. You know most of the sounds that letters can represent in English. When letters are combined, however, it is not always so easy to know what sound is represented. In English, there are some rules and patterns that will help you determine how to pronounce a word. This chart shows you some of the vowel digraphs, which are combinations like *ea* and *oa*. Two vowels together are called vowel digraphs. Usually, vowel digraphs represent the long sound of the first vowel.

Vowel Diagraphs	Examples of Unusual Sounds	Exceptions
ee and *ea*	steep, each, treat, sea	head, sweat, dread
ai and *ay*	plain, paid, may, betray	plaid
oa, ow, and *oe*	soak, slow, doe	now, shoe
ie and *igh*	lie, night, delight	friend, eight

As you read, sometimes the only way to know how to pronounce a word with an ea spelling is to see if the word makes sense in the sentence. Look at this example:

The water pipes were made of *lead*.

First, try out the long sound "ee." Ask yourself if it sounds right. It does not. Then, try the short sound "e." You will find that the short sound is correct in that sentence.

Now try this example.

Where you *lead*, I will follow.

Word Patterns

Recognizing different vowel-consonant patterns will help you read longer words. In the following sections, the **V** stands for "vowel" and the **C** stands for "consonant."

Single-syllable Words

CV – go: In two letter words with a consonant followed by a vowel, the vowel is usually long. For example, the word *go* is pronounced with a long *o* sound.

In a single syllable word, a vowel followed only by a single consonant is usually short.

CVC – got: If you add a consonant to the word *go*, such as the *t* in *got*, the vowel sound is a short *o*. Say the words *go* and *got* aloud and notice the difference in pronunciation.

Multi-syllable words

In words of more than one syllable, notice the letters that follow a vowel.

VCCV – robber: A single vowel followed by two consonants is usually short.

VCV — begin: A single vowel followed by a single consonant is usually long.

VCe — beside: An extension of the VCV pattern is vowel-consonant-silent *e*. In these words, the vowel is long and the *e* is not pronounced.

When you see a word with the VCV pattern, try the long vowel sound first. If the word does not make sense, try the short sound. Pronounce the words *model, camel,* and *closet*. First, try the long vowel sound. That does not sound correct, so try the short vowel sound. The short vowel sound is correct in those words.

Remember that patterns help you get started on figuring out a word. You will sometimes need to try a different sound or find the word in a dictionary.

As you read and find unfamiliar words, look the pronunciations up in a dictionary. Write the words in this chart in the correct column to help you notice patterns and remember pronunciations.

Syllables	Example	New words	Vowel
CV	go		long
CVC	got		short
VCC	robber		short
V/CV	begin open		long long
VC/V	closet		short

Mnemonics are devices, or methods, that help you remember things. The basic strategy is to link something you do not know with something that you *do* know. Here are some common mnemonic devices:

Visualizing Create a picture in your head that will help you remember the meaning of a vocabulary word. For example, the first four letters of the word *significance* spell *sign.* Picture a sign with the word *meaning* written on it to remember that significance means "meaning" or "importance."

Spelling The way a word is spelled can help you remember its meaning. For example, you might remember that *clarify* means to "make clear" if you notice that both *clarify* and *clear* start with the letters *cl.*

To help you remember how to spell certain words, look for a familiar word within the difficult word. For example:

Believe has a *lie* in it.

Separate is *a rat* of a word to spell.

Your *principal* is your *pal.*

Rhyming Here is a popular rhyme that helps people figure out how to spell *ei* and *ie* words.

_i_ before **_e_** — except after **_c_** *or when sounding like* **_a_** *as in neighbor and weigh.*

List words here that you need help remembering. Work with a group to create mnemonic devices to help you remember each word.

_____   _____

_____   _____

_____   _____

_____   _____

List words here that you need help remembering. Work with a group to create
mnemonic devices to help you remember each word.

_____   _____

_____   _____

_____   _____

_____   _____

_____   _____

_____   _____

_____   _____

_____   _____

_____   _____

_____   _____

_____   _____

_____   _____

Use these sentence starters to help you express yourself clearly in different classroom situations.

Expressing an Opinion

I think that _____

I believe that _____

In my opinion, _____

Agreeing

I agree with _____ that _____

I see what you mean.

That's an interesting idea.

My idea is similar to _____'s idea.

My idea builds upon _____'s idea.

Disagreeing

I don't completely agree with you because _____

My opinion is different than yours.

I got a different answer than you.

I see it a different way.

Reporting a Group's Ideas

We agreed that _____

We decided that _____

We had a different approach.

We had a similar idea.

Predicting

I predict that _____

I imagine that _____

Based on _____ I predict that _____

Paraphrasing

So you are saying that _____

In other words, you think _____

What I hear you saying is _____

Offering a Suggestion

Maybe we could _____

What if we _____

Here's something we might try.

Asking for Clarification

I have a question about that.

Could you explain that another way?

Can you give me another example of that?

Asking for a Response

What do you think?

Do you agree?

What answer did you get?

VOCABULARY BOOKMARKS

Cut out each bookmark to use as a handy word list when you are reading. On the lines, jot down words you want to learn and remember. You can also use the bookmark as a placeholder in your book.

TITLE		
Word		**Page #**

TITLE		
Word		**Page #**

TITLE		
Word		**Page #**

Cut out each bookmark to use as -a handy word list when you are reading.
On the lines, jot down words you want to learn and remember. You can also
use the bookmark as a placeholder in your book.

TITLE		TITLE		TITLE	
Word	**Page #**	**Word**	**Page #**	**Word**	**Page #**
_____		_____		_____	
_____		_____		_____	
_____		_____		_____	
_____		_____		_____	
_____		_____		_____	
_____		_____		_____	
_____		_____		_____	
_____		_____		_____	
_____		_____		_____	
_____		_____		_____	
_____		_____		_____	
_____		_____		_____	

Use these cards to record words you want to remember. Write the word, the title of the story or article in which it appears, its part of speech, and its definition. Then, use the word in an original sentence that shows its meaning

Word: _____ Page _____

Selection: _____

Part of Speech: _____

Definition: _____

My Sentence _____

_____

Word: _____ Page _____

Selection: _____

Part of Speech: _____

Definition: _____

_____

My Sentence _____

_____

Word: _____ Page _____

Selection: _____

Part of Speech: _____

Definition: _____

_____

My Sentence _____

_____

VOCABULARY BUILDER CARDS

Use these cards to record words you want to remember. Write the word, the title of the story or article in which it appears, its part of speech, and its definition. Then, use the word in an original sentence that shows its meaning

Word: _____ Page _____

Selection: _____

Part of Speech: _____

Definition: _____

_____

My Sentence _____

_____

Word: _____ Page _____

Selection: _____

Part of Speech: _____

Definition: _____

_____

My Sentence _____

_____

Word: _____ Page _____

Selection: _____

Part of Speech: _____

Definition: _____

_____

My Sentence _____

_____

Using the Personal Thesaurus

The Personal Thesaurus provides students with the opportunity to make connections between words academic words, familiar words, and even slang words. Students can use the Personal Thesaurus to help them understand the importance of using words in the proper context and also avoid overusing words in their writing.

Use the following routine to foster frequent use of the Personal Thesaurus.

1. After students have read a selection or done some writing, have them turn to the Personal Thesaurus.

2. Encourage students to add new entries. Help them to understand the connection between their personal language, which might include familiar words and even slang, and the academic language of their reading and writing.

3. Call on volunteers to read a few entries aloud. Point out that writers have many choices of words when they write. Help students see that audience often determines word choice.

N

nice

admirable

friendly

agreeable

pleasant

cool

phat

A

B

C

D

E

F

G

H

I

J

K

L

M

N

O

P

Q

R

S

T

U

V

W

X

Y

Z

(Acknowledgments continued from page ii)

Dell Publishing, a division of Random House, Inc.
"The Tail" Copyright © 1992 by Joyce Hansen from *Funny You Should Ask* by David Gale, Editor. Used by permission of Dell Publishing, a division of Random House, Inc.

Dial Books for Young Readers, a division of Penguin Young Readers Group
Black Cowboy, Wild Horses written by Julius Lester and illustrated by Jerry Pinkney. Text copyright © 1998 by Julius Lester. Illustrations copyright © 1998 by Jerry Pinkney. "Gluskabe and Old Man Winter: Abenaki" by Joseph Bruchac from *Pushing Up the Sky*. Copyright © 2000 by Joseph Bruchac, text. Used by permission of Dial Books for Young Readers, A Division of Penguin Young Readers Group, A Member of Penguin Group (USA).

Encyclopedia Brittanica
"How to Read a Road Map" from *Britannica Student Encyclopaedia Online www.britannica.com/ebi/article-199642*. Copyright © 2007 Encyclopaedia Brittanica, Inc. Used with permission from Britannica Student Encyclopedia.

Paul S. Eriksson
"My Papa, Mark Twain" by Susy Clemens from *Small Voices* by Josef and Dorothy Berger. Copyright © 1966 by Josef and Dorothy Berger in arrangement with Paul S. Eriksson, Publisher. Used by permission.

Florida Fish and Wildlife Conservation Commission
Manatee Decal Art Contest from *http://myfwc.com/manatee/decals/contest2007.htm*. Copyright © 2007 Florida Fish and Wildlife Conservation Commission. Used by permission.

Forsyth County Public Library
Forsyth County Public Library Card Application from *www.forsyth.public.lib.ga.us/librarycard.htm*. Copyright © 2007 Sarasota County Library.

Samuel French, Inc.
"The Phantom Tollbooth" from *The Phantom Tollbooth: A Children's Play in Two Acts* by Susan Nanus and Norton Juster. Copyright © 1977 by Susan Nanus and Norton Juster. Used by permission of Samuel French, Inc. All rights reserved. CAUTION: Professionals and amateurs are hereby warned that "The Phantom Tollbooth," being fully protected under the copyright laws of the United States of America, the British Commonwealth countries, including Canada, and the other countries of the Copyright Union, is subject to royalty. All rights, including professional, amateur, motion picture, recitation, lecturing, public reading, radio, television and cable broadcasting, and the rights of translation into foreign languages, are strictly reserved. Any inquiry regarding the availability of performance rights, or the purchase of individual copies of the authorized acting edition, must be directed to Samuel French, Inc., 45 West 25th Street, NY, NY 10010 with other locations in Hollywood and Toronto, Canada.

Greenwillow Books, a division of HarperCollins
"Ankylosaurus" by Jack Prelutsky from *Tyrannosaurus Was A Beast*. Text copyright © 1988 by Jack Prelutsky. Used by permission of HarperCollins Publishers.

Harcourt, Inc.
"Ode to Family Photographs" from *Neighborhood Odes,* copyright © 1992 by Gary Soto. Used by permission of Harcourt, Inc.

HarperCollins Publishers, Inc.
From *The Wounded Wolf* by Jean Craighead George. Text copyright © 1978 by Jean Craighead George. Used by permission of HarperCollins Publishers.

Harper's Magazine
"Preserving a Great American Symbol," (originally titled "Desecrating America") by Richard Durbin from *Harper's Magazine, October 1989, p.32*. Copyright © 1989 by Harper's Magazine. All rights reserved. Reproduced from the October issue by special permission.

Harvard University Press
"Fame Is a bee" (#1763) by Emily Dickinson is used by permission of the publishers and the Trustees of Amherst College from *The Poems of Emily Dickinson,* Thomas H. Johnson, editor, Cambridge, Mass.: The Belknap Press of Harvard University Press, Copyright © 1951, 1955, 1979, 1983 by the President and Fellows of Harvard College.

The Barbara Hogenson Agency, Inc.
"The Tiger Who Would Be King" by James Thurber, from *Further Fables for Our Time*. Copyright © 1956 James Thurber. Copyright © renewed 1984 by Rosemary A. Thurber. Used by arrangement with Rosemary A. Thurber and The Barbara Hogenson Agency, Inc.

Houghton Mifflin Company, Inc.
"Arachne" from *Greek Myths*. Copyright © 1949 by Olivia E. Coolidge; copyright © renewed 1977 by Olivia E. Coolidge. Used by permission of Houghton Mifflin Company. All rights reserved.

Imaginova c/o Space.com
"NASA Finally Goes Metric" from *www.space.com/news/070108_moon_metric.html*. Copyright © 2007 Space.com.

Information Please
"The Seven Wonders of the World" from *www.infoplease.com*. Information Please® Database, Copyright © 2006 Pearson Education, Inc. All rights reserved.

Dr. Francisco Jiménez
"The Circuit" by Francisco Jiménez from *America Street: A Mulicultural Anthology Of Stories*. Copyright © 1993 by Anne Mazer. Used with permission of the author Francisco Jiménez.

Rachel Katz
"Origami with Rachel Katz: Apatosauras" by Rachel Katz from *www.geocities.com/rachel_katz*. Copyright © 2001–2004 Rachel Katz. All Rights Reserved. Used by permission.

© Pearson Education

PHOTO AND ART CREDITS

Greyling: Corel Professional Photos CD-ROM™; *My Heart is in the Highlands*: Silver Burdett Ginn; *Stray*: istockphoto.com; *The Homecoming*: Pearson Education; *The Drive-In Movies*: CORBIS; *The Market Square Dog*: Corel Professional Photos CD-ROM™; *My Papa, Mark Twain*: National Archives and Records Administration; *Stage Fright*: Phillip Dvorak/Getty Images, Inc.; *The Lady and the Spider*: istockphoto.com; *The Caribbean*: © Dorling Kindersley; *The Wounded Wolf*: Corel Professional Photos CD-ROM™; *The Tail*: Corel Professional Photos CD-ROM™; *Dragon, Dragon*: istockphoto.com; *Zlateh the Goat*: Shutterstock, Inc.; *The Old Woman Who Lived With the Wolves*: Library of Congress; *The Seven Wonders of the World*: Archives Charmet, The Hanging Gardens of Babylon, from a series of the 'Seven Wonders of the World' published in 'Munchener Bilderbogen', 1886 (colour litho), Knab, Ferdinand (1834-1902) / Private Collection, Archives Charmet / The Bridgeman Art Library International, The Statue of Olympian Zeus by Phidias, plate 5 from 'Entwurf einer historischen Architektur', engraved by Johann Adam Delsenbach (1687-1765) 1721 (engraving) (later colouration), Fischer von Erlach, Johann Bernhard (1656-1723) (after) / Private Collection, The Stapleton Collection / The Bridgeman Art Library International, Temple of Diana at Ephesus from a series of the 'Seven Wonders of the Ancient World' published in 'Muenchener Bilderbogen', 1886 (colour engraving), Knab, Ferdinand (1834-1902) / Private Collection, Archives Charmet / The Bridgeman Art Library International, The Mausoleum of Halicarnassus, from a series of the 'Seven Wonders of the Ancient world' published in 'Muenchnener Bilderbogen'. 1886 (colour engraving), Knab, Ferdinand (1834-1902) / Private Collection, Archives Charmet / The Bridgeman Art Library International, The Art Archive / Egyptian Museum Cairo / Gianni Dagli Orti; *The All-American Slurp*: Corel Professional Photos CD-ROM™; *The Circuit*: National Archives and Records Administration; *The King of Mazy May*: Library of Congress; *Aaron's Gift*: istockphoto.com; *Race to the End of the Earth*: Bettmann/CORBIS; *Zlata's Diary*: Sipa www.sipa.com; *Water*: istockphoto.com; *Hard as Nails*: istockphoto.com; *Jackie Robinson: Justice at Last*: Library of Congress; *The Shutout*: Library of Congress; *Preserving a Great American Symbol*: AP/Wide World Photos; *Turkeys*: Corel Professional Photos CD-ROM™; *Langston Terrace*: Used by permission of HarperCollins Publishers: *La Lena Buena*: Ken Samuelsen/Getty Images, Inc.; from *The Pigman & Me*: Bob Daemmrich Photography; *Advertisments*: Image of The Advertising Archive; *Oranges, Ode to Family Photographs*: istockphoto.com; *Poetry Collection 1*: Library of Congress; *Poetry Collection 2*: Pearson Education; *Poetry Collection 3*: istockphoto.com; *Poetry Collection 4*: NASA; *Origami*: Instructions, diagram and models ©1998 by Steve and Megumi Biddle. Models photograph by Les Morsillo. Photograph ©1998 The Metropolitan Museum; *Poetry Collection 5*: istockphoto.com; *Poetry Collection 6*: Corel Professional Photos CD-ROM™; *Poetry Collection 7*: Corel Professional Photos CD-ROM™; *Poetry Collection 8*: Corel Professional Photos CD-ROM™; *NASA Finally Goes Metric*: NASA / Photo Researchers, Inc. *Black Cowboy, Wild Horses*: istockphoto.com; *The Tiger Who Would Be King, The Ant and the Dove*: Corel Professional Photos CD-ROM™; *The Lion and the Bulls, A Crippled Boy*: Corel Professional Photos CD-ROM™; *Arachne*: Pearson Education; *Prologue from The Whale Rider*: istockphoto.com; *Satellites and Sea Lions*: Sea World of California/CORBIS, DLILLC/CORBIS; *Red Cross Helps Florida Residens Recover From Tornadoes*: Gene Rhoden/Peter Arnold, Inc. *Why the Tortoise's Shell is Not Smooth*: Corel Professional Photos CD-ROM™; *He Lion, Bruh Bear, and Bruh Rabbit*: Corel Professional Photos CD-ROM™; *The Three Wishes*: Mitch Hrdlicka/Getty Images, Inc.; *The Stone*: istockphoto.com